* * * * * * * * * *

Written by
Jen Van Meter

Illustrated
& lettered by

W9-BMZ-993

* * * * * *

Chapter 1 flashback illustrated
& lettered by Andi Watson

Chapter 2 flashback and
chapter 4 television sequences
illustrated by Christine Norrie

Chapter 3 flashback illustrated
by Chynna Clugston-Major

Chapter 3 main story inked by
Catherine & Christine Norrie

Chapter breaks by
Terry Dodson

Edited by Jamie S. Rich

Book design by K. Seda

HOPELESS SAVAGES

Ground Zero

Front Cover by
Christine Norrie & Guy Major

Hopeless Savages logo based on a logo designed by
Andi Watson

Chapter 2 flashback, chapter 4 television sequences lettered by
Spookoo (Christine Norrie, Matty Ryan, & Andrew Lis)

Chapter 3 flashback lettered by
Bryan Lee O'Malley

Published by Oni Press, Inc.
Joe Nozemack, publisher
Jamie S. Rich, editor in chief
James Lucas Jones, associate editor

This book collects all four issues of the Oni Press comic
book series Hopeless Savages: Ground Zero.

Hopeless Savages ™ & ° 2002, 2003 Jen Van Meter. Unless otherwise specified,
all other material ° 2003 Oni Press, Inc. Oni Press logo and icon are ™ & ° 2003
Oni Press, Inc. All rights reserved. Oni Press logo and icon artwork created by
Dave Gibbons. The events, institutions, and characters presented in this book
are fictional. Any resemblance to actual persons, living, dead, or undead, is
purely coincidental. No portion of this publication may be reproduced, by any
means, without the express written permission of the copyright holders.

ONI PRESS, INC.
6336 SE Milwaukie Avenue, PMB30
Portland, OR 97202
USA

www.onipress.com
www.spookoo.com

Second Oni Press edition: February 2004.
ISBN 1-929998-99-6

3 5 7 9 10 8 6 4 2
PRINTED IN CANADA.

There aren't a lot of good songs about superheroes.

There's "Waiting For Superman" by The Flaming Lips, "Ghostrider" by the Henry Rollins Band, and...well, that's pretty much it, unless you're a fan of "Magneto and Titanium Man" by Wings, or "Captain America" by Jimmy Buffet.

♥INTRODUCTION♥

It's therefore perhaps only right and proper that there are so few good comics about love. It's the cultural exchange programme that never was. Pop music doesn't get to have any great adolescent power fantasies (well, apart from the one about being rock music), and comics don't get to express the mysteries of the human heart. Sure, there are lots of comics about relationships, and even a few that flirt with subtler emotions than "grrr"and "argh," but love? Romance comics died out in the '50s.

Which makes *Hopeless Savages* either a glorious throwback, or the first of some strange new hyphen-ated sub-genre, like retro-post-romantic comics lit. Or, it just is what it is, and what it is is something incredibly rare: a really great comic about love.

It must be rare, because frankly, I hate love, and I love this comic.

I am, of course, single. I resent all couples, with their constant inseparability and their cutesy insufferability. I detest their snuggling and their moony-eyed staring and their banal chitter-chatter. And most of all, I bitterly resent their ability to find happiness in the arms of another. Damn them.

As I write this, it's mere days away from Valentine's Day, so my dander is up. The TV is full of ads for Greatest Love Song compilations that can drain the soul and destroy any right thinking man's faith in humanity. The track listings mix in bona fide classics by Marvin Gaye and Carole King with Celine Dion's "Think Twice" and Michael Bolton's "How Am I Supposed To Live Without You." The most offensive thing being, to some people, Michael Bolton and Celine Dion really do speak of love. Because if you're in love, even Mariah Carey seems passionate and sincere.

Any love song can seem profound if it's "your song." Even "Your Song," though it beggars belief that anyone can be moved by the lyric, "If I were a sculptor - but then again no." These songs are designed to be banal, so that anyone who hears them at the right moment can impose their own emotions over the top and give them a cod-profundity. With the right lighting and the proper amount of wine, "Girl On TV" by the Lyte Funky Ones could resonate.

Truly great love songs don't need to find the mood; they set the mood. Great love songs capture some truth about love that really expresses the author's experience, and, with any luck, reflects on the listener's experience as well. Even if the listener is single, bitter and drunk. Well, especially if he's drunk.

Real love songs have something more interesting to say than, "It's a little bit funny, this feeling inside."

Songs that really say something about love, while certainly more common than songs about superheroes, are rare enough. *Comics* that really say something about love are gold dust.

Thankfully, Jen Van Meter is a soppy old romantic, and she knows how to create something special. Something that can even touch someone like me. *Ground Zero* is a tale that reminds us all of the days when we were idealists, and it finds that little spark of faith and blows on the embers to get the flames of hope flickering again. Whether you've found love or you're still looking, *Ground Zero* is a story that reminds you that love is worth finding and worth hanging on to.

And most importantly, it reminds us that to feel love takes courage. Now, there's a million stories about love against the odds, and how it takes courage to overcome obstacles – both those imposed by the constraints of social acceptability and those imposed by the best intentions of the people who care most about us and want to see us protected. *Ground Zero* covers that ground, but it has something more to say. It tells us that the most courageous thing of all is simply to fall in love. The bravest thing to do is to place your heart in someone else's hands.

It's Zero's love story, of course, but for me the real key to the book is Twitch. If anyone knows about the courage it takes to love, it's someone who can say at such an early age that *who* they can love should not be constrained by old-fashioned concepts of normality. Twitch may have made some missteps on the road to happiness, but at least he was brave enough to take any steps at all.

I should confess, though, when it comes to Twitch, I'm terribly biased. Last year, while Jen Van Meter was still working on the book, she visited London. She and I went for dinner at Jimmy the Greek's in Soho, and over calamari and grilled halloumi, I told her how desperate I was to see greater representation of the diversity of sexuality in comics. It's a plea I've brought to the doorstep of many publishers, including some of the industry's most heavyweight carbuncles, with some apparently positive (and some not so positive) results.

In Jen's case, I was preaching to the converted, of course. In Twitch, she had already created one of the most unforced and natural gay characters in comics. Still, I told Jen that what I really wanted to see was a gay character who was not only permitted a love life, but permitted a kiss, and not only permitted a kiss, but permitted a love story.

I didn't realise quite what a receptive audience I'd found. I'm forever grateful to Jen for her heart and courage.

I should add, though, that the book's great passion and veracity isn't solely due to Jen. It boasts an impressive line-up of richly idiosyncratic artists that really make it sing with sincerity. Andi Watson, Chynna Clugston-Major, and Christine Norrie, all pop stars in the finest sense, never lose the beat as they provide their wonderful evocations of the family's romantic misadventures, while Bryan O'Malley's insolent pug-nosed faces and wide eyes provide the unmistakable refrain. There's a sense of adolescence to 'Malley's wonderful character depictions that perfectly captures the youthful flush of love. With a team like this, you're a million miles away from Celine Dion – which is a great place to be.

In closing, I should note that for two of my friends, *Hopeless Savages* really is the comics equivalent of "our song." Though friends for a while, it was over a shared love for *Hopeless Savages* that they bonded, and during a conversation about the series that one finally found the courage to ask the other out. They'll be spending Valentine's Day at the theatre, watching Sean Bean in leather pants.

I'll spend my Valentine's Day miserable and alone, thinking about Sean Bean in leather pants. That will be my sole concession to romance.

Oh, by the way, if you do get teary-eyed over Mariah Carey, it's not such a bad thing. I'll leave you with some sage advice from the Hopeless-Savages, and my favourite line from the series;

"We don't care *what* music you kids love, so long as you *have* music to love."

Andrew Wheeler
London, 12th February 2003

Andrew Wheeler is a professional entertainment journalist and editor of Ninth Art [www.ninthart.com], the comics journalism website for the discerning reader. GWM with GSOH, he enjoys pina coladas and taking walks in the rain…

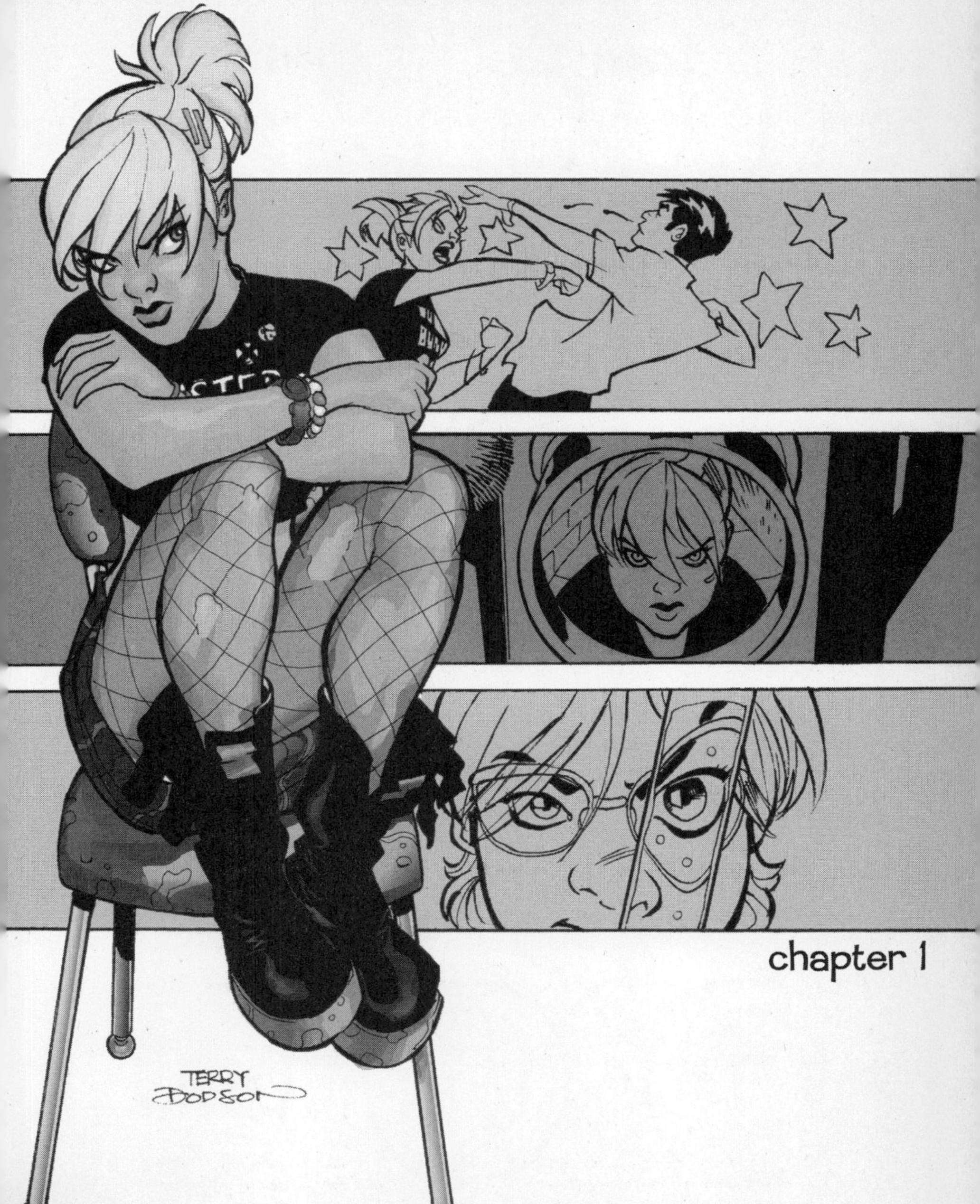
TERRY
DODSON

chapter 1

THE HOPELESS-SAVAGE FAMILY

Dirk Hopeless
a.k.a. David Sterling

Nikki Savage

Rat Bastard
Hopeless-Savage

Arsenal Fierce
Hopeless-Savage

Twitch Strummer
Hopeless-Savage

Skank Zero
Hopeless Savage

EXTENDED FAMILY

Norwegian "Weej" Blue
The family's long-time manager

Dusted Bunnies – Zero's band

Emma, bass

Toby, guitar

Flora, drums

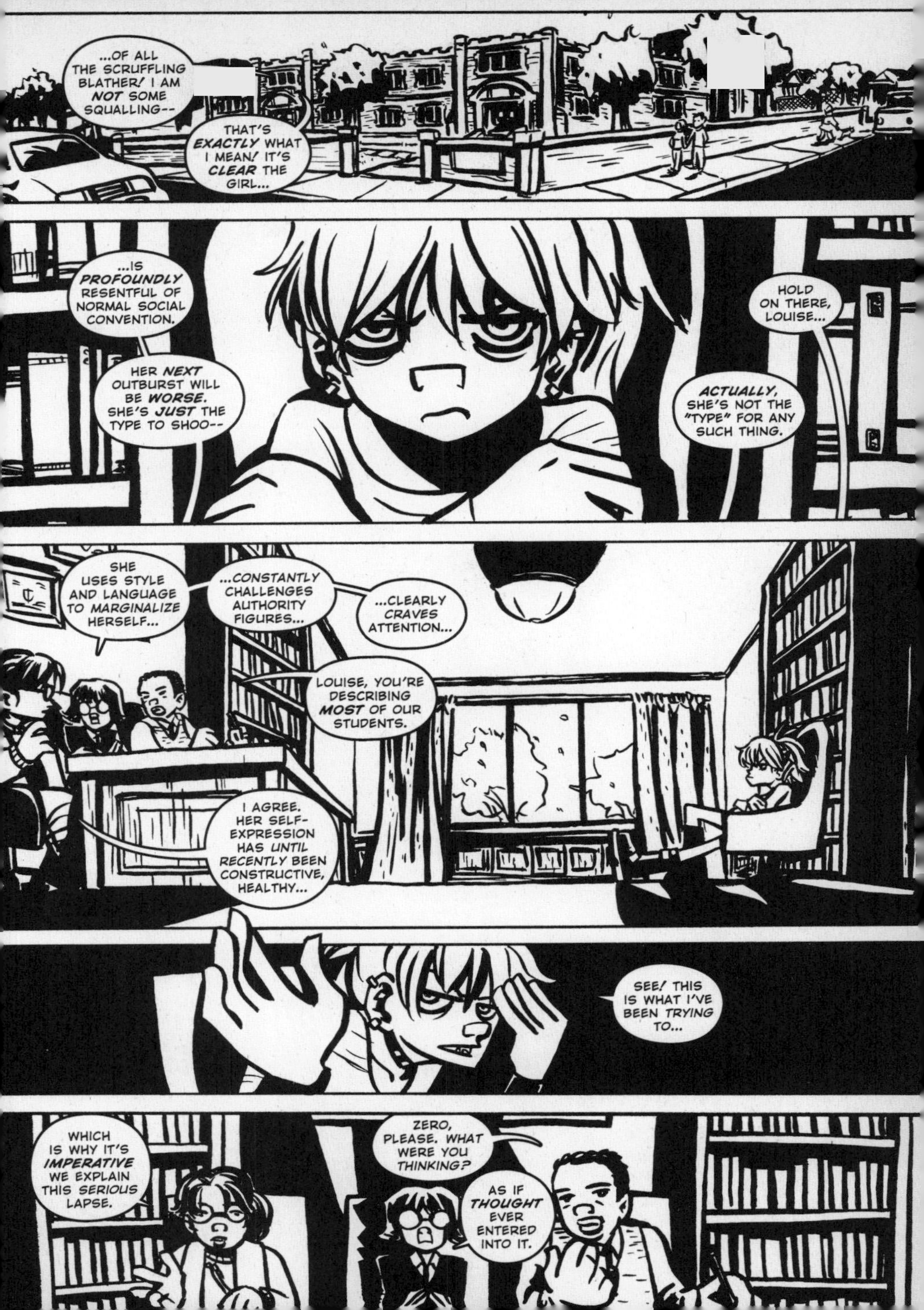
...OF ALL THE SCRUFFLING BLATHER! I AM NOT SOME SQUALLING--
THAT'S EXACTLY WHAT I MEAN! IT'S CLEAR THE GIRL...
...IS PROFOUNDLY RESENTFUL OF NORMAL SOCIAL CONVENTION.
HER NEXT OUTBURST WILL BE WORSE. SHE'S JUST THE TYPE TO SHOO--
HOLD ON THERE, LOUISE...
ACTUALLY, SHE'S NOT THE "TYPE" FOR ANY SUCH THING.
SHE USES STYLE AND LANGUAGE TO MARGINALIZE HERSELF...
...CONSTANTLY CHALLENGES AUTHORITY FIGURES...
...CLEARLY CRAVES ATTENTION...
LOUISE, YOU'RE DESCRIBING MOST OF OUR STUDENTS.
I AGREE. HER SELF-EXPRESSION HAS UNTIL RECENTLY BEEN CONSTRUCTIVE, HEALTHY...
SEE! THIS IS WHAT I'VE BEEN TRYING TO...
WHICH IS WHY IT'S IMPERATIVE WE EXPLAIN THIS SERIOUS LAPSE.
ZERO, PLEASE. WHAT WERE YOU THINKING?
AS IF THOUGHT EVER ENTERED INTO IT.

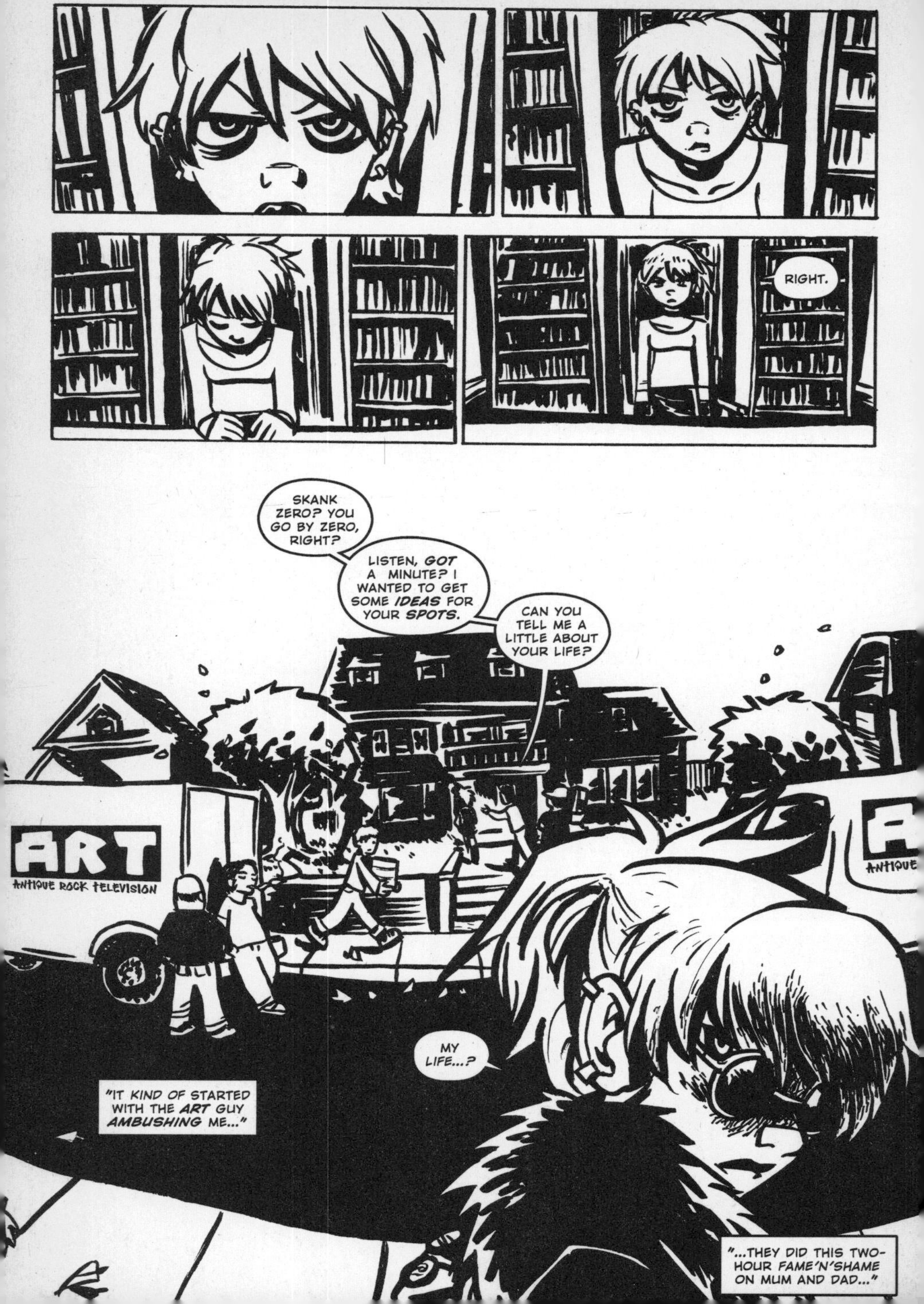
RIGHT.
SKANK ZERO? YOU GO BY ZERO, RIGHT?
LISTEN, GOT A MINUTE? I WANTED TO GET SOME IDEAS FOR YOUR SPOTS.
CAN YOU TELL ME A LITTLE ABOUT YOUR LIFE?
ART
ANTIQUE ROCK TELEVISION
MY LIFE...?
"IT KIND OF STARTED WITH THE ART GUY AMBUSHING ME..."
"...THEY DID THIS TWO-HOUR FAME'N'SHAME ON MUM AND DAD..."

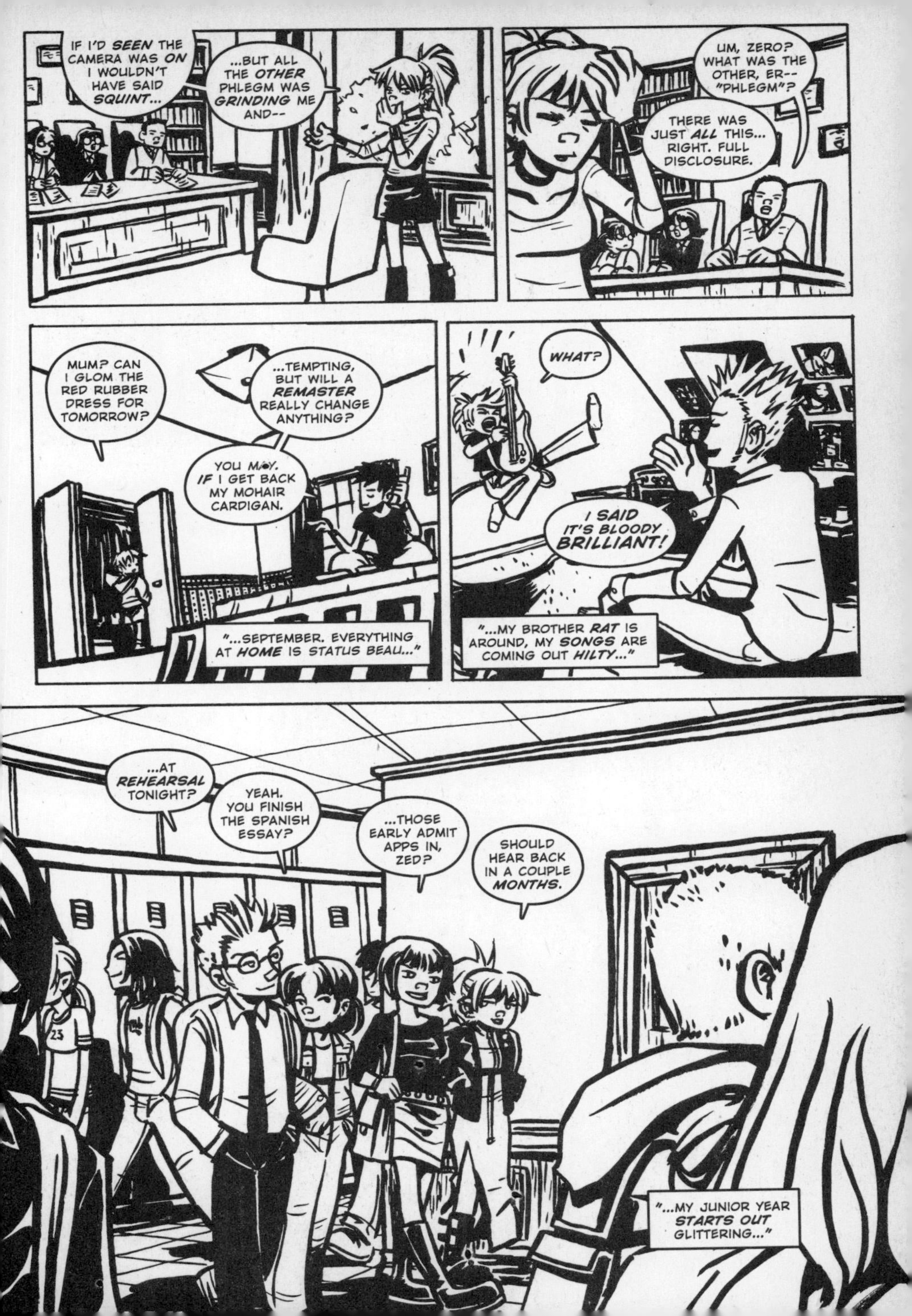
IF I'D SEEN THE CAMERA WAS ON I WOULDN'T HAVE SAID SQUINT...
...BUT ALL THE OTHER PHLEGM WAS GRINDING ME AND--
UM, ZERO? WHAT WAS THE OTHER, ER-- "PHLEGM"?
THERE WAS JUST ALL THIS... RIGHT. FULL DISCLOSURE.
MUM? CAN I GLOM THE RED RUBBER DRESS FOR TOMORROW?
...TEMPTING, BUT WILL A REMASTER REALLY CHANGE ANYTHING?
YOU MAY. IF I GET BACK MY MOHAIR CARDIGAN.
"...SEPTEMBER. EVERYTHING AT HOME IS STATUS BEAU..."
WHAT?
I SAID IT'S BLOODY BRILLIANT!
"...MY BROTHER RAT IS AROUND, MY SONGS ARE COMING OUT HILTY..."
...AT REHEARSAL TONIGHT?
YEAH. YOU FINISH THE SPANISH ESSAY?
...THOSE EARLY ADMIT APPS IN, ZED?
SHOULD HEAR BACK IN A COUPLE MONTHS.
23
"...MY JUNIOR YEAR STARTS OUT GLITTERING..."

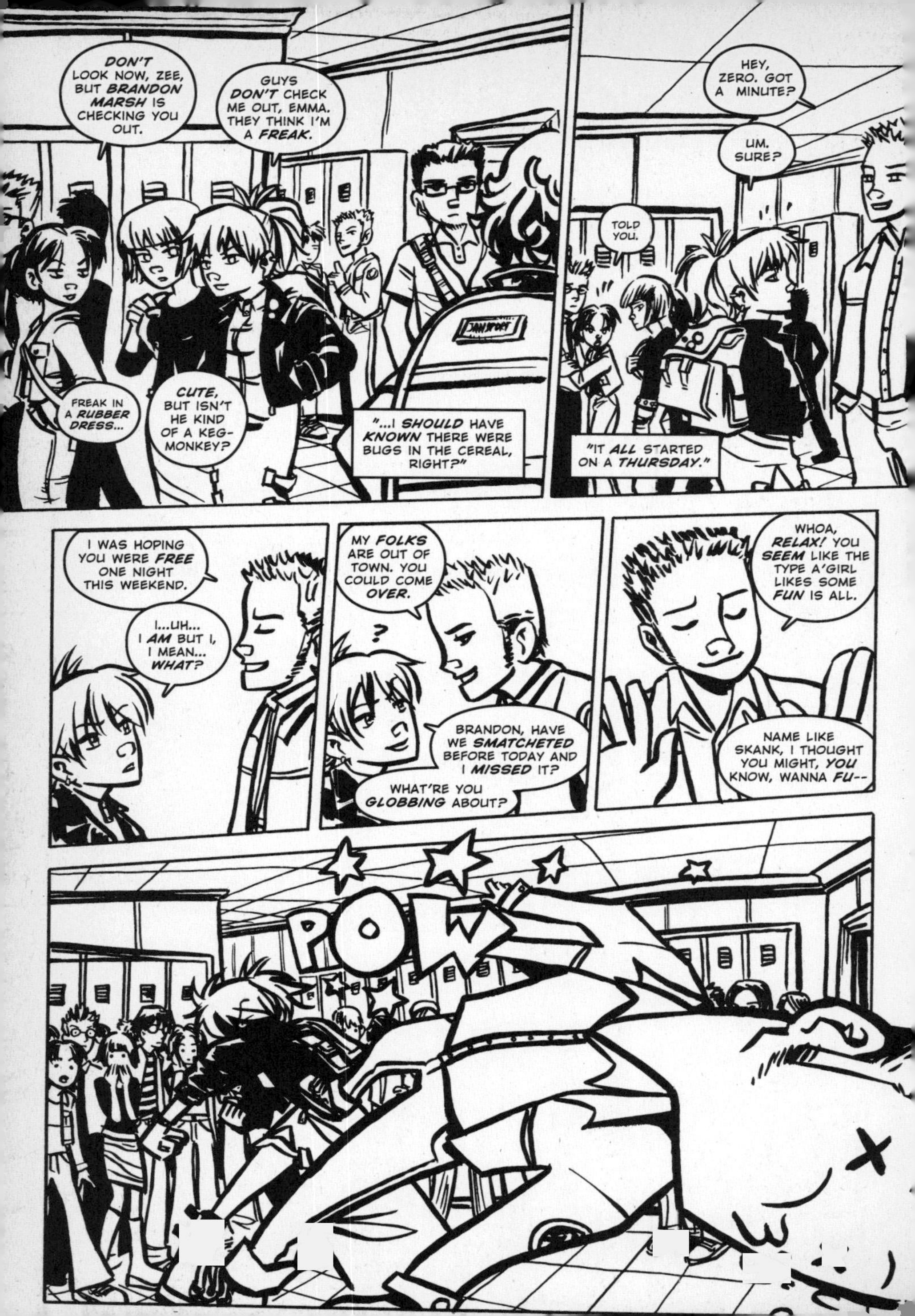

DON'T LOOK NOW, ZEE, BUT BRANDON MARSH IS CHECKING YOU OUT.
GUYS DON'T CHECK ME OUT, EMMA. THEY THINK I'M A FREAK.
FREAK IN A RUBBER DRESS...
CUTE, BUT ISN'T HE KIND OF A KEG-MONKEY?
"...I SHOULD HAVE KNOWN THERE WERE BUGS IN THE CEREAL, RIGHT?"
"IT ALL STARTED ON A THURSDAY."
HEY, ZERO. GOT A MINUTE?
UM. SURE?
TOLD YOU.
I WAS HOPING YOU WERE FREE ONE NIGHT THIS WEEKEND.
I...UH... I AM BUT I, I MEAN... WHAT?
MY FOLKS ARE OUT OF TOWN. YOU COULD COME OVER.
?
BRANDON, HAVE WE SMATCHETED BEFORE TODAY AND I MISSED IT?
WHAT'RE YOU GLOBBING ABOUT?
WHOA, RELAX! YOU SEEM LIKE THE TYPE A'GIRL LIKES SOME FUN IS ALL.
NAME LIKE SKANK, I THOUGHT YOU MIGHT, YOU KNOW, WANNA FU--
POW

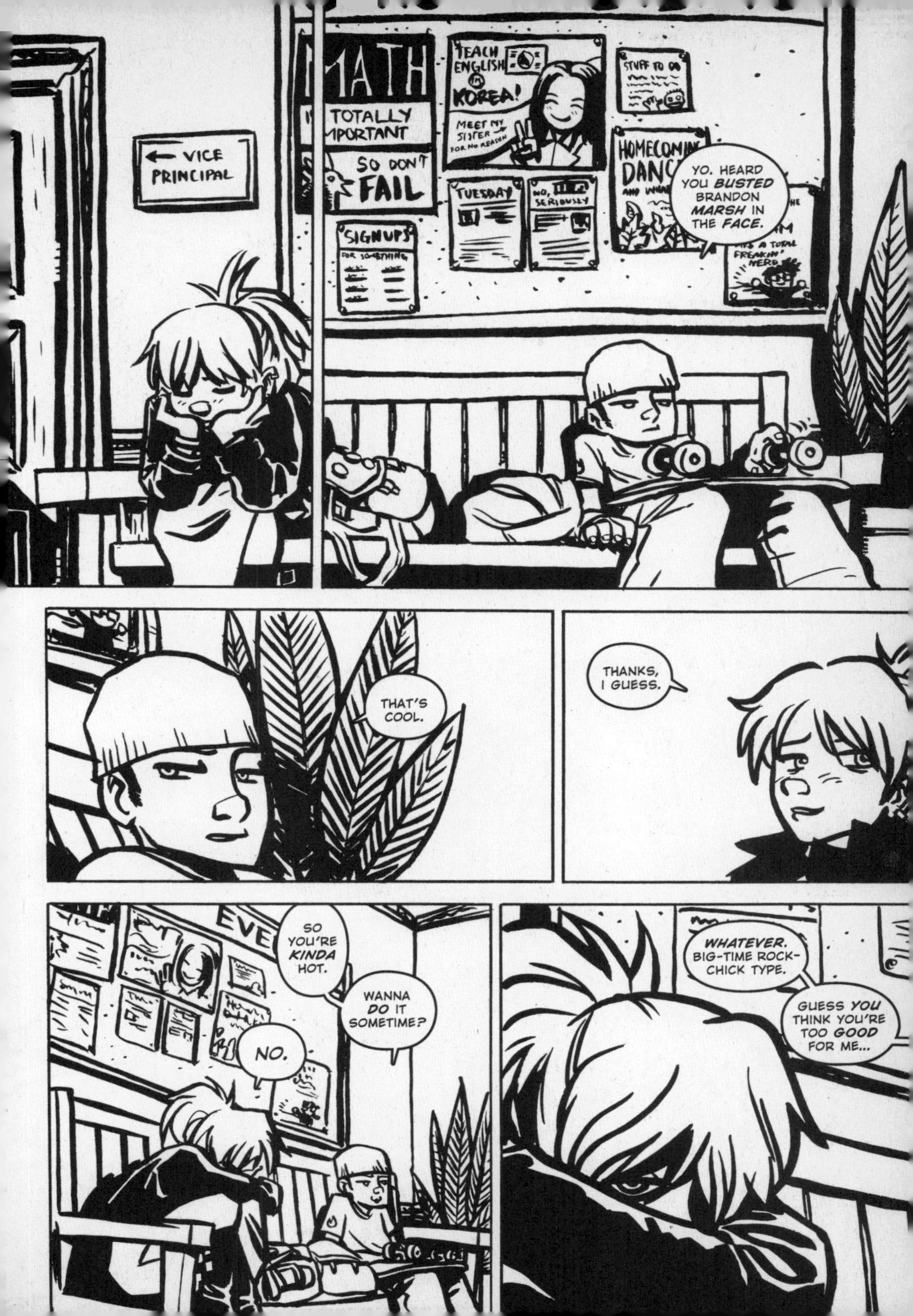
← VICE PRINCIPAL
MATH
TOTALLY
MPORTANT
SO DON'T FAIL
SIGNUPS
FOR SOMETHING
TEACH ENGLISH IN KOREA!
MEET MY SISTER FOR NO REASON
TUESDAY
NO, SERIOUSLY
STUFF TO DO
YO. HEARD YOU **BUSTED** BRANDON **MARSH** IN THE **FACE.**
THAT'S COOL.
THANKS, I GUESS.
SO YOU'RE **KINDA** HOT.
WANNA **DO** IT SOMETIME?
NO.
WHATEVER. BIG-TIME ROCK-CHICK TYPE.
GUESS **YOU** THINK YOU'RE TOO **GOOD** FOR ME...

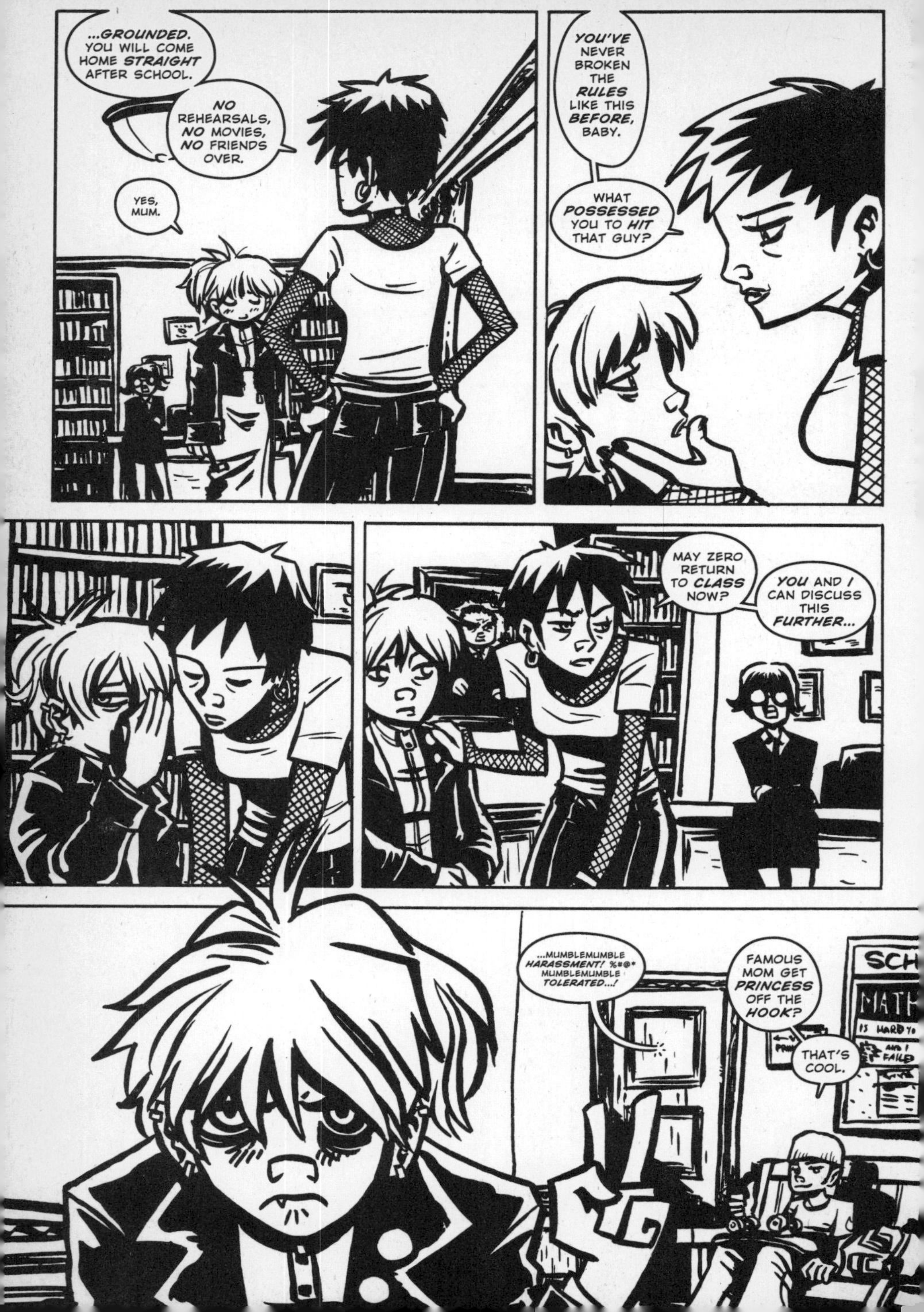
...GROUNDED. YOU WILL COME HOME STRAIGHT AFTER SCHOOL.
NO REHEARSALS, NO MOVIES, NO FRIENDS OVER.
YES, MUM.
YOU'VE NEVER BROKEN THE RULES LIKE THIS BEFORE, BABY.
WHAT POSSESSED YOU TO HIT THAT GUY?
MAY ZERO RETURN TO CLASS NOW?
YOU AND I CAN DISCUSS THIS FURTHER...
...MUMBLEMUMBLE HARASSMENT! %#@* MUMBLEMUMBLE TOLERATED...!
FAMOUS MOM GET PRINCESS OFF THE HOOK?
THAT'S COOL.

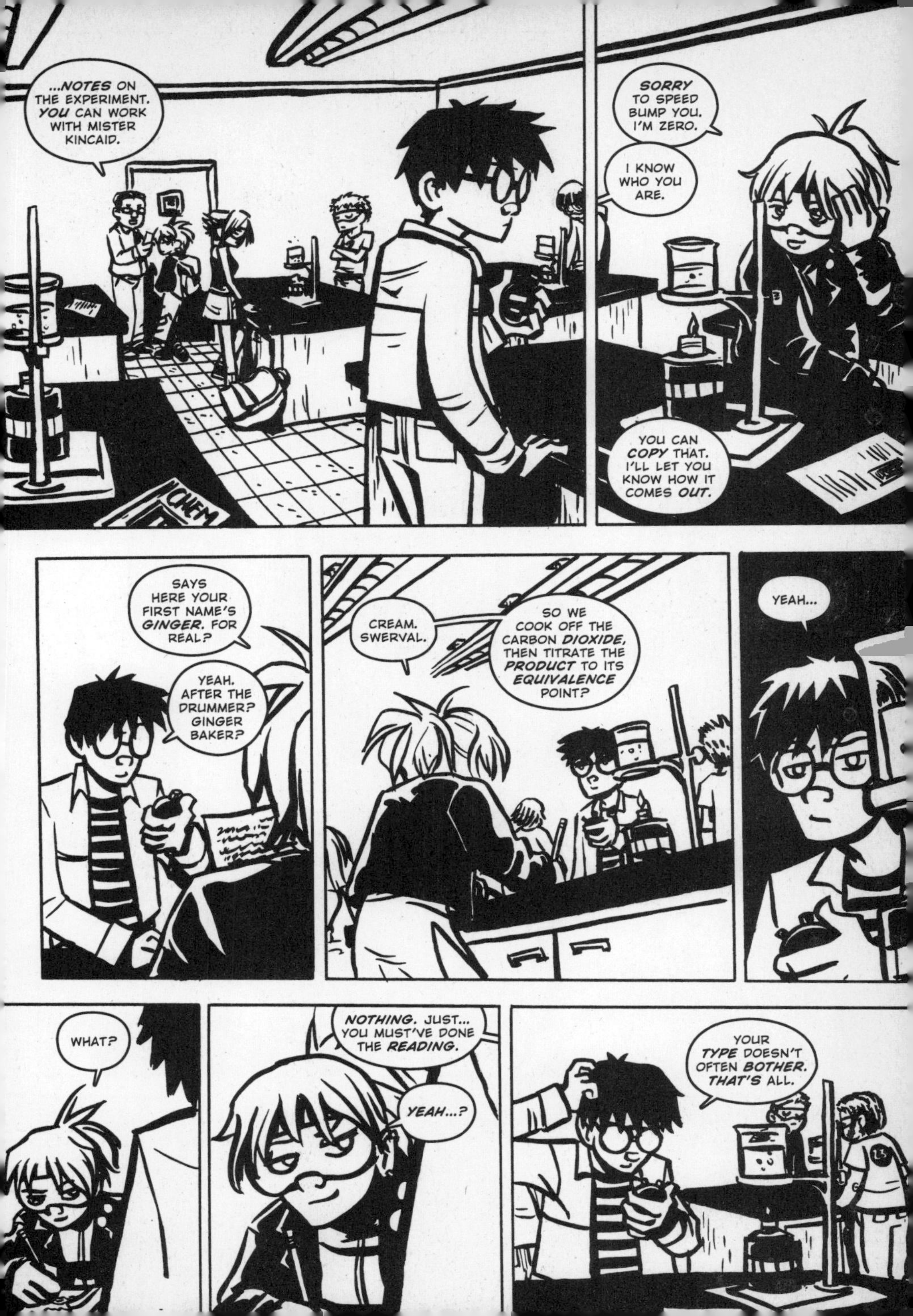
...NOTES ON THE EXPERIMENT. YOU CAN WORK WITH MISTER KINCAID.
CHEM
SORRY TO SPEED BUMP YOU. I'M ZERO.
I KNOW WHO YOU ARE.
YOU CAN COPY THAT. I'LL LET YOU KNOW HOW IT COMES OUT.
SAYS HERE YOUR FIRST NAME'S GINGER. FOR REAL?
YEAH. AFTER THE DRUMMER? GINGER BAKER?
CREAM. SWERVAL.
SO WE COOK OFF THE CARBON DIOXIDE, THEN TITRATE THE PRODUCT TO ITS EQUIVALENCE POINT?
YEAH...
WHAT?
NOTHING. JUST... YOU MUST'VE DONE THE READING.
YEAH...?
YOUR TYPE DOESN'T OFTEN BOTHER. THAT'S ALL.

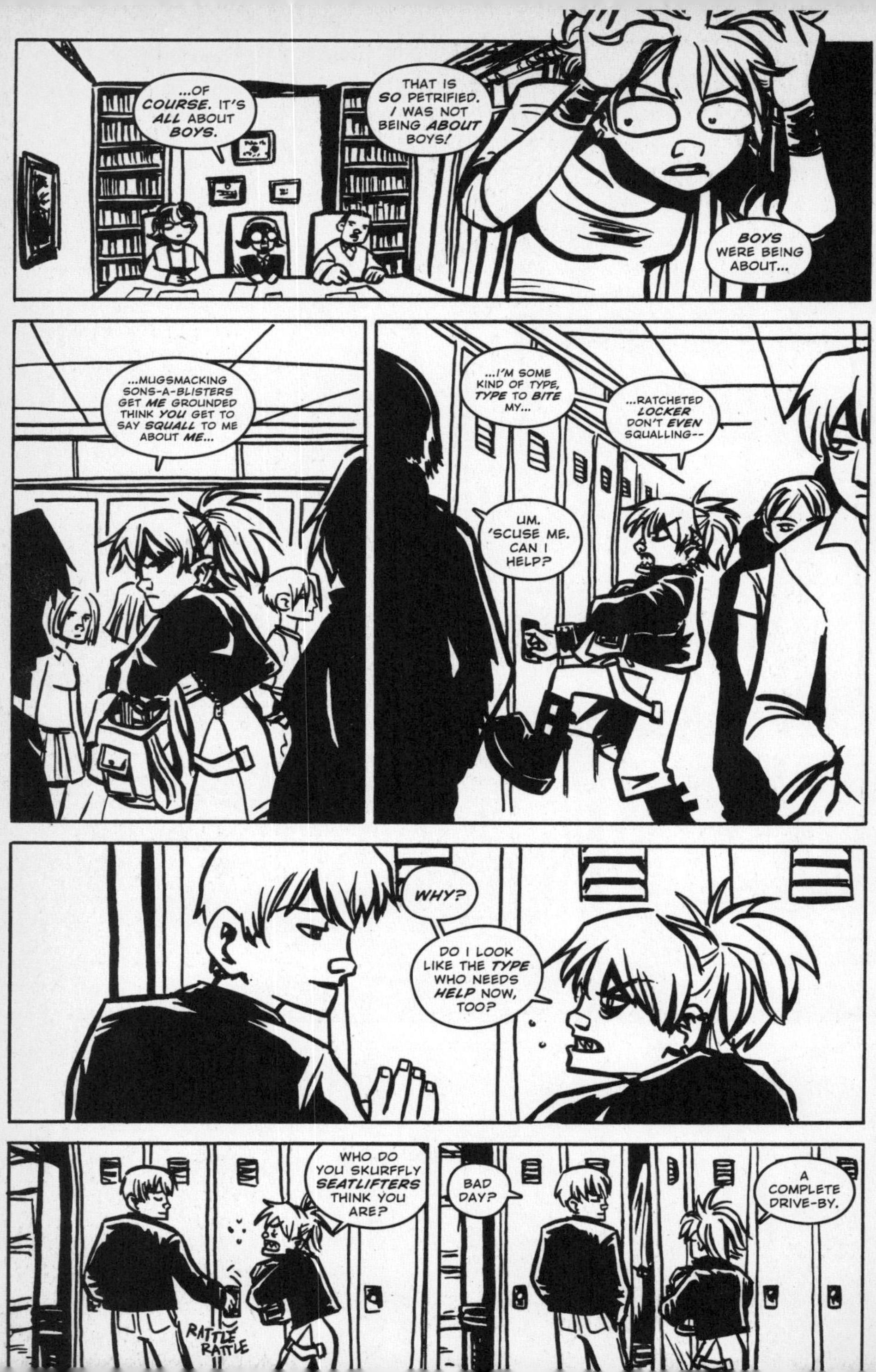
...OF COURSE. IT'S ALL ABOUT BOYS.
THAT IS SO PETRIFIED. I WAS NOT BEING ABOUT BOYS!
BOYS WERE BEING ABOUT...
...MUGSMACKING SONS-A-BLISTERS GET ME GROUNDED THINK YOU GET TO SAY SQUALL TO ME ABOUT ME...
...I'M SOME KIND OF TYPE, TYPE TO BITE MY...
...RATCHETED LOCKER DON'T EVEN SQUALLING--
UM. 'SCUSE ME. CAN I HELP?
WHY?
DO I LOOK LIKE THE TYPE WHO NEEDS HELP NOW, TOO?
WHO DO YOU SKURFFLY SEATLIFTERS THINK YOU ARE?
RATTLE RATTLE
BAD DAY?
A COMPLETE DRIVE-BY.

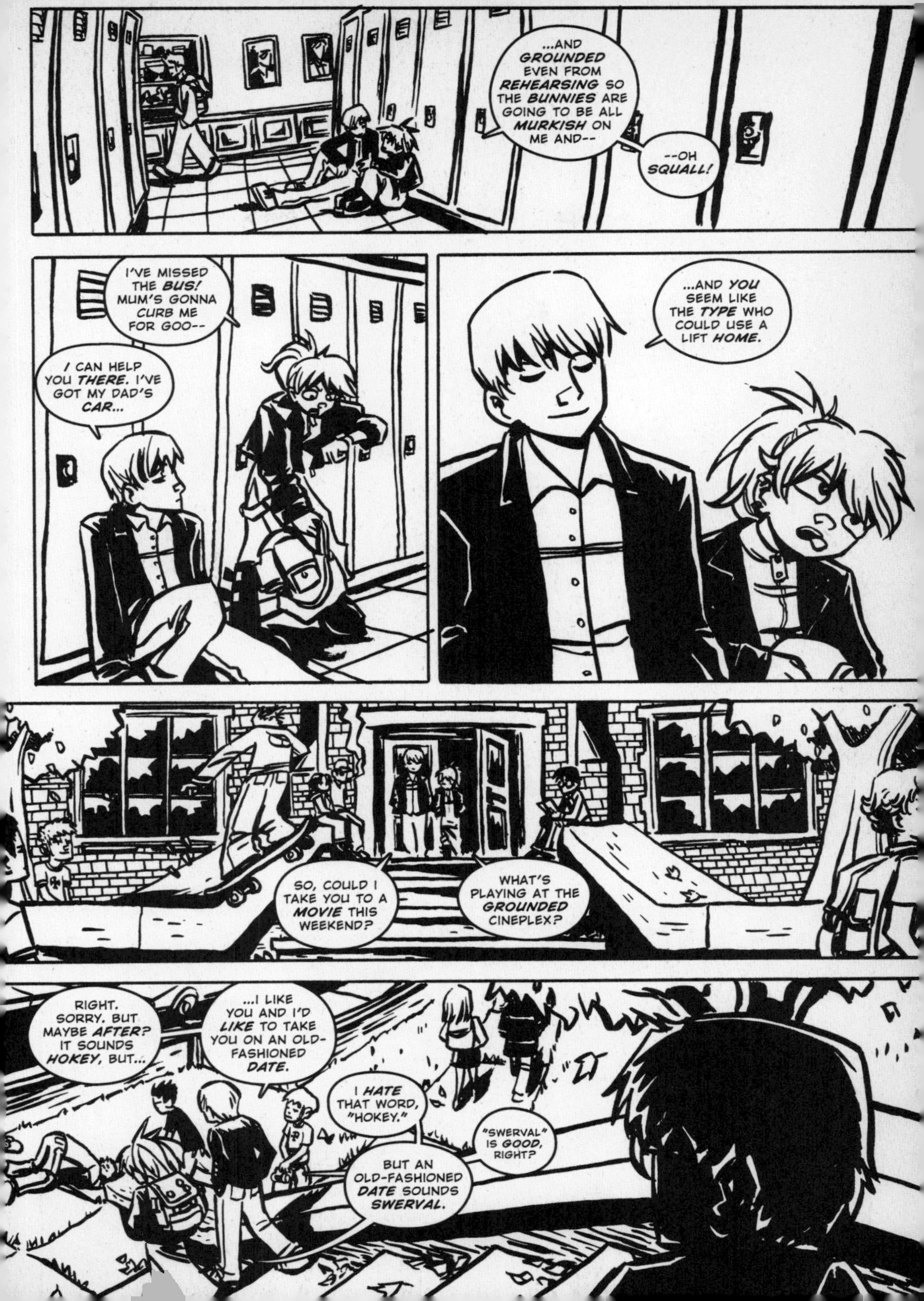
...AND GROUNDED EVEN FROM REHEARSING SO THE BUNNIES ARE GOING TO BE ALL MURKISH ON ME AND--
--OH SQUALL!
I'VE MISSED THE BUS! MUM'S GONNA CURB ME FOR GOO--
I CAN HELP YOU THERE. I'VE GOT MY DAD'S CAR...
...AND YOU SEEM LIKE THE TYPE WHO COULD USE A LIFT HOME.
SO, COULD I TAKE YOU TO A MOVIE THIS WEEKEND?
WHAT'S PLAYING AT THE GROUNDED CINEPLEX?
RIGHT. SORRY. BUT MAYBE AFTER? IT SOUNDS HOKEY, BUT...
...I LIKE YOU AND I'D LIKE TO TAKE YOU ON AN OLD-FASHIONED DATE.
I HATE THAT WORD, "HOKEY."
BUT AN OLD-FASHIONED DATE SOUNDS SWERVAL.
"SWERVAL" IS GOOD, RIGHT?

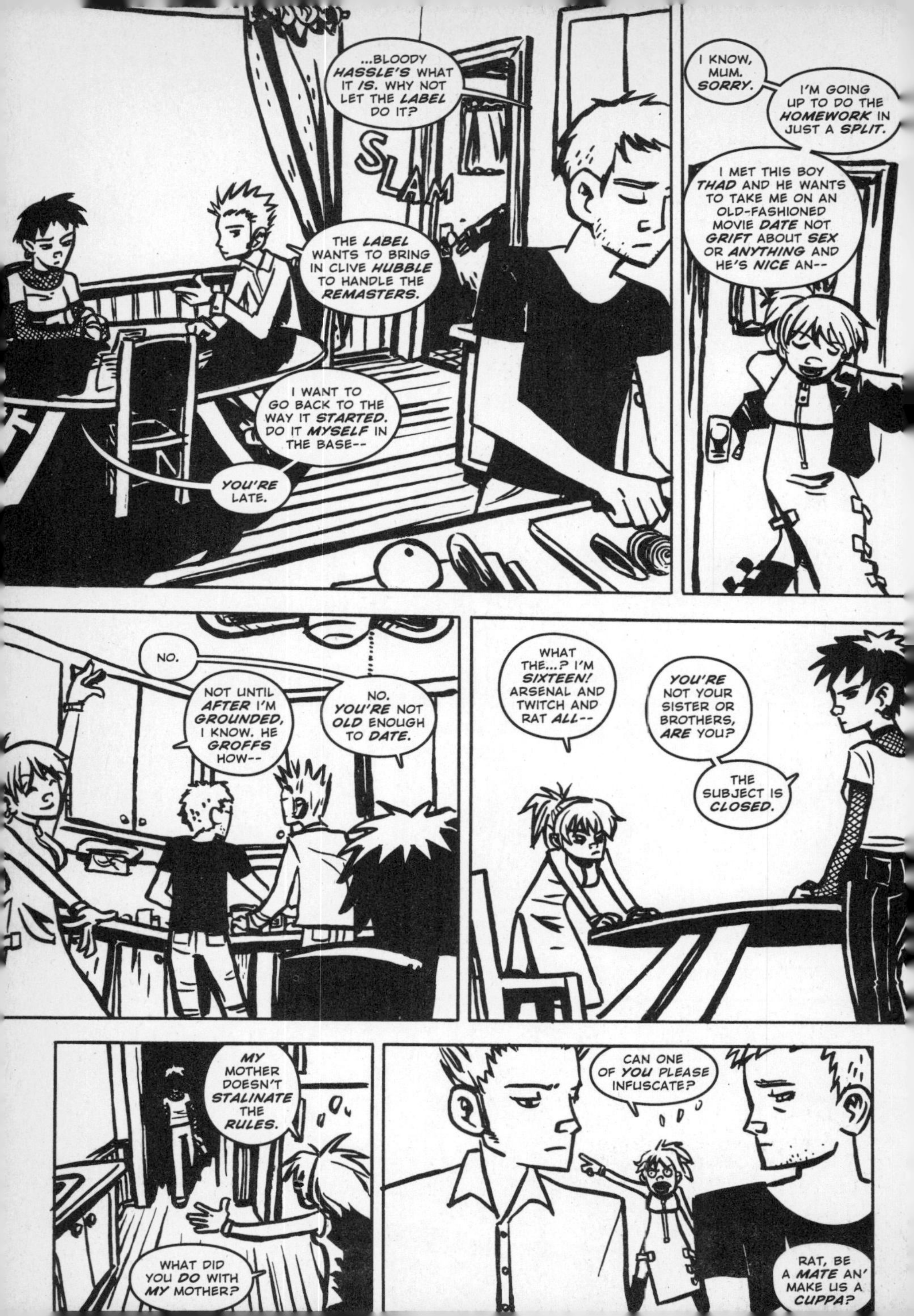
...BLOODY HASSLE'S WHAT IT IS. WHY NOT LET THE LABEL DO IT?
SLAM
THE LABEL WANTS TO BRING IN CLIVE HUBBLE TO HANDLE THE REMASTERS.
I WANT TO GO BACK TO THE WAY IT STARTED. DO IT MYSELF IN THE BASE--
YOU'RE LATE.
I KNOW, MUM. SORRY.
I'M GOING UP TO DO THE HOMEWORK IN JUST A SPLIT.
I MET THIS BOY THAD AND HE WANTS TO TAKE ME ON AN OLD-FASHIONED MOVIE DATE NOT GRIFT ABOUT SEX OR ANYTHING AND HE'S NICE AN--
NO.
NOT UNTIL AFTER I'M GROUNDED, I KNOW. HE GROFFS HOW--
NO. YOU'RE NOT OLD ENOUGH TO DATE.
WHAT THE...? I'M SIXTEEN! ARSENAL AND TWITCH AND RAT ALL--
YOU'RE NOT YOUR SISTER OR BROTHERS, ARE YOU?
THE SUBJECT IS CLOSED.
MY MOTHER DOESN'T STALINATE THE RULES.
WHAT DID YOU DO WITH MY MOTHER?
CAN ONE OF YOU PLEASE INFUSCATE?
RAT, BE A MATE AN' MAKE US A CUPPA?

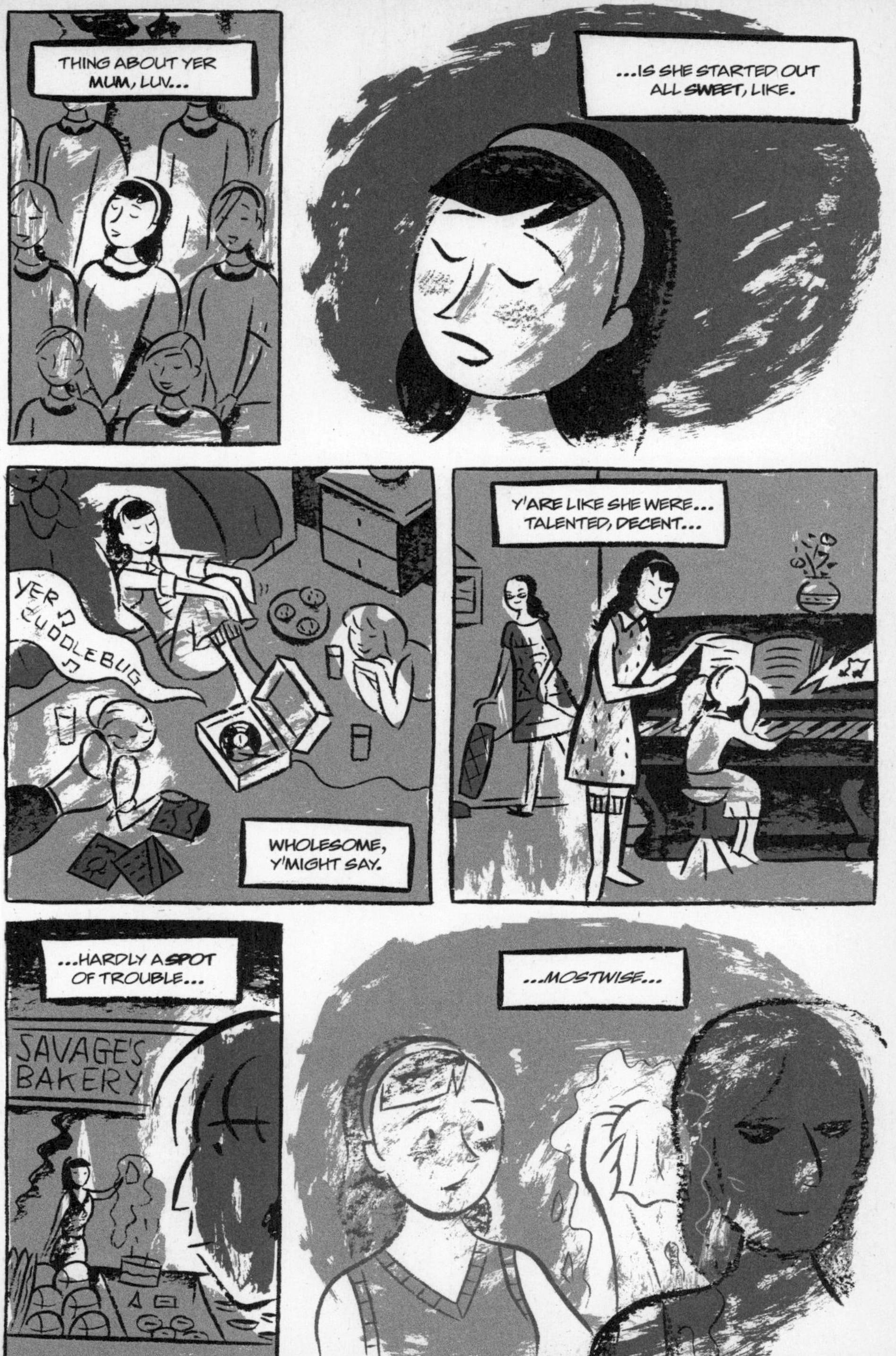
THING ABOUT YER MUM, LUV...
...IS SHE STARTED OUT ALL SWEET, LIKE.
YER CUDDLEBUG
WHOLESOME, Y'MIGHT SAY.
Y'ARE LIKE SHE WERE... TALENTED, DECENT...
...HARDLY A SPOT OF TROUBLE...
SAVAGE'S BAKERY
...MOSTWISE...

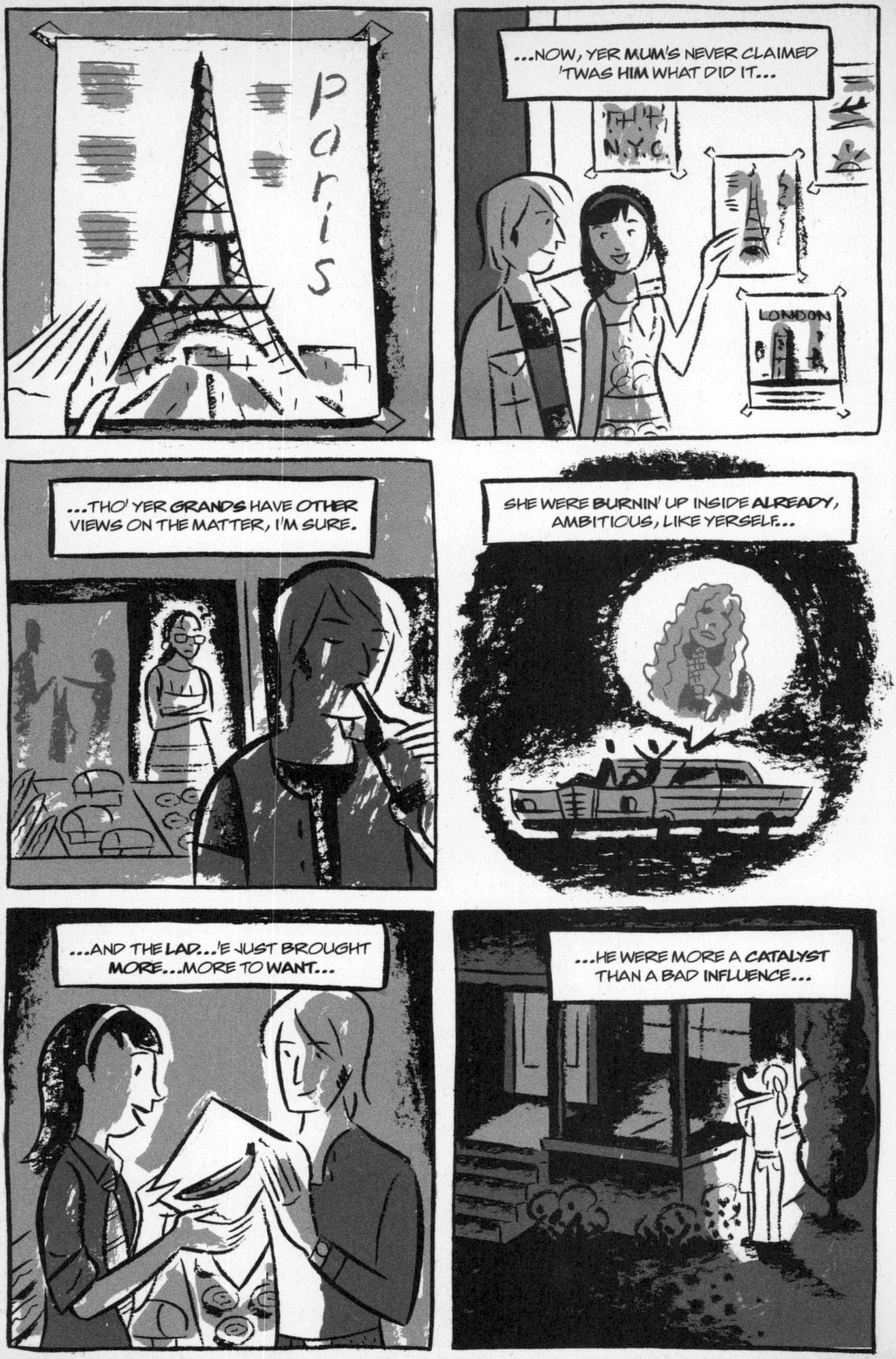
Paris
...NOW, YER MUM'S NEVER CLAIMED 'TWAS HIM WHAT DID IT...
N.Y.C.
LONDON
...THO' YER GRANDS HAVE OTHER VIEWS ON THE MATTER, I'M SURE.
SHE WERE BURNIN' UP INSIDE ALREADY, AMBITIOUS, LIKE YERSELF...
...AND THE LAD...'E JUST BROUGHT MORE...MORE TO WANT...
...HE WERE MORE A CATALYST THAN A BAD INFLUENCE...

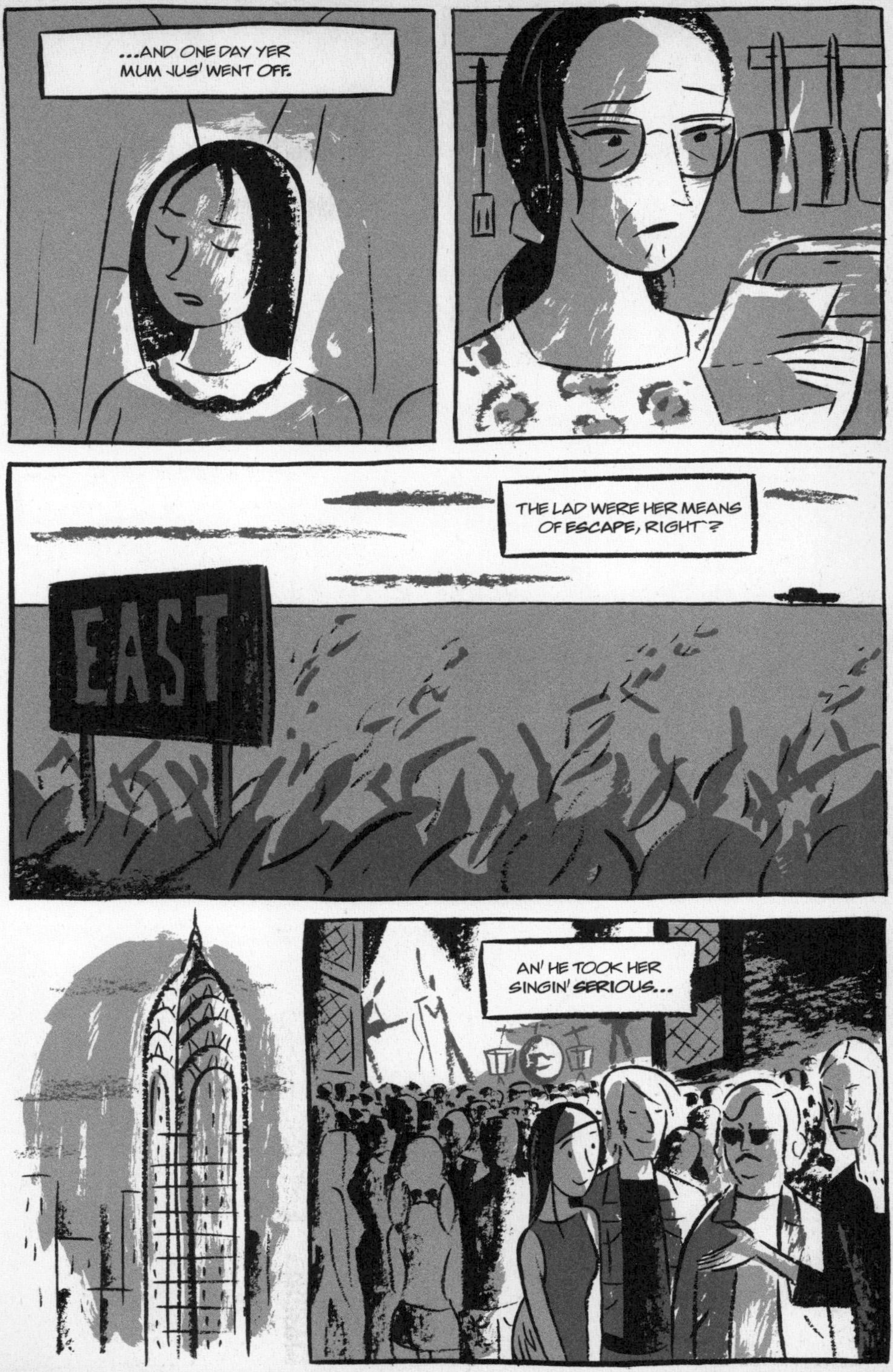
...AND ONE DAY YER MUM JUS' WENT OFF.
THE LAD WERE HER MEANS OF ESCAPE, RIGHT?
EAST
AN' HE TOOK HER SINGIN' SERIOUS...

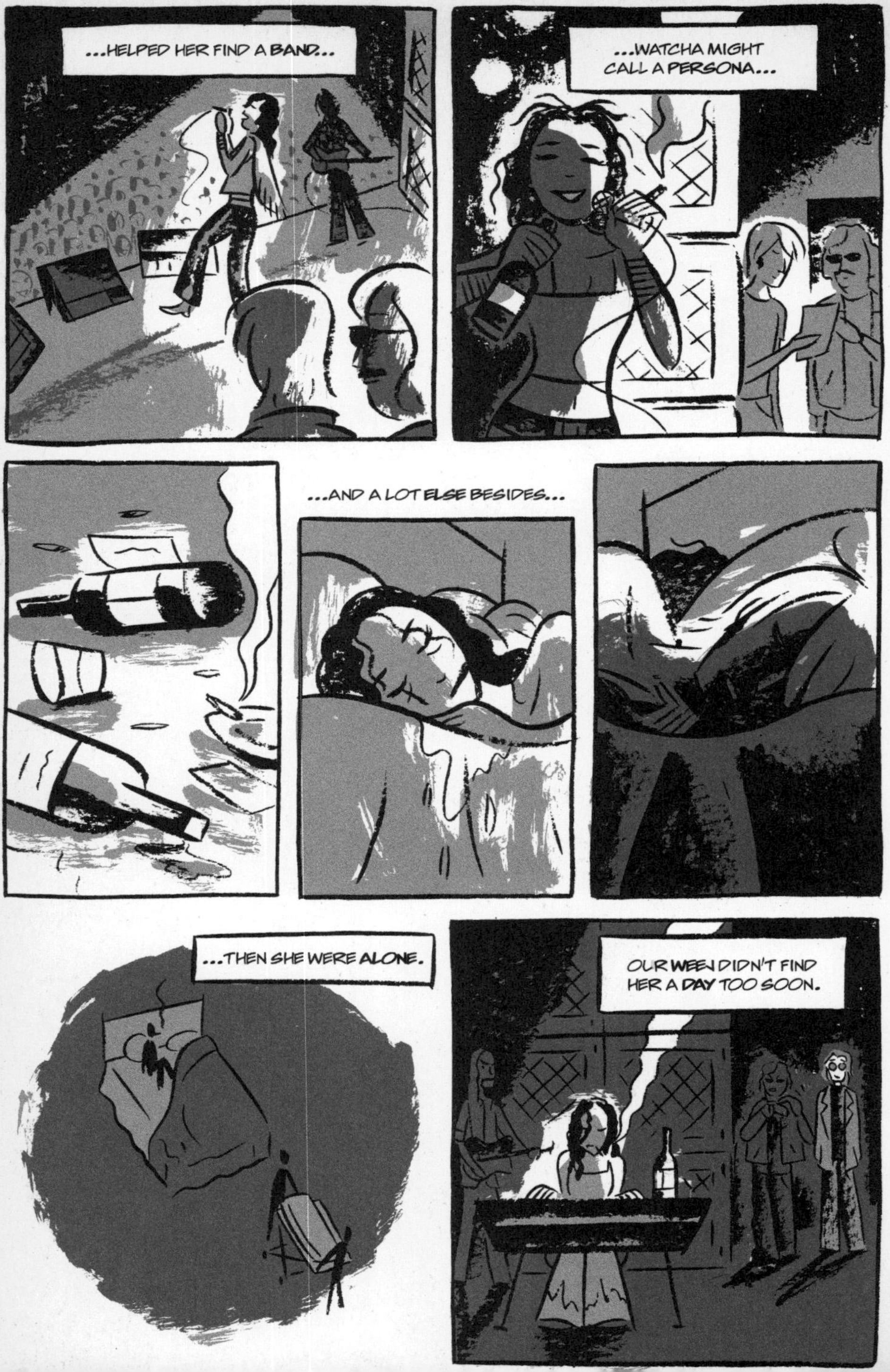
...HELPED HER FIND A BAND...
...WATCHA MIGHT CALL A PERSONA...
...AND A LOT ELSE BESIDES...
...THEN SHE WERE ALONE.
OUR WEEN DIDN'T FIND HER A DAY TOO SOON.

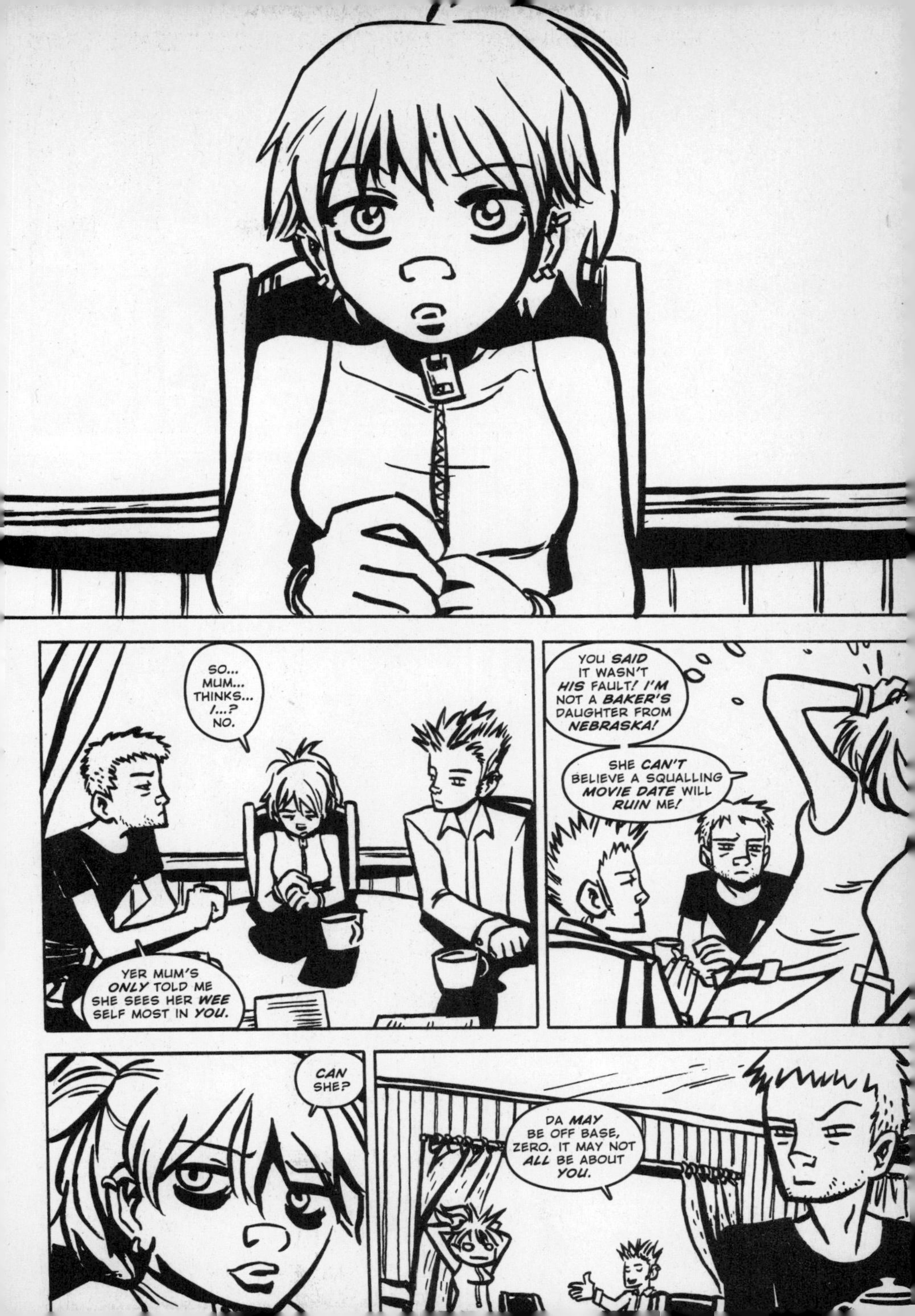
SO... MUM... THINKS... I...? NO.
YER MUM'S ONLY TOLD ME SHE SEES HER WEE SELF MOST IN YOU.
YOU SAID IT WASN'T HIS FAULT! I'M NOT A BAKER'S DAUGHTER FROM NEBRASKA!
SHE CAN'T BELIEVE A SQUALLING MOVIE DATE WILL RUIN ME!
CAN SHE?
DA MAY BE OFF BASE, ZERO. IT MAY NOT ALL BE ABOUT YOU.

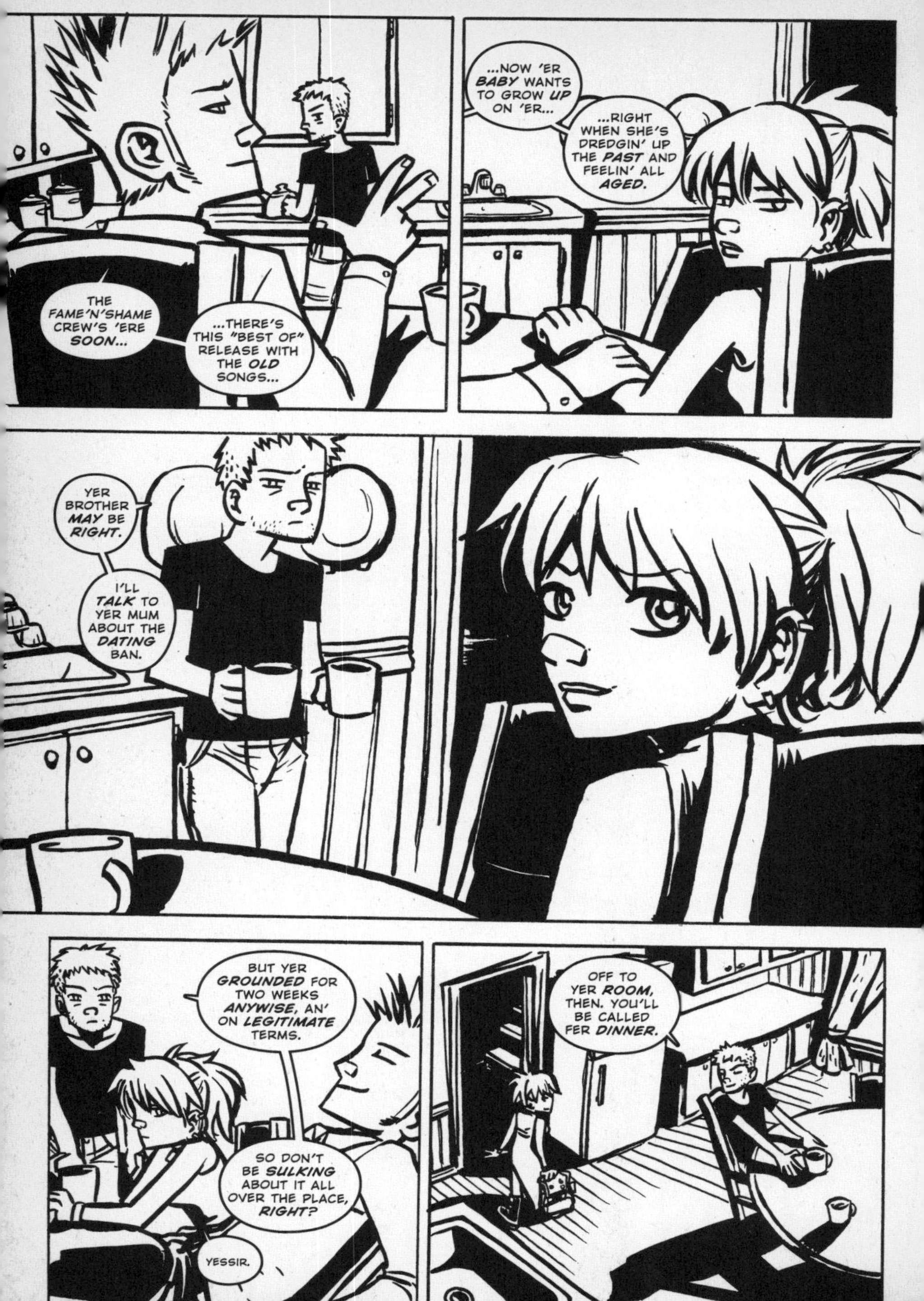
THE FAME'N'SHAME CREW'S 'ERE SOON...
...THERE'S THIS "BEST OF" RELEASE WITH THE OLD SONGS...
...NOW 'ER BABY WANTS TO GROW UP ON 'ER...
...RIGHT WHEN SHE'S DREDGIN' UP THE PAST AND FEELIN' ALL AGED.
YER BROTHER MAY BE RIGHT.
I'LL TALK TO YER MUM ABOUT THE DATING BAN.
BUT YER GROUNDED FOR TWO WEEKS ANYWISE, AN' ON LEGITIMATE TERMS.
SO DON'T BE SULKING ABOUT IT ALL OVER THE PLACE, RIGHT?
YESSIR.
OFF TO YER ROOM, THEN. YOU'LL BE CALLED FER DINNER.

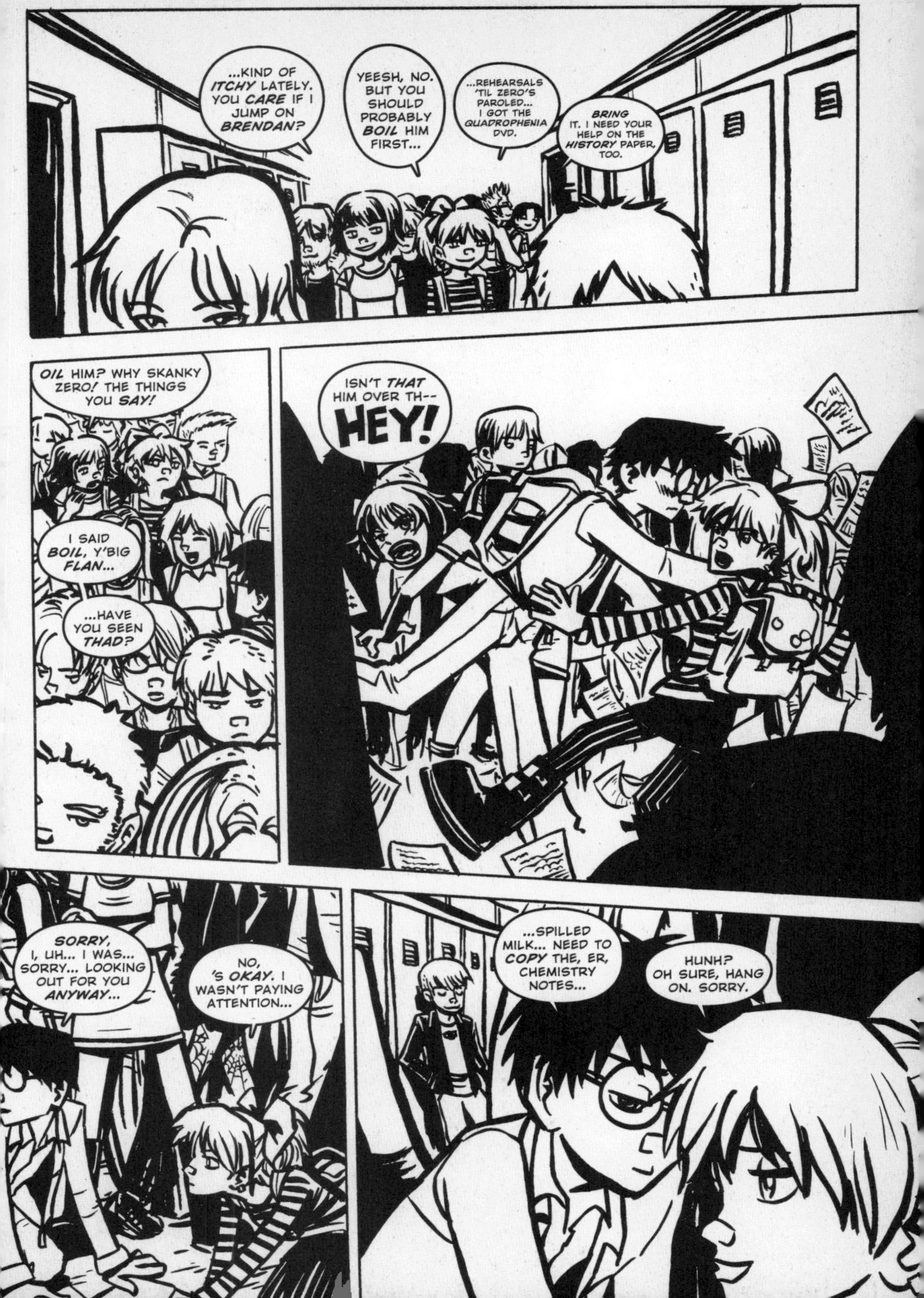

...KIND OF ITCHY LATELY. YOU CARE IF I JUMP ON BRENDAN?
YEESH, NO. BUT YOU SHOULD PROBABLY BOIL HIM FIRST...
...REHEARSALS 'TIL ZERO'S PAROLED... I GOT THE QUADROPHENIA DVD.
BRING IT. I NEED YOUR HELP ON THE HISTORY PAPER, TOO.
OIL HIM? WHY SKANKY ZERO! THE THINGS YOU SAY!
I SAID BOIL, Y'BIG FLAN...
...HAVE YOU SEEN THAD?
ISN'T THAT HIM OVER TH-- HEY!
SORRY, I, UH... I WAS... SORRY... LOOKING OUT FOR YOU ANYWAY...
NO, 'S OKAY. I WASN'T PAYING ATTENTION...
...SPILLED MILK... NEED TO COPY THE, ER, CHEMISTRY NOTES...
HUNH? OH SURE, HANG ON. SORRY.

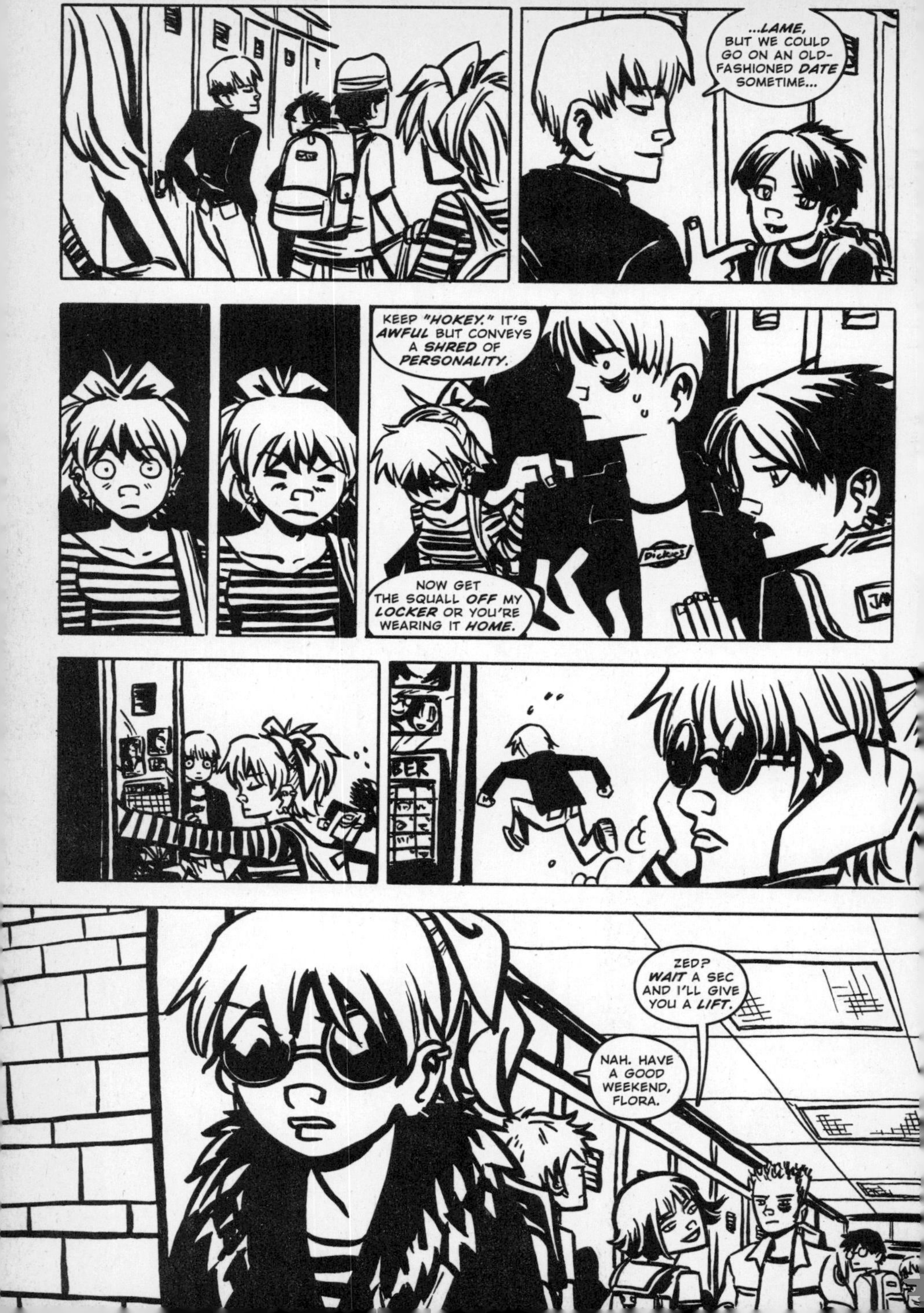
...LAME, BUT WE COULD GO ON AN OLD-FASHIONED DATE SOMETIME...
KEEP "HOKEY." IT'S AWFUL BUT CONVEYS A SHRED OF PERSONALITY.
NOW GET THE SQUALL OFF MY LOCKER OR YOU'RE WEARING IT HOME.
ZED? WAIT A SEC AND I'LL GIVE YOU A LIFT.
NAH. HAVE A GOOD WEEKEND, FLORA.

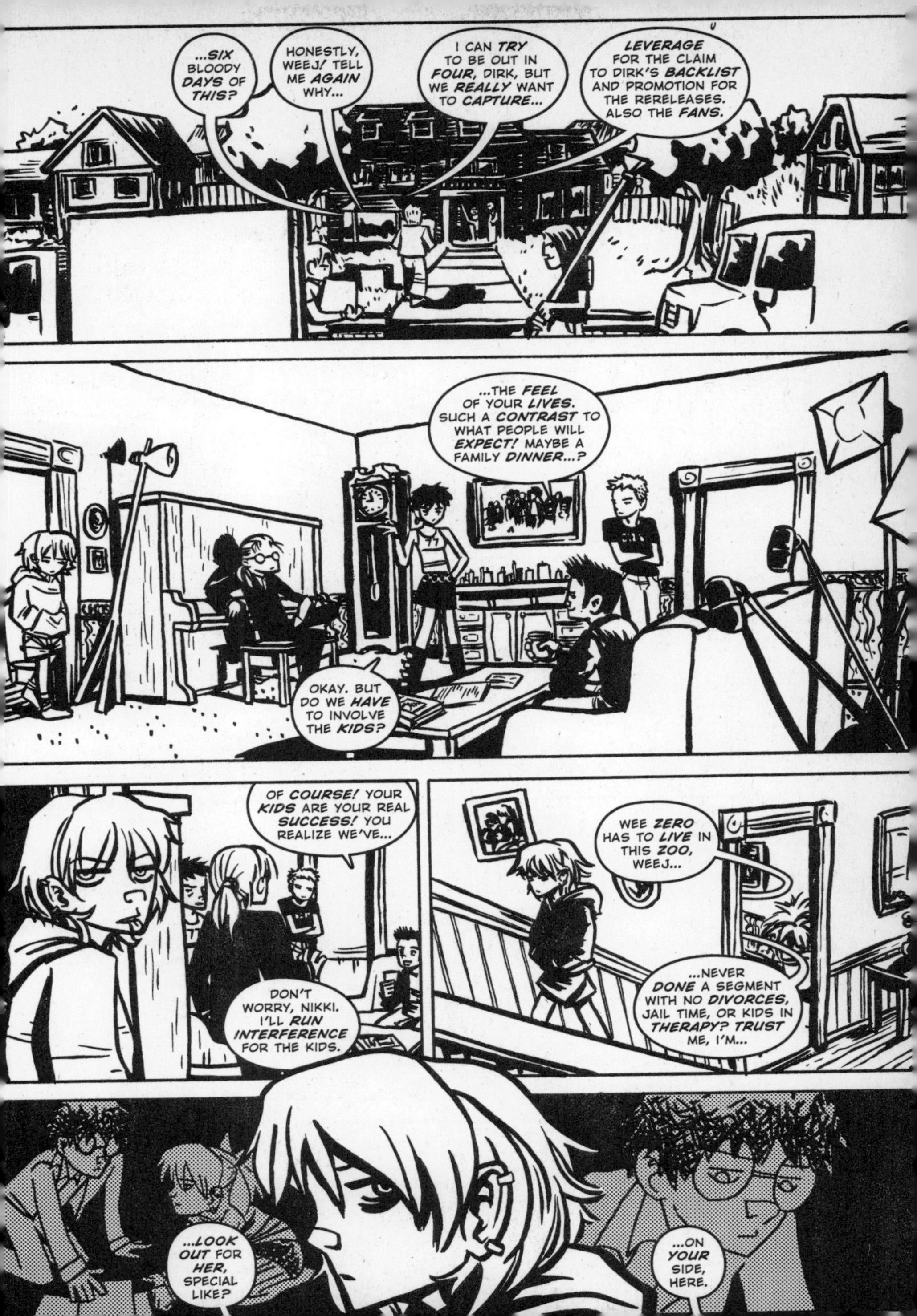
...SIX BLOODY DAYS OF THIS?
HONESTLY, WEEJ! TELL ME AGAIN WHY...
I CAN TRY TO BE OUT IN FOUR, DIRK, BUT WE REALLY WANT TO CAPTURE...
LEVERAGE FOR THE CLAIM TO DIRK'S BACKLIST AND PROMOTION FOR THE RERELEASES. ALSO THE FANS.
...THE FEEL OF YOUR LIVES. SUCH A CONTRAST TO WHAT PEOPLE WILL EXPECT! MAYBE A FAMILY DINNER...?
OKAY. BUT DO WE HAVE TO INVOLVE THE KIDS?
OF COURSE! YOUR KIDS ARE YOUR REAL SUCCESS! YOU REALIZE WE'VE...
DON'T WORRY, NIKKI. I'LL RUN INTERFERENCE FOR THE KIDS.
WEE ZERO HAS TO LIVE IN THIS ZOO, WEEJ...
...NEVER DONE A SEGMENT WITH NO DIVORCES, JAIL TIME, OR KIDS IN THERAPY? TRUST ME, I'M...
...LOOK OUT FOR HER, SPECIAL LIKE?
...ON YOUR SIDE, HERE.

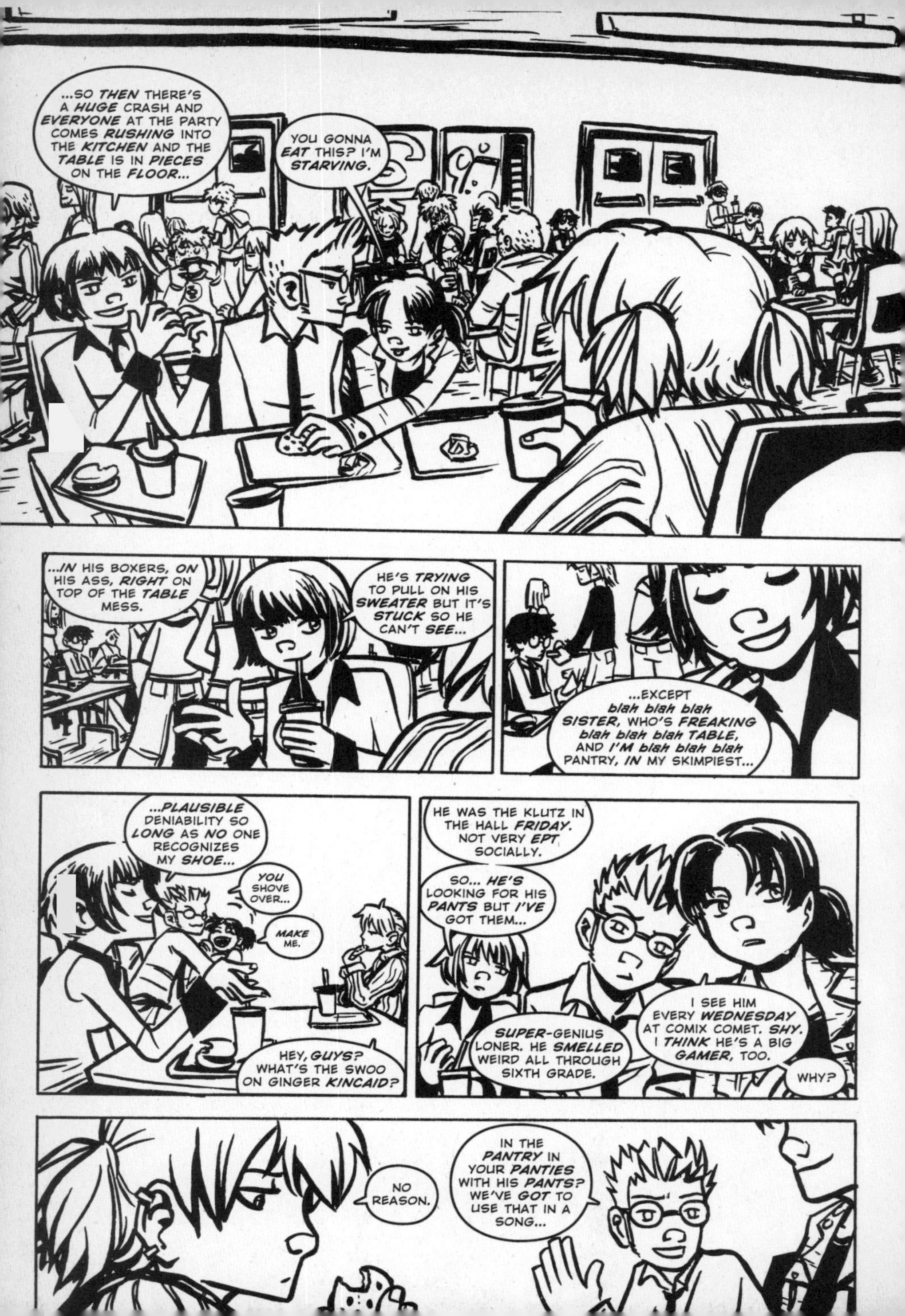
...SO THEN THERE'S A HUGE CRASH AND EVERYONE AT THE PARTY COMES RUSHING INTO THE KITCHEN AND THE TABLE IS IN PIECES ON THE FLOOR...
YOU GONNA EAT THIS? I'M STARVING.
...IN HIS BOXERS, ON HIS ASS, RIGHT ON TOP OF THE TABLE MESS.
HE'S TRYING TO PULL ON HIS SWEATER BUT IT'S STUCK SO HE CAN'T SEE...
...EXCEPT blah blah blah SISTER, WHO'S FREAKING blah blah blah TABLE, AND I'M blah blah blah PANTRY, IN MY SKIMPIEST...
...PLAUSIBLE DENIABILITY SO LONG AS NO ONE RECOGNIZES MY SHOE...
YOU SHOVE OVER...
MAKE ME.
HEY, GUYS? WHAT'S THE SWOO ON GINGER KINCAID?
HE WAS THE KLUTZ IN THE HALL FRIDAY. NOT VERY EPT SOCIALLY.
SO... HE'S LOOKING FOR HIS PANTS BUT I'VE GOT THEM...
SUPER-GENIUS LONER. HE SMELLED WEIRD ALL THROUGH SIXTH GRADE.
I SEE HIM EVERY WEDNESDAY AT COMIX COMET. SHY. I THINK HE'S A BIG GAMER, TOO.
WHY?
NO REASON.
IN THE PANTRY IN YOUR PANTIES WITH HIS PANTS? WE'VE GOT TO USE THAT IN A SONG...

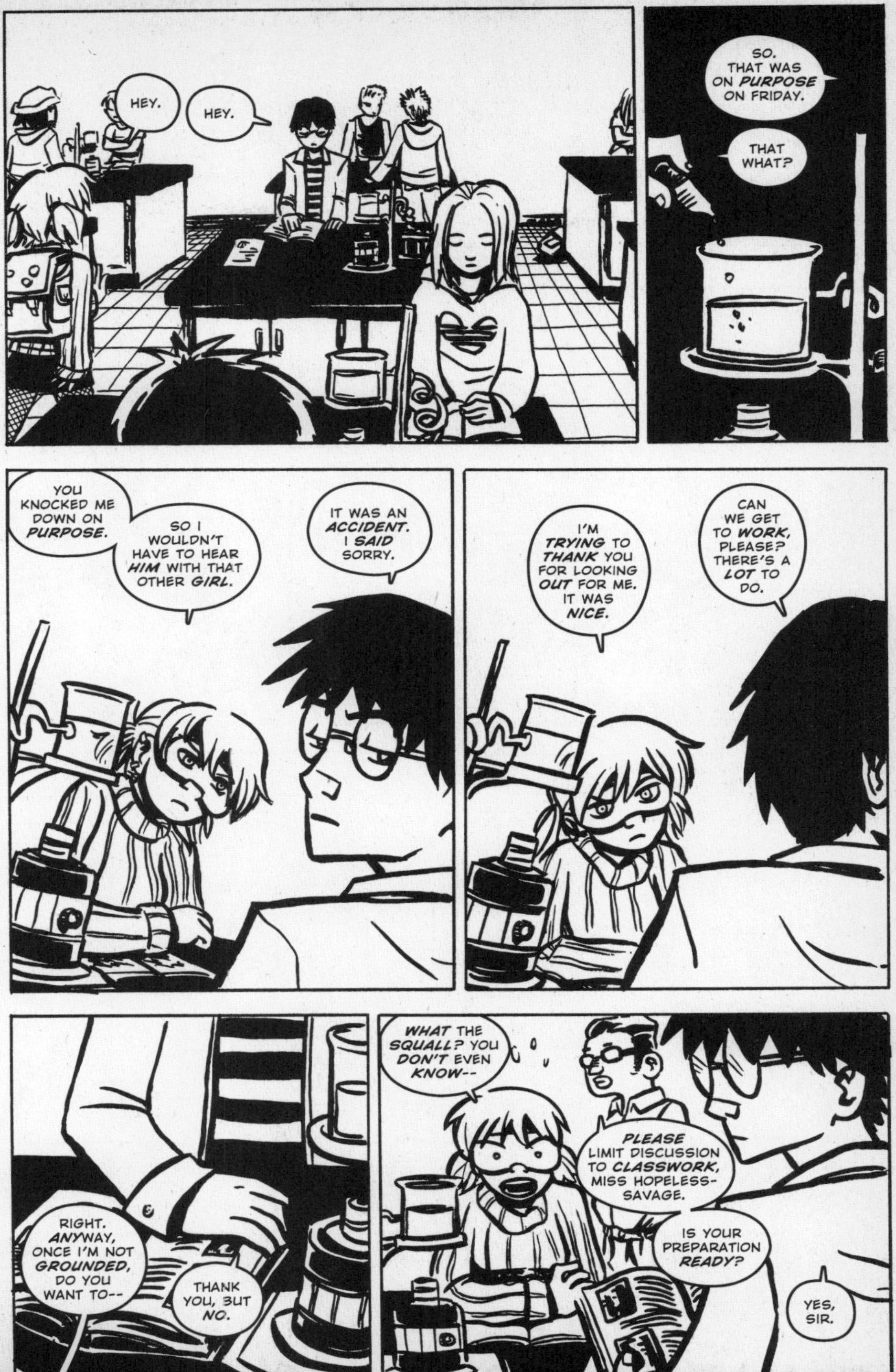
HEY.
HEY.
SO. THAT WAS ON PURPOSE ON FRIDAY.
THAT WHAT?
YOU KNOCKED ME DOWN ON PURPOSE.
SO I WOULDN'T HAVE TO HEAR HIM WITH THAT OTHER GIRL.
IT WAS AN ACCIDENT. I SAID SORRY.
I'M TRYING TO THANK YOU FOR LOOKING OUT FOR ME. IT WAS NICE.
CAN WE GET TO WORK, PLEASE? THERE'S A LOT TO DO.
RIGHT. ANYWAY, ONCE I'M NOT GROUNDED, DO YOU WANT TO--
THANK YOU, BUT NO.
WHAT THE SQUALL? YOU DON'T EVEN KNOW--
PLEASE LIMIT DISCUSSION TO CLASSWORK, MISS HOPELESS-SAVAGE.
IS YOUR PREPARATION READY?
YES, SIR.

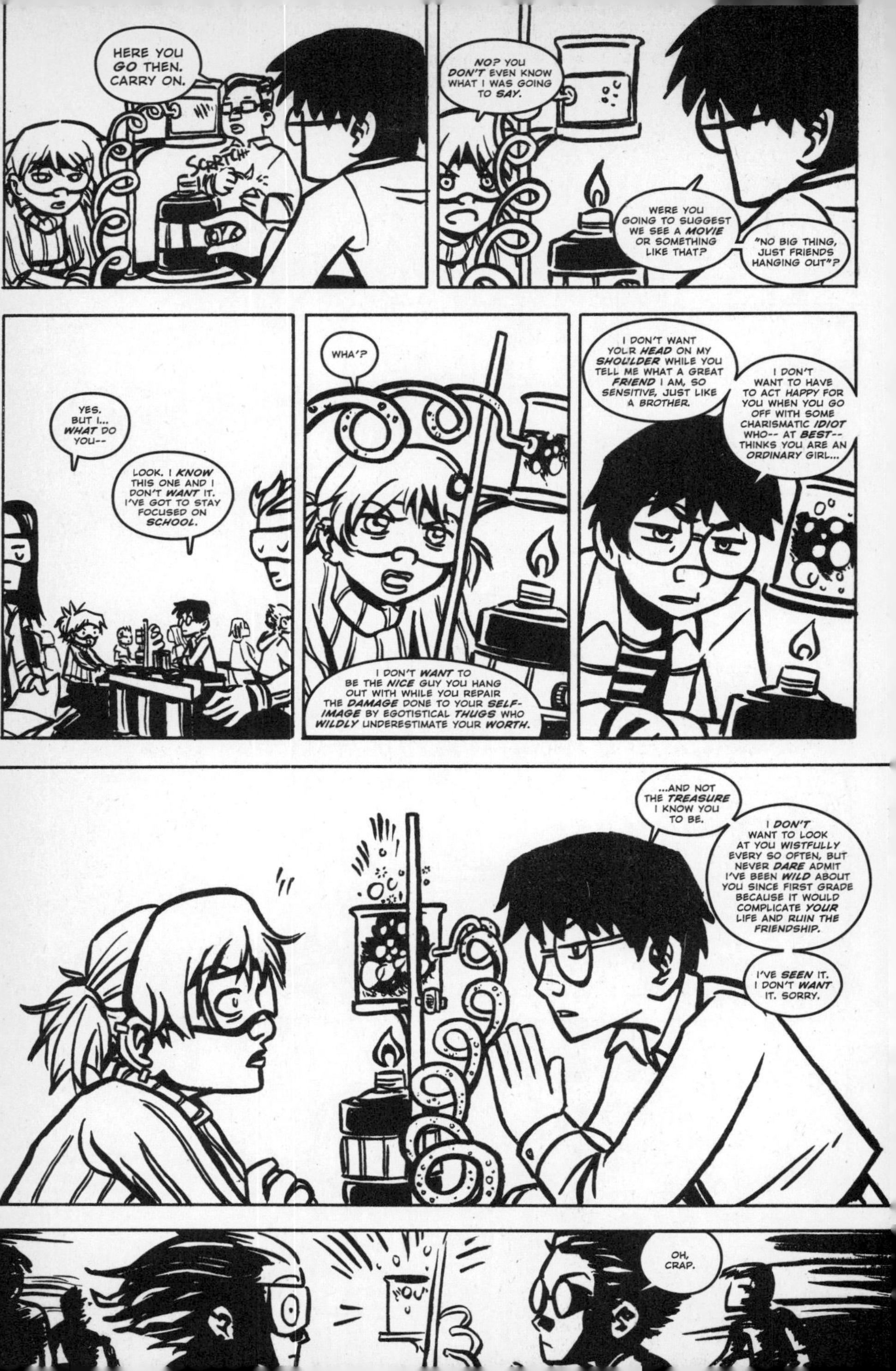
HERE YOU GO THEN. CARRY ON.
SCRRTCH
NO? YOU DON'T EVEN KNOW WHAT I WAS GOING TO SAY.
WERE YOU GOING TO SUGGEST WE SEE A MOVIE OR SOMETHING LIKE THAT?
"NO BIG THING, JUST FRIENDS HANGING OUT"?
YES. BUT I... WHAT DO YOU--
LOOK. I KNOW THIS ONE AND I DON'T WANT IT. I'VE GOT TO STAY FOCUSED ON SCHOOL.
WHA'?
I DON'T WANT TO BE THE NICE GUY YOU HANG OUT WITH WHILE YOU REPAIR THE DAMAGE DONE TO YOUR SELF-IMAGE BY EGOTISTICAL THUGS WHO WILDLY UNDERESTIMATE YOUR WORTH.
I DON'T WANT YOUR HEAD ON MY SHOULDER WHILE YOU TELL ME WHAT A GREAT FRIEND I AM, SO SENSITIVE, JUST LIKE A BROTHER.
I DON'T WANT TO HAVE TO ACT HAPPY FOR YOU WHEN YOU GO OFF WITH SOME CHARISMATIC IDIOT WHO-- AT BEST-- THINKS YOU ARE AN ORDINARY GIRL...
...AND NOT THE TREASURE I KNOW YOU TO BE.
I DON'T WANT TO LOOK AT YOU WISTFULLY EVERY SO OFTEN, BUT NEVER DARE ADMIT I'VE BEEN WILD ABOUT YOU SINCE FIRST GRADE BECAUSE IT WOULD COMPLICATE YOUR LIFE AND RUIN THE FRIENDSHIP.
I'VE SEEN IT. I DON'T WANT IT. SORRY.
OH, CRAP.

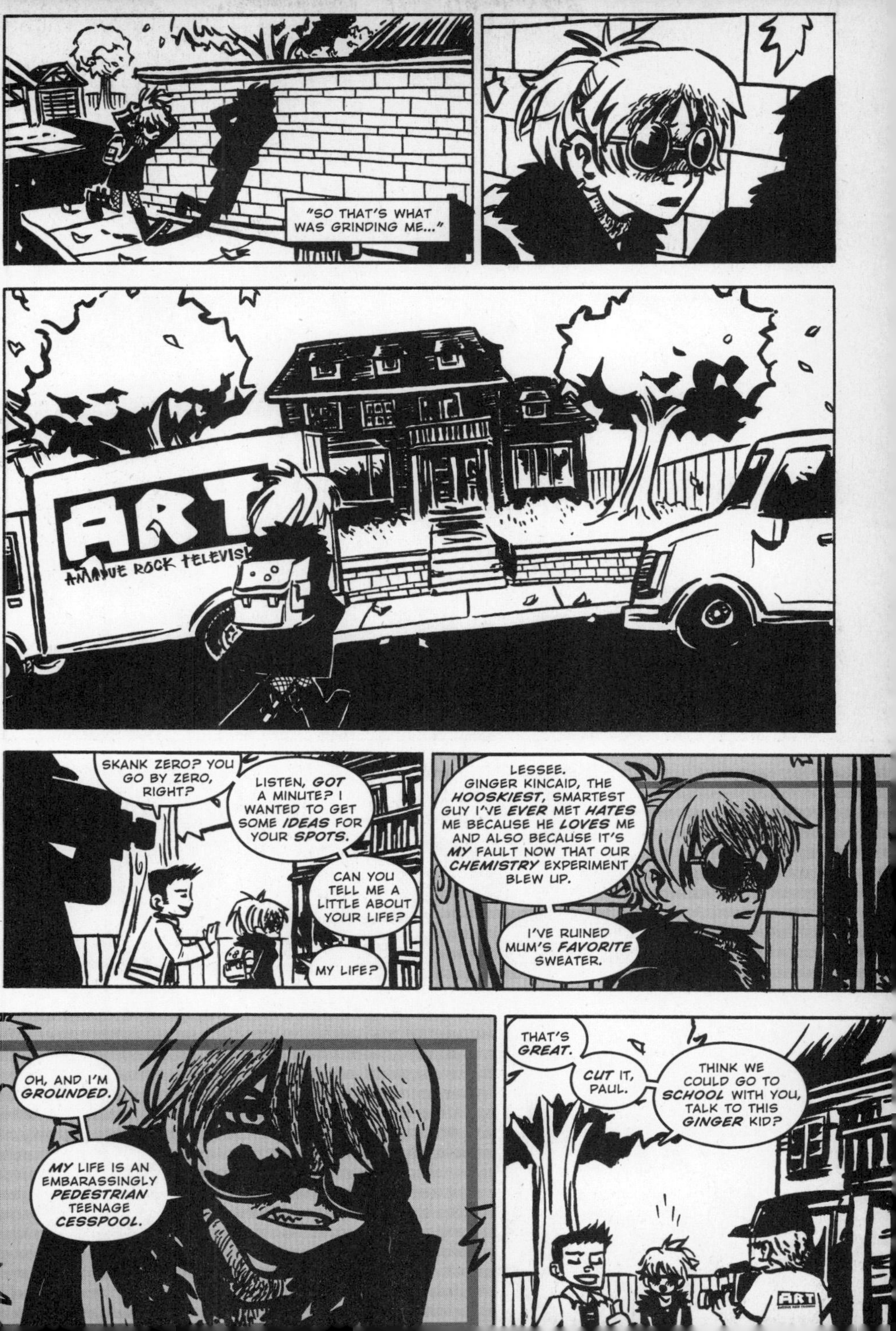
"SO THAT'S WHAT WAS GRINDING ME..."
ART
AMADUE ROCK TELEVIS
SKANK ZERO? YOU GO BY ZERO, RIGHT?
LISTEN, GOT A MINUTE? I WANTED TO GET SOME IDEAS FOR YOUR SPOTS.
CAN YOU TELL ME A LITTLE ABOUT YOUR LIFE?
MY LIFE?
LESSEE. GINGER KINCAID, THE HOOSKIEST, SMARTEST GUY I'VE EVER MET HATES ME BECAUSE HE LOVES ME AND ALSO BECAUSE IT'S MY FAULT NOW THAT OUR CHEMISTRY EXPERIMENT BLEW UP.
I'VE RUINED MUM'S FAVORITE SWEATER.
OH, AND I'M GROUNDED.
MY LIFE IS AN EMBARASSINGLY PEDESTRIAN TEENAGE CESSPOOL.
THAT'S GREAT.
CUT IT, PAUL.
THINK WE COULD GO TO SCHOOL WITH YOU, TALK TO THIS GINGER KID?
ART

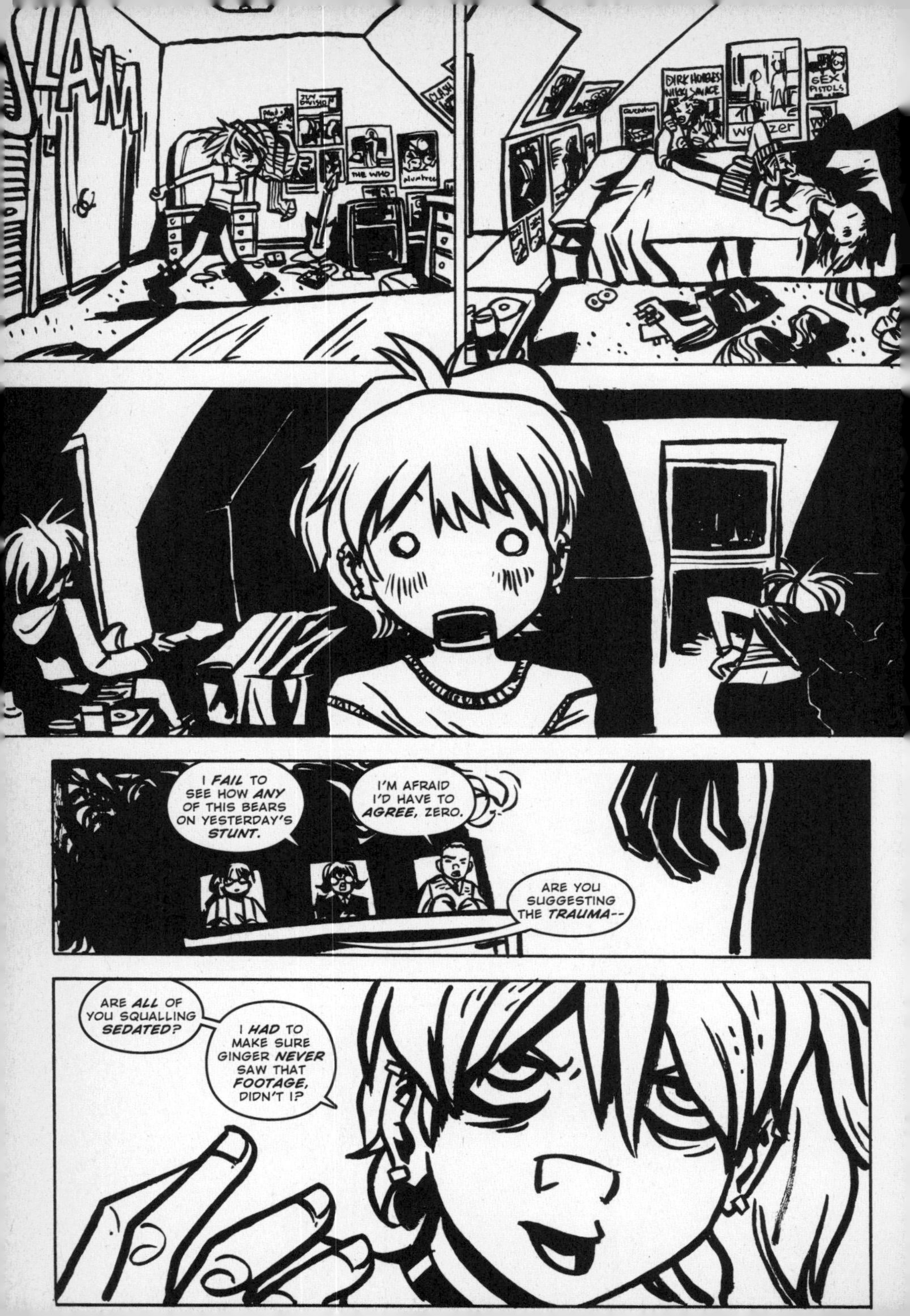
SLAM
CLASH
THE WHO
DIRK HOBBES / NIKKI SAVAGE
SEX PISTOLS
weezer
I FAIL TO SEE HOW ANY OF THIS BEARS ON YESTERDAY'S STUNT.
I'M AFRAID I'D HAVE TO AGREE, ZERO.
ARE YOU SUGGESTING THE TRAUMA--
ARE ALL OF YOU SQUALLING SEDATED?
I HAD TO MAKE SURE GINGER NEVER SAW THAT FOOTAGE, DIDN'T I?

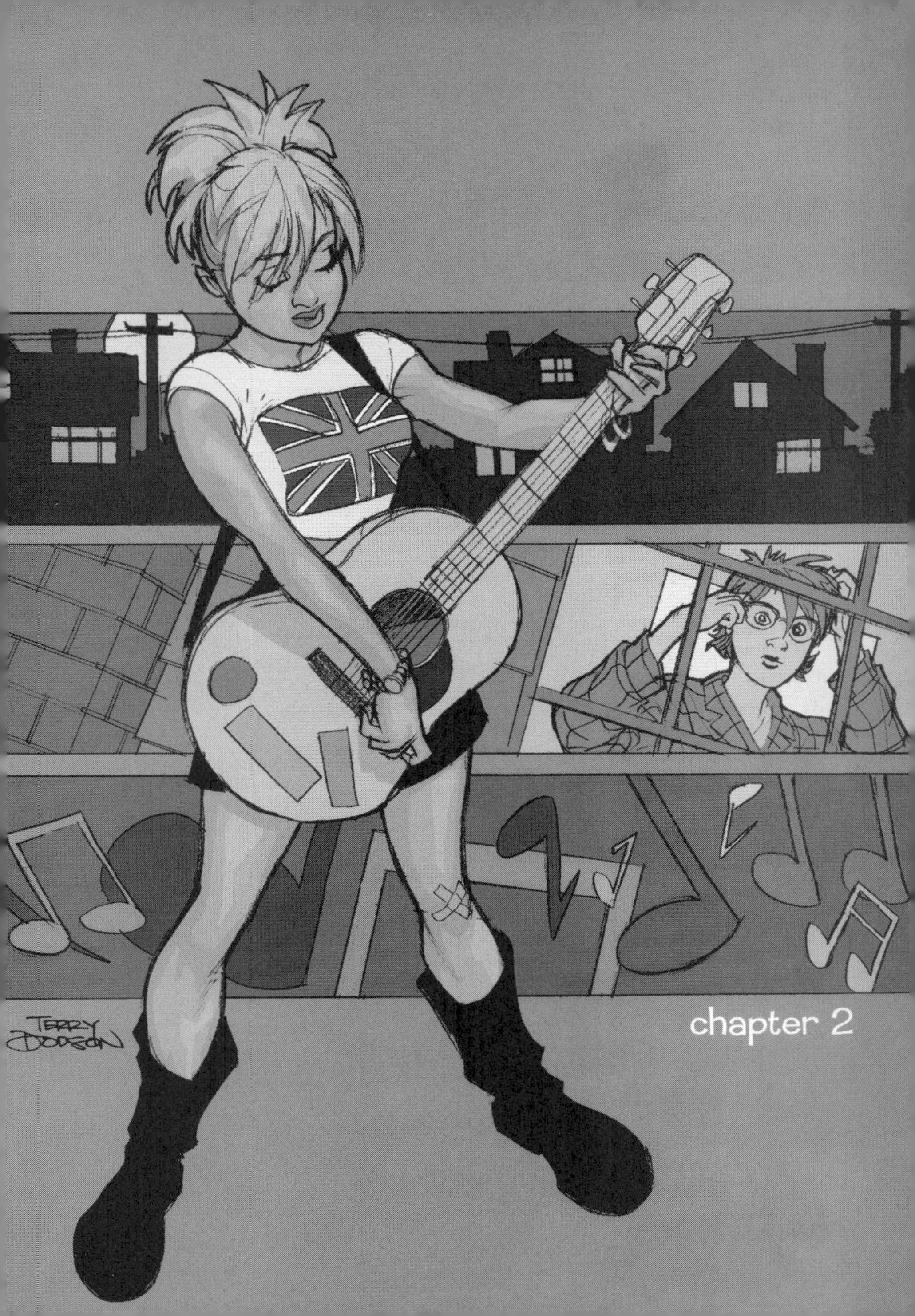
TERRY DODSON
chapter 2

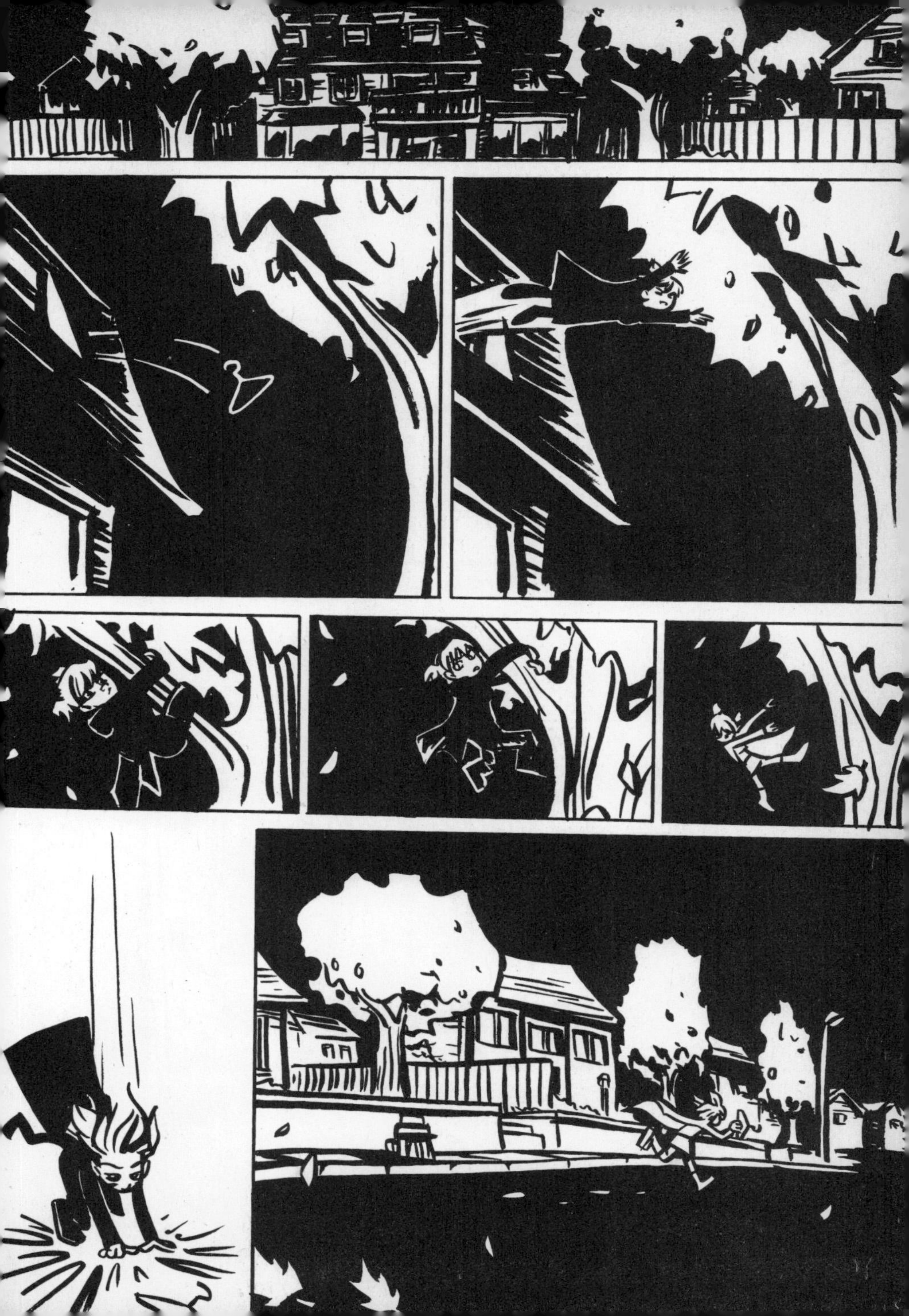

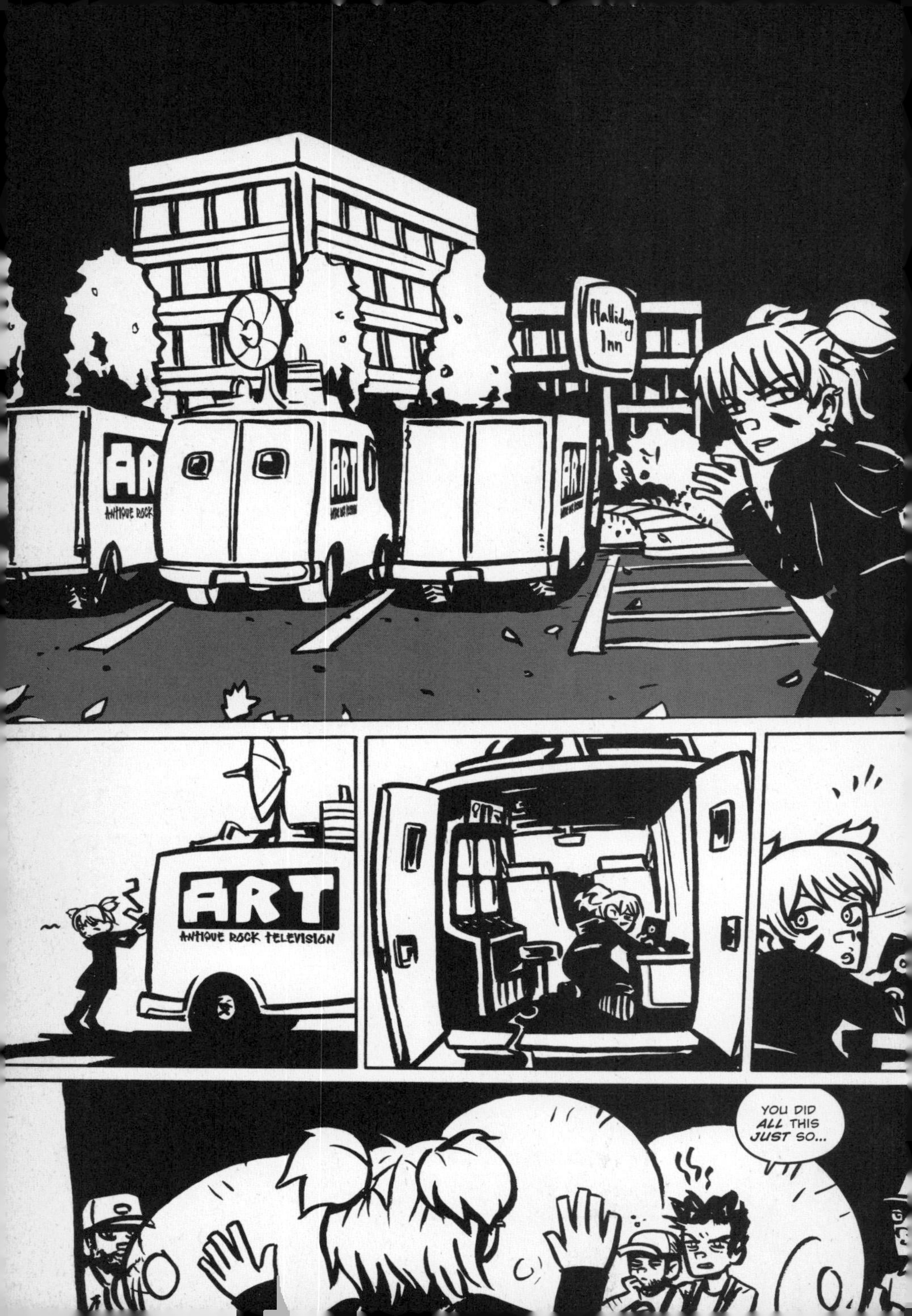
Halliday Inn
ART
ANTIQUE ROCK
ART
ART
ANTIQUE ROCK TELEVISION
YOU DID ***ALL*** THIS ***JUST*** SO...

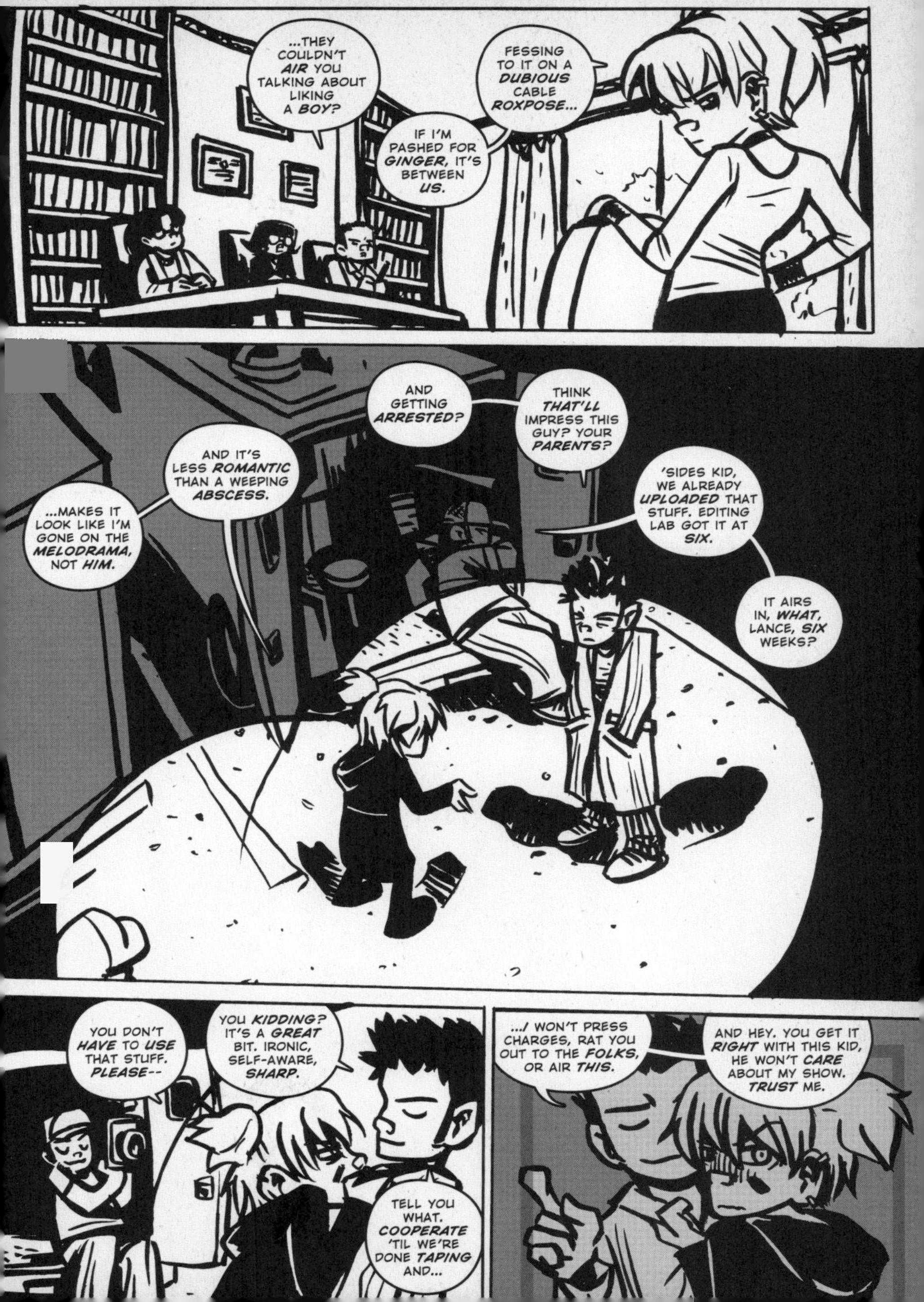
...THEY COULDN'T AIR YOU TALKING ABOUT LIKING A BOY?
FESSING TO IT ON A DUBIOUS CABLE ROXPOSE...
IF I'M PASHED FOR GINGER, IT'S BETWEEN US.
AND GETTING ARRESTED?
THINK THAT'LL IMPRESS THIS GUY? YOUR PARENTS?
AND IT'S LESS ROMANTIC THAN A WEEPING ABSCESS.
...MAKES IT LOOK LIKE I'M GONE ON THE MELODRAMA, NOT HIM.
'SIDES KID, WE ALREADY UPLOADED THAT STUFF. EDITING LAB GOT IT AT SIX.
IT AIRS IN, WHAT, LANCE, SIX WEEKS?
YOU DON'T HAVE TO USE THAT STUFF. PLEASE--
YOU KIDDING? IT'S A GREAT BIT. IRONIC, SELF-AWARE, SHARP.
TELL YOU WHAT. COOPERATE 'TIL WE'RE DONE TAPING AND...
...I WON'T PRESS CHARGES, RAT YOU OUT TO THE FOLKS, OR AIR THIS.
AND HEY. YOU GET IT RIGHT WITH THIS KID, HE WON'T CARE ABOUT MY SHOW. TRUST ME.

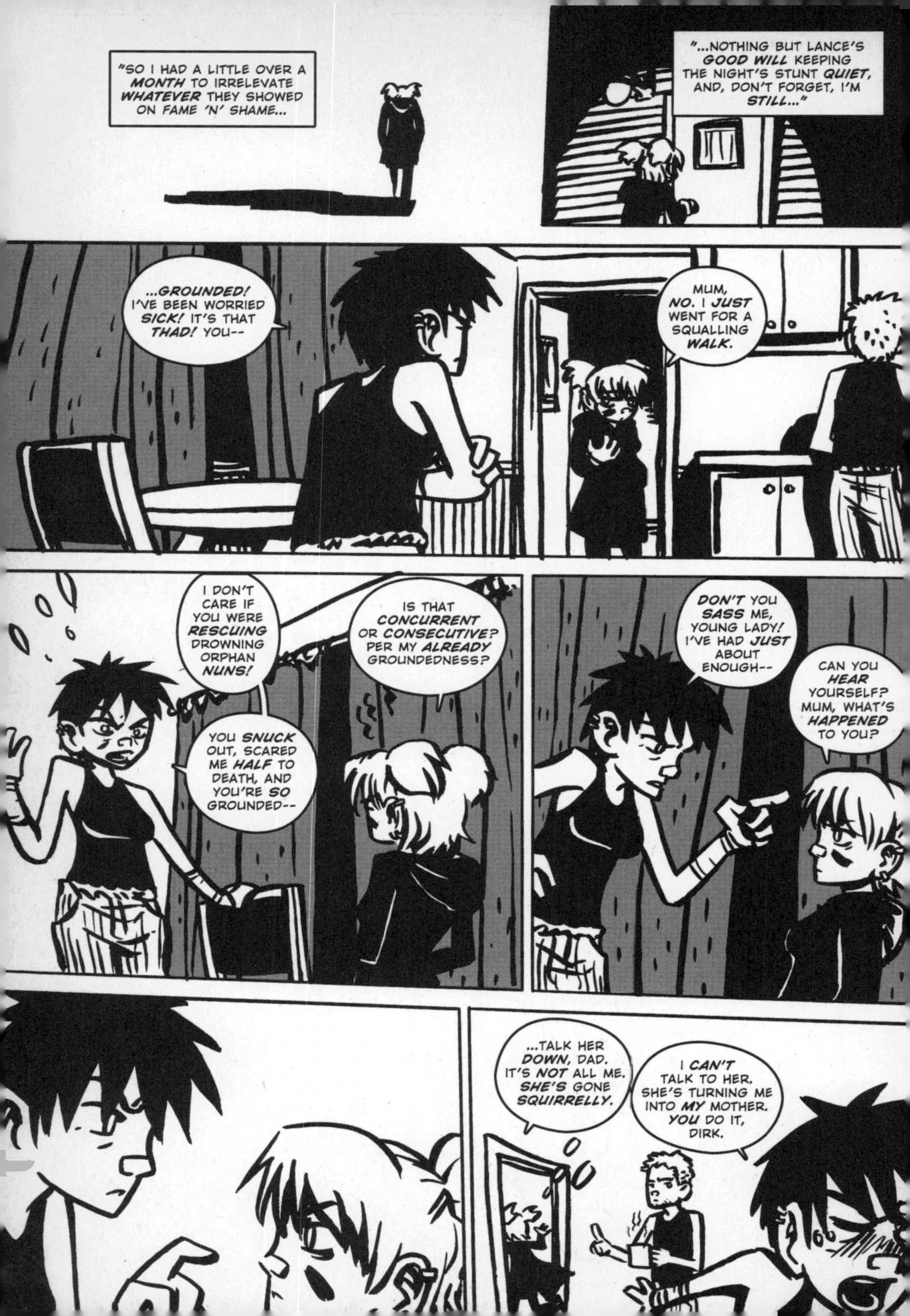
"SO I HAD A LITTLE OVER A MONTH TO IRRELEVATE WHATEVER THEY SHOWED ON FAME 'N' SHAME...
"...NOTHING BUT LANCE'S GOOD WILL KEEPING THE NIGHT'S STUNT QUIET, AND, DON'T FORGET, I'M STILL..."
...GROUNDED! I'VE BEEN WORRIED SICK! IT'S THAT THAD! YOU--
MUM, NO. I JUST WENT FOR A SQUALLING WALK.
I DON'T CARE IF YOU WERE RESCUING DROWNING ORPHAN NUNS!
IS THAT CONCURRENT OR CONSECUTIVE? PER MY ALREADY GROUNDEDNESS?
YOU SNUCK OUT, SCARED ME HALF TO DEATH, AND YOU'RE SO GROUNDED--
DON'T YOU SASS ME, YOUNG LADY! I'VE HAD JUST ABOUT ENOUGH--
CAN YOU HEAR YOURSELF? MUM, WHAT'S HAPPENED TO YOU?
...TALK HER DOWN, DAD. IT'S NOT ALL ME. SHE'S GONE SQUIRRELLY.
I CAN'T TALK TO HER. SHE'S TURNING ME INTO MY MOTHER. YOU DO IT, DIRK.

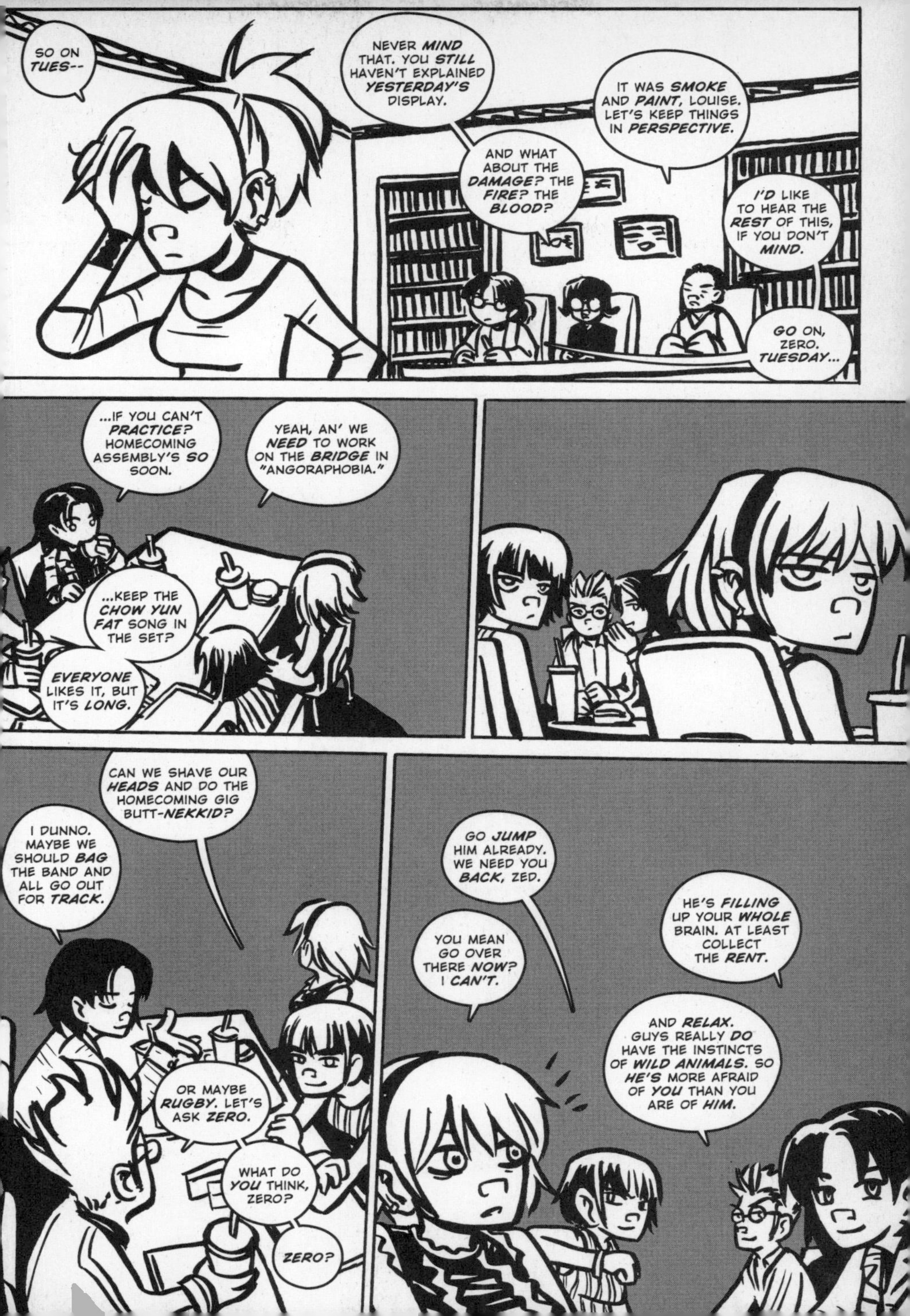
SO ON TUES--
NEVER MIND THAT. YOU STILL HAVEN'T EXPLAINED YESTERDAY'S DISPLAY.
AND WHAT ABOUT THE DAMAGE? THE FIRE? THE BLOOD?
IT WAS SMOKE AND PAINT, LOUISE. LET'S KEEP THINGS IN PERSPECTIVE.
I'D LIKE TO HEAR THE REST OF THIS, IF YOU DON'T MIND.
GO ON, ZERO. TUESDAY...
...IF YOU CAN'T PRACTICE? HOMECOMING ASSEMBLY'S SO SOON.
YEAH, AN' WE NEED TO WORK ON THE BRIDGE IN "ANGORAPHOBIA."
...KEEP THE CHOW YUN FAT SONG IN THE SET?
EVERYONE LIKES IT, BUT IT'S LONG.
I DUNNO. MAYBE WE SHOULD BAG THE BAND AND ALL GO OUT FOR TRACK.
CAN WE SHAVE OUR HEADS AND DO THE HOMECOMING GIG BUTT-NEKKID?
OR MAYBE RUGBY. LET'S ASK ZERO.
WHAT DO YOU THINK, ZERO?
ZERO?
GO JUMP HIM ALREADY. WE NEED YOU BACK, ZED.
YOU MEAN GO OVER THERE NOW? I CAN'T.
HE'S FILLING UP YOUR WHOLE BRAIN. AT LEAST COLLECT THE RENT.
AND RELAX. GUYS REALLY DO HAVE THE INSTINCTS OF WILD ANIMALS. SO HE'S MORE AFRAID OF YOU THAN YOU ARE OF HIM.

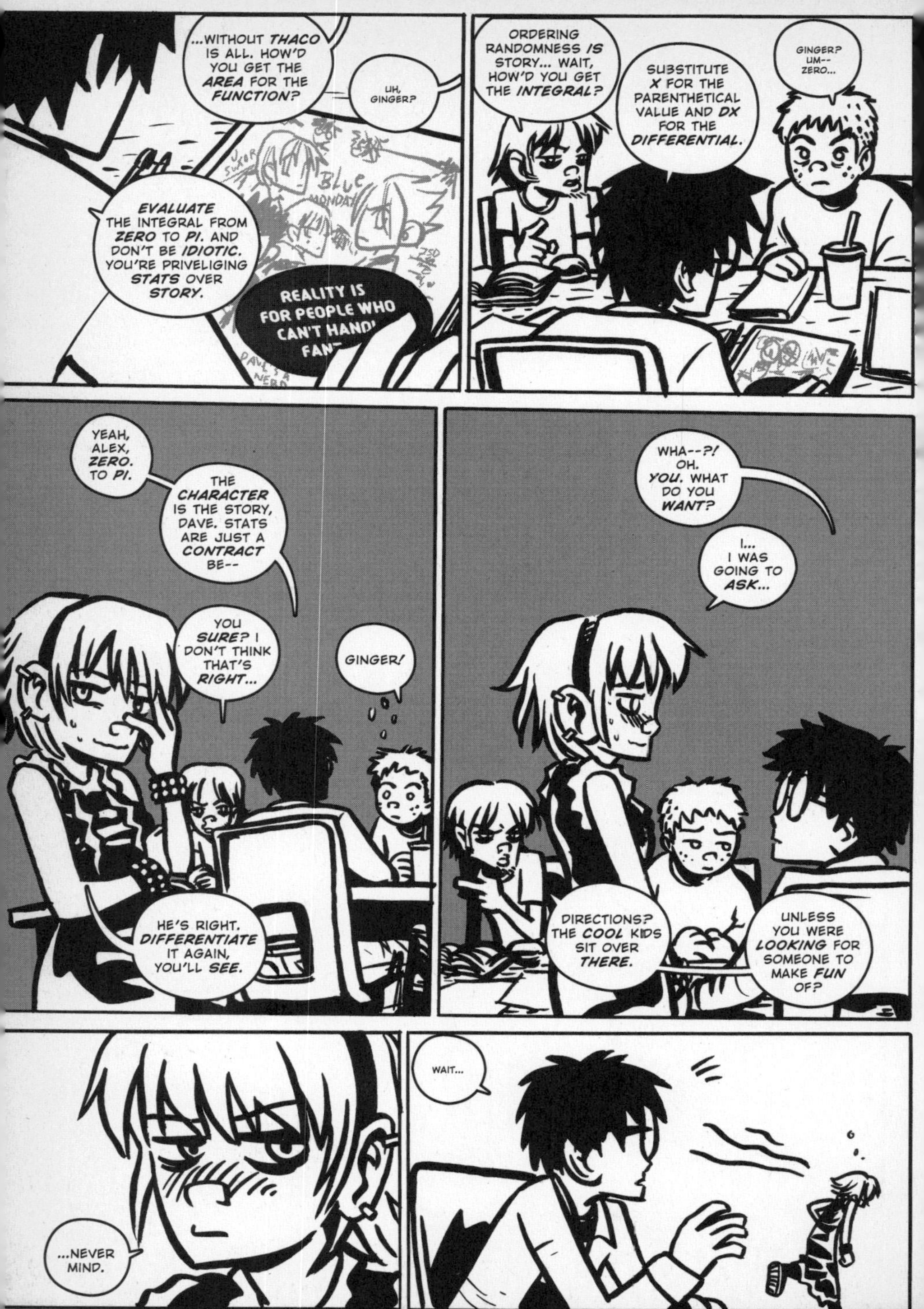
...WITHOUT THACO IS ALL. HOW'D YOU GET THE AREA FOR THE FUNCTION?
UH, GINGER?
EVALUATE THE INTEGRAL FROM ZERO TO PI. AND DON'T BE IDIOTIC. YOU'RE PRIVELIGING STATS OVER STORY.
REALITY IS FOR PEOPLE WHO CAN'T HAND FAN
ORDERING RANDOMNESS IS STORY... WAIT, HOW'D YOU GET THE INTEGRAL?
SUBSTITUTE X FOR THE PARENTHETICAL VALUE AND DX FOR THE DIFFERENTIAL.
GINGER? UM-- ZERO...
YEAH, ALEX, ZERO. TO PI.
THE CHARACTER IS THE STORY, DAVE. STATS ARE JUST A CONTRACT BE--
YOU SURE? I DON'T THINK THAT'S RIGHT...
GINGER!
HE'S RIGHT. DIFFERENTIATE IT AGAIN, YOU'LL SEE.
WHA--?! OH. YOU. WHAT DO YOU WANT?
I... I WAS GOING TO ASK...
DIRECTIONS? THE COOL KIDS SIT OVER THERE.
UNLESS YOU WERE LOOKING FOR SOMEONE TO MAKE FUN OF?
...NEVER MIND.
WAIT...

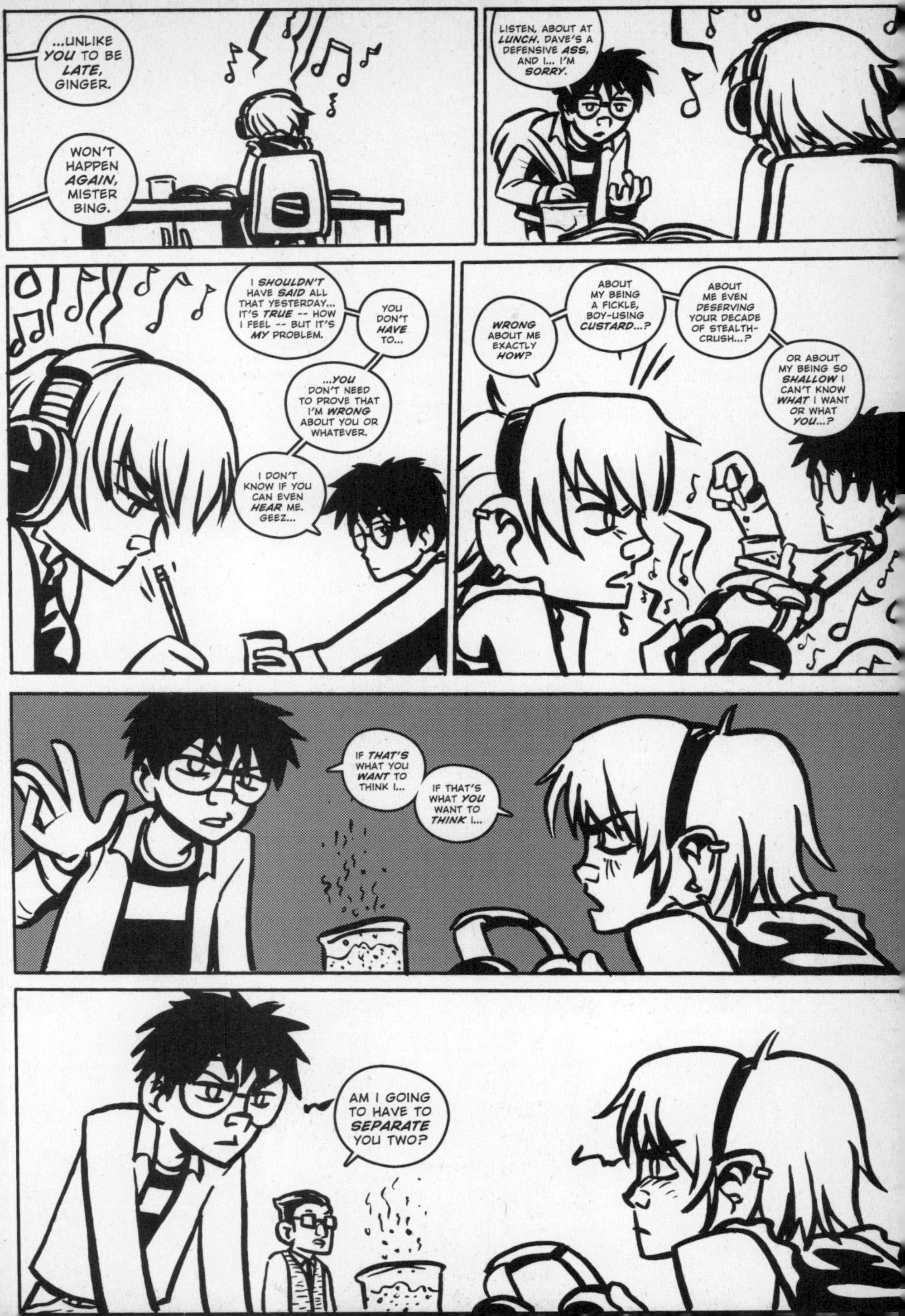
...UNLIKE *YOU* TO BE *LATE*, GINGER.
WON'T HAPPEN *AGAIN*, MISTER BING.
LISTEN, ABOUT AT *LUNCH*. DAVE'S A DEFENSIVE *ASS*, AND I... I'M *SORRY*.
I *SHOULDN'T* HAVE *SAID* ALL THAT YESTERDAY... IT'S *TRUE* -- HOW I FEEL -- BUT IT'S *MY* PROBLEM.
YOU DON'T *HAVE* TO...
...*YOU* DON'T NEED TO PROVE THAT I'M *WRONG* ABOUT YOU OR WHATEVER.
I DON'T KNOW IF YOU CAN EVEN *HEAR* ME. GEEZ...
WRONG ABOUT ME EXACTLY *HOW*?
ABOUT MY BEING A FICKLE, BOY-USING *CUSTARD*...?
ABOUT ME EVEN DESERVING YOUR DECADE OF STEALTH-CRUSH...?
OR ABOUT MY BEING SO *SHALLOW* I CAN'T KNOW *WHAT* I WANT OR WHAT *YOU*...?
IF *THAT'S* WHAT YOU *WANT* TO THINK I...
IF THAT'S WHAT *YOU* WANT TO *THINK* I...
AM I GOING TO HAVE TO *SEPARATE* YOU TWO?

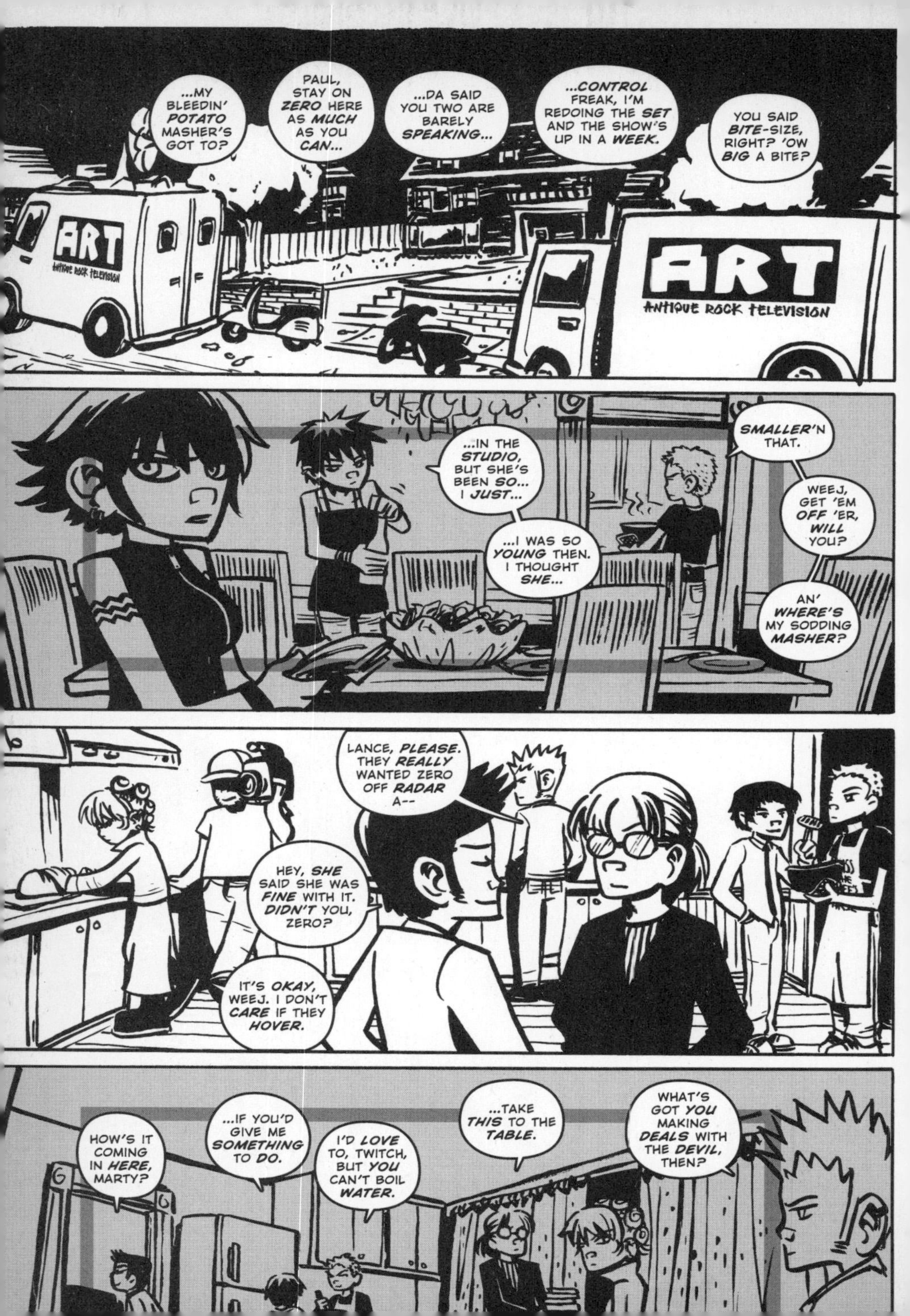

...MY BLEEDIN' POTATO MASHER'S GOT TO?
PAUL, STAY ON ZERO HERE AS MUCH AS YOU CAN...
...DA SAID YOU TWO ARE BARELY SPEAKING...
...CONTROL FREAK, I'M REDOING THE SET AND THE SHOW'S UP IN A WEEK.
YOU SAID BITE-SIZE, RIGHT? 'OW BIG A BITE?
ART
ANTIQUE ROCK TELEVISION
ART
ANTIQUE ROCK TELEVISION
...IN THE STUDIO, BUT SHE'S BEEN SO... I JUST...
...I WAS SO YOUNG THEN. I THOUGHT SHE...
SMALLER'N THAT.
WEEJ, GET 'EM OFF 'ER, WILL YOU?
AN' WHERE'S MY SODDING MASHER?
LANCE, PLEASE. THEY REALLY WANTED ZERO OFF RADAR A--
HEY, SHE SAID SHE WAS FINE WITH IT. DIDN'T YOU, ZERO?
IT'S OKAY, WEEJ. I DON'T CARE IF THEY HOVER.
HOW'S IT COMING IN HERE, MARTY?
...IF YOU'D GIVE ME SOMETHING TO DO.
I'D LOVE TO, TWITCH, BUT YOU CAN'T BOIL WATER.
...TAKE THIS TO THE TABLE.
WHAT'S GOT YOU MAKING DEALS WITH THE DEVIL, THEN?

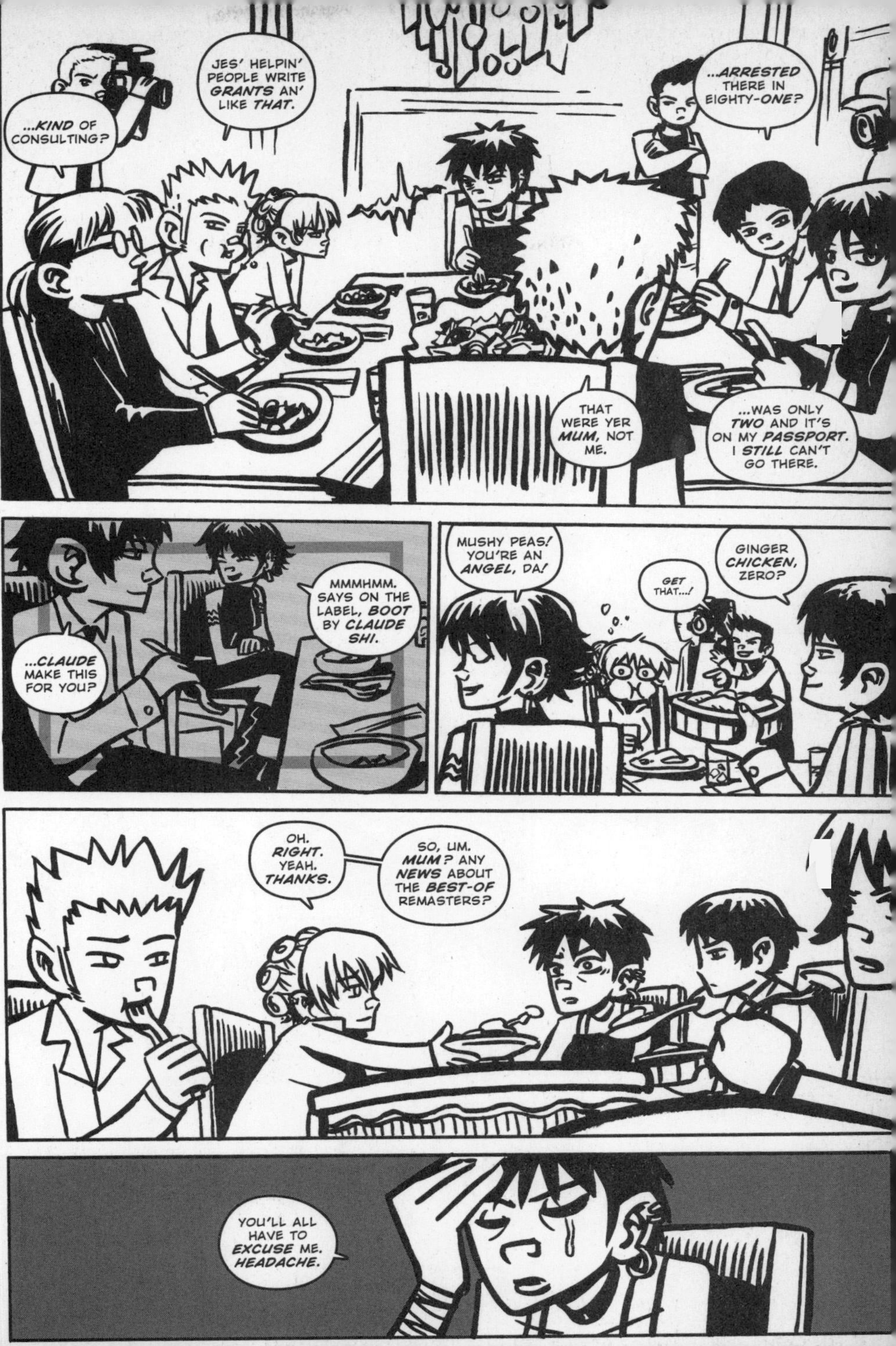
...KIND OF CONSULTING?
JES' HELPIN' PEOPLE WRITE GRANTS AN' LIKE THAT.
...ARRESTED THERE IN EIGHTY-ONE?
THAT WERE YER MUM, NOT ME.
...WAS ONLY TWO AND IT'S ON MY PASSPORT. I STILL CAN'T GO THERE.
...CLAUDE MAKE THIS FOR YOU?
MMMHMM. SAYS ON THE LABEL, BOOT BY CLAUDE SHI.
MUSHY PEAS! YOU'RE AN ANGEL, DA!
GET THAT...!
GINGER CHICKEN, ZERO?
OH. RIGHT. YEAH. THANKS.
SO, UM. MUM? ANY NEWS ABOUT THE BEST-OF REMASTERS?
YOU'LL ALL HAVE TO EXCUSE ME. HEADACHE.

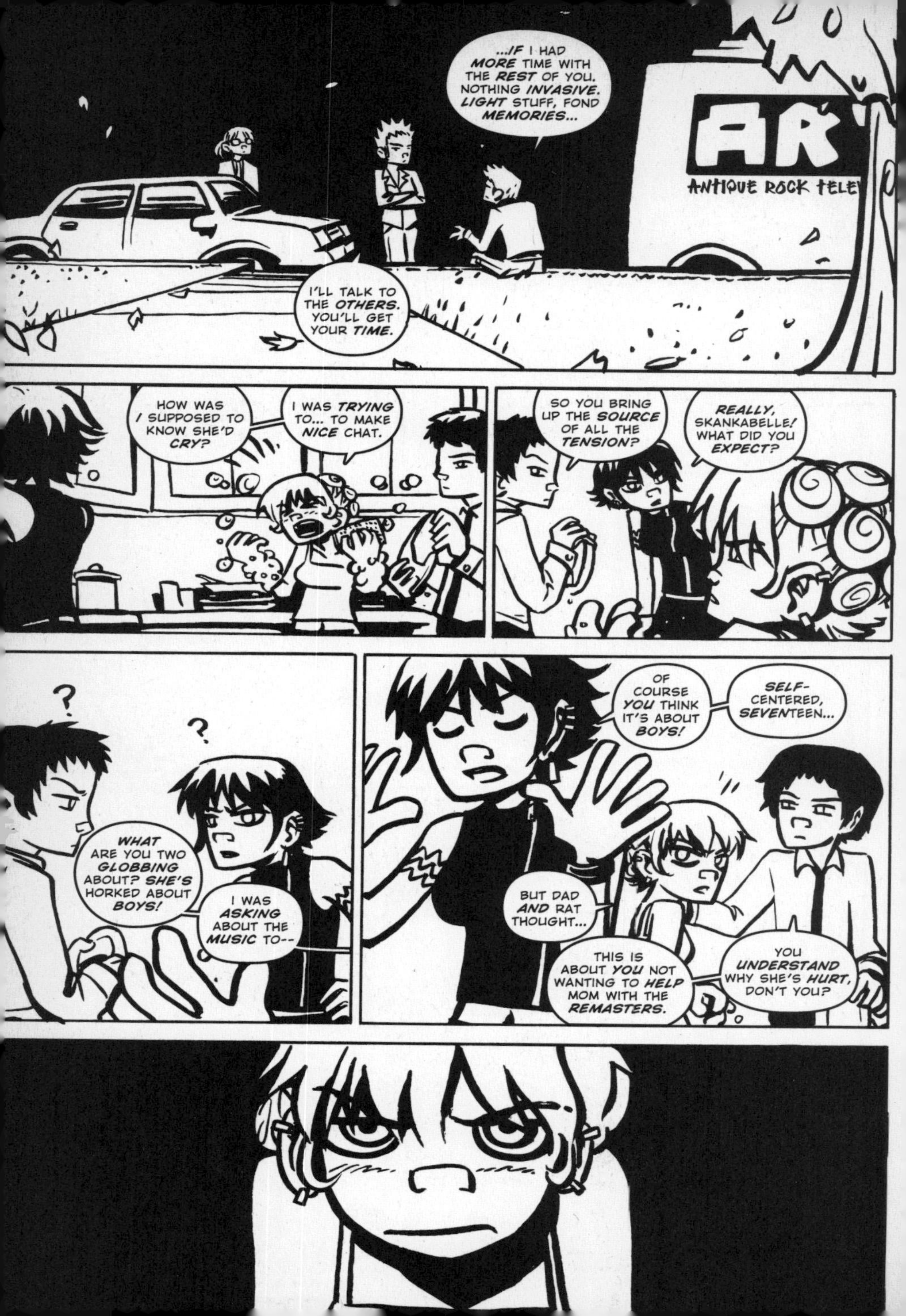
...IF I HAD MORE TIME WITH THE REST OF YOU. NOTHING INVASIVE. LIGHT STUFF, FOND MEMORIES...
AR
ANTIQUE ROCK TELE
I'LL TALK TO THE OTHERS. YOU'LL GET YOUR TIME.
HOW WAS I SUPPOSED TO KNOW SHE'D CRY?
I WAS TRYING TO... TO MAKE NICE CHAT.
SO YOU BRING UP THE SOURCE OF ALL THE TENSION?
REALLY, SKANKABELLE! WHAT DID YOU EXPECT?
?
?
WHAT ARE YOU TWO GLOBBING ABOUT? SHE'S HORKED ABOUT BOYS!
I WAS ASKING ABOUT THE MUSIC TO--
OF COURSE YOU THINK IT'S ABOUT BOYS!
SELF-CENTERED, SEVENTEEN...
BUT DAD AND RAT THOUGHT...
THIS IS ABOUT YOU NOT WANTING TO HELP MOM WITH THE REMASTERS.
YOU UNDERSTAND WHY SHE'S HURT, DON'T YOU?

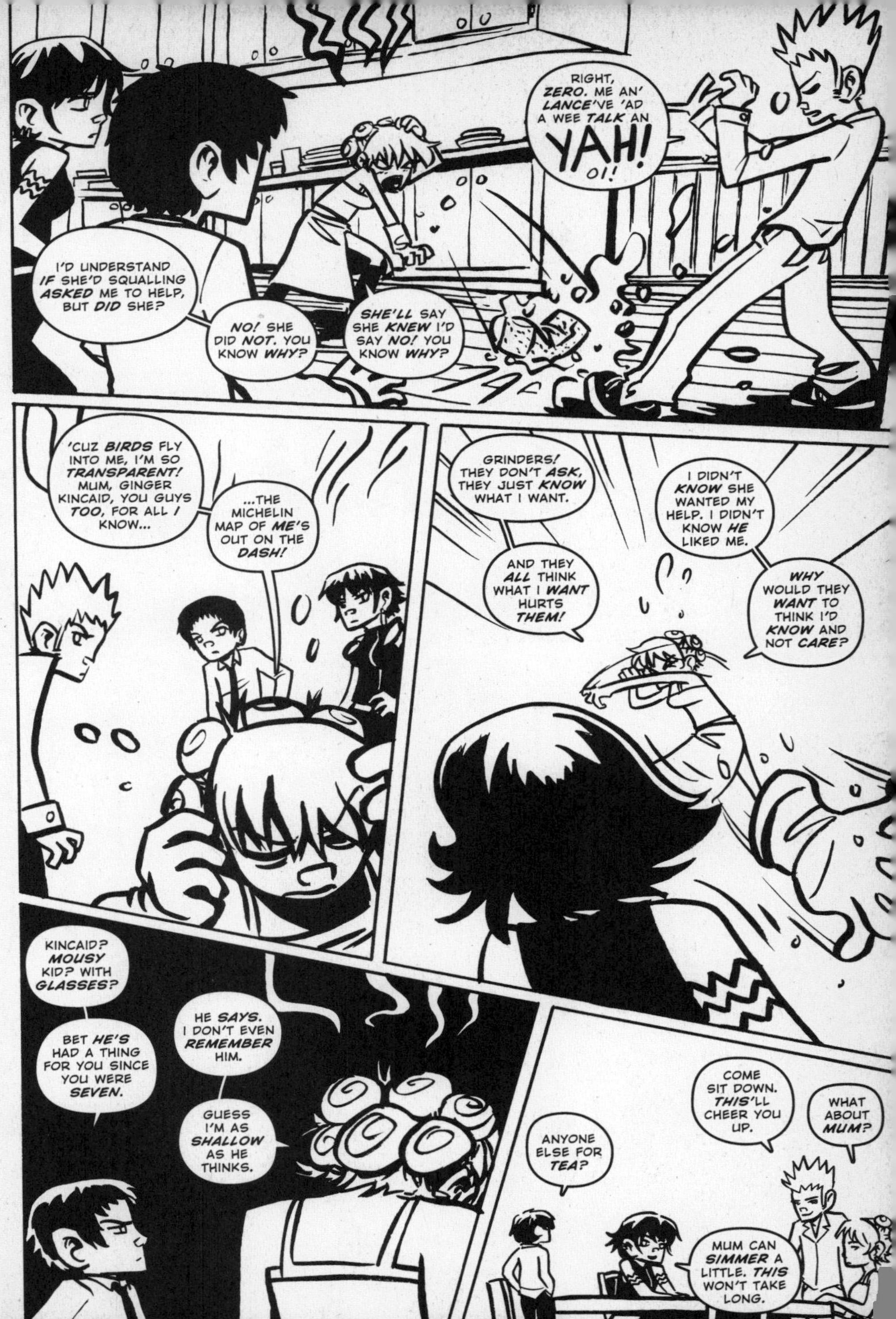
RIGHT, ZERO. ME AN' LANCE'VE 'AD A WEE TALK AN
YAH!
OI!
I'D UNDERSTAND IF SHE'D SQUALLING ASKED ME TO HELP, BUT DID SHE?
NO! SHE DID NOT. YOU KNOW WHY?
SHE'LL SAY SHE KNEW I'D SAY NO! YOU KNOW WHY?
'CUZ BIRDS FLY INTO ME, I'M SO TRANSPARENT! MUM, GINGER KINCAID, YOU GUYS TOO, FOR ALL I KNOW...
...THE MICHELIN MAP OF ME'S OUT ON THE DASH!
GRINDERS! THEY DON'T ASK, THEY JUST KNOW WHAT I WANT.
AND THEY ALL THINK WHAT I WANT HURTS THEM!
I DIDN'T KNOW SHE WANTED MY HELP. I DIDN'T KNOW HE LIKED ME.
WHY WOULD THEY WANT TO THINK I'D KNOW AND NOT CARE?
KINCAID? MOUSY KID? WITH GLASSES?
BET HE'S HAD A THING FOR YOU SINCE YOU WERE SEVEN.
HE SAYS. I DON'T EVEN REMEMBER HIM.
GUESS I'M AS SHALLOW AS HE THINKS.
ANYONE ELSE FOR TEA?
COME SIT DOWN. THIS'LL CHEER YOU UP.
WHAT ABOUT MUM?
MUM CAN SIMMER A LITTLE. THIS WON'T TAKE LONG.

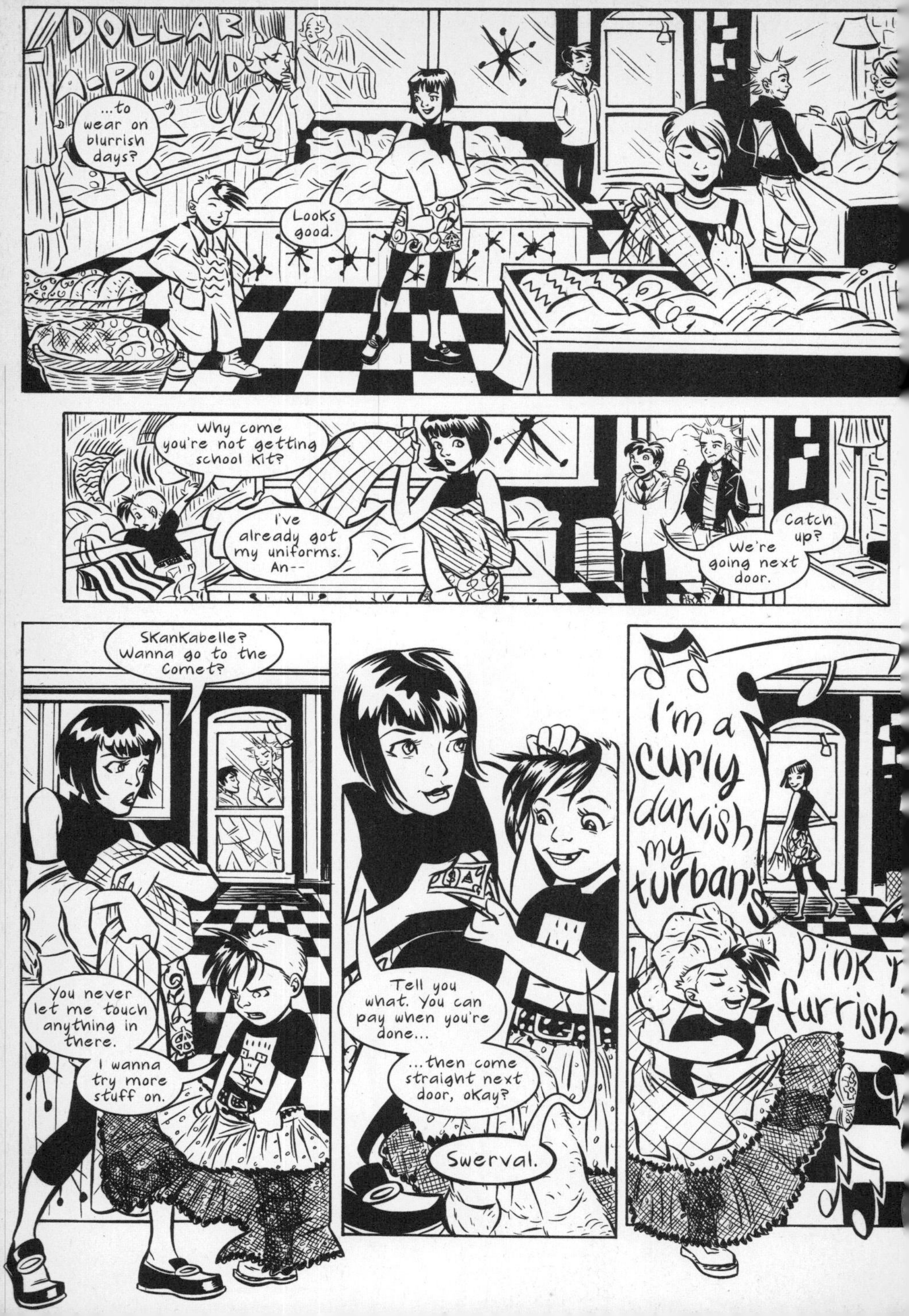
DOLLAR A-POUND
...to wear on blurrish days?
Looks good.
Why come you're not getting school kit?
I've already got my uniforms. An--
We're going next door.
Catch up?
SKanKabelle? Wanna go to the Comet?
You never let me touch anything in there.
I wanna try more stuff on.
Tell you what. You can pay when you're done...
...then come straight next door, oKay?
Swerval.
I'm a curly durvish my turban's PINK 'n furrish.

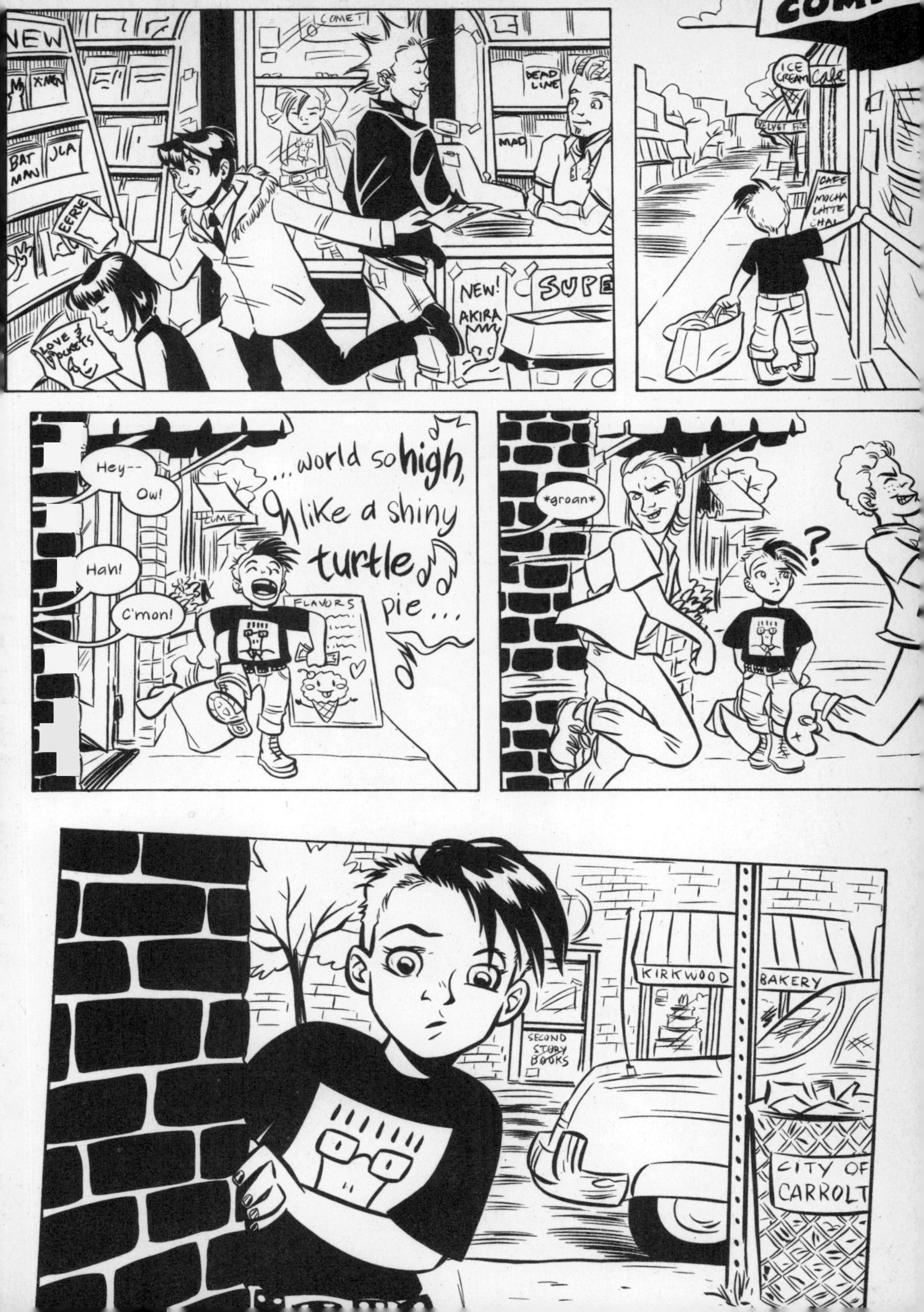

NEW
X-MEN
BATMAN
JLA
LOVE & ROCKETS
COMET
DEAD LINE
MAD
NEW! AKIRA
SUPE
COMICS
ICE CREAM
Cafe
CAFE MOCHA LATTE CHAI
Hey--
Ow!
Hah!
C'mon!
...world so high, like a shiny turtle pie...
COMET
FLAVORS
groan
?
SECOND STORY BOOKS
KIRKWOOD
BAKERY
CITY OF CARROLT

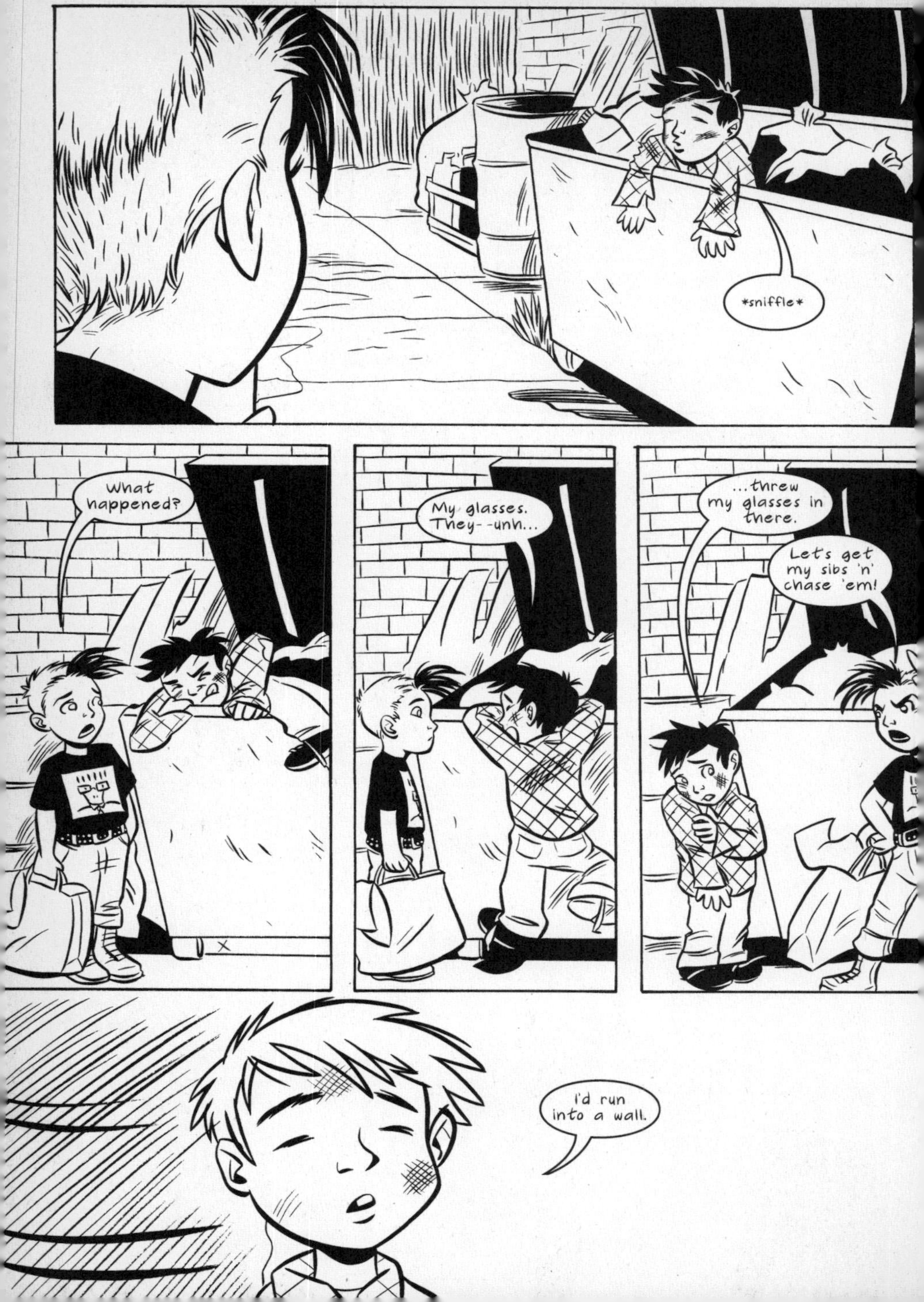
sniffle
What happened?
My glasses. They--unh...
...threw my glasses in there.
Let's get my sibs 'n' chase 'em!
I'd run into a wall.

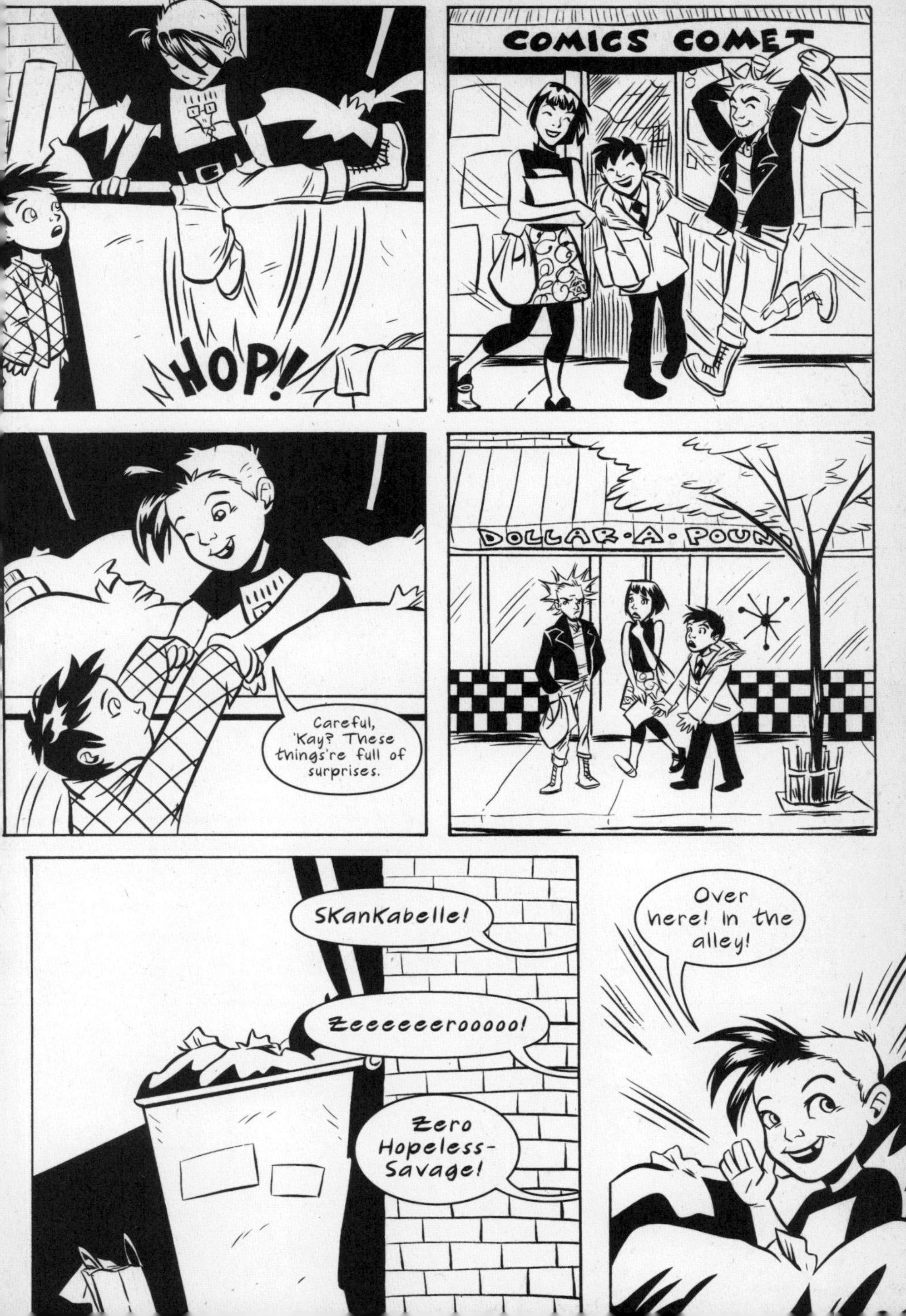
HOP!
COMICS COMET
Careful, 'Kay? These things're full of surprises.
DOLLAR·A·POUN
SKanKabelle!
Zeeeeeeroooo!
Zero Hopeless-Savage!
Over here! In the alley!

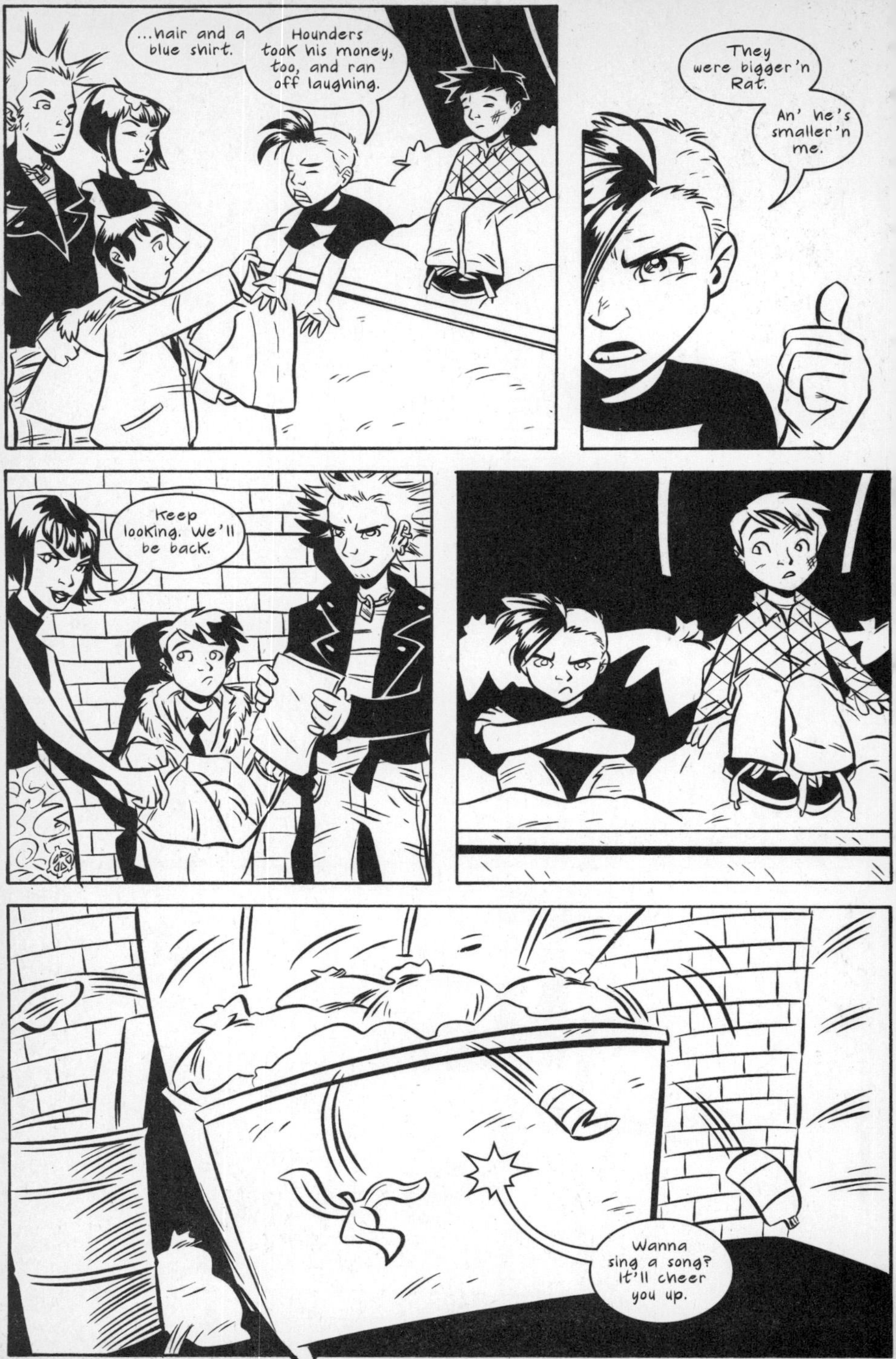
...hair and a blue shirt.
Hounders took his money, too, and ran off laughing.
They were bigger'n Rat.
An' he's smaller'n me.
Keep looking. We'll be back.
Wanna sing a song? It'll cheer you up.

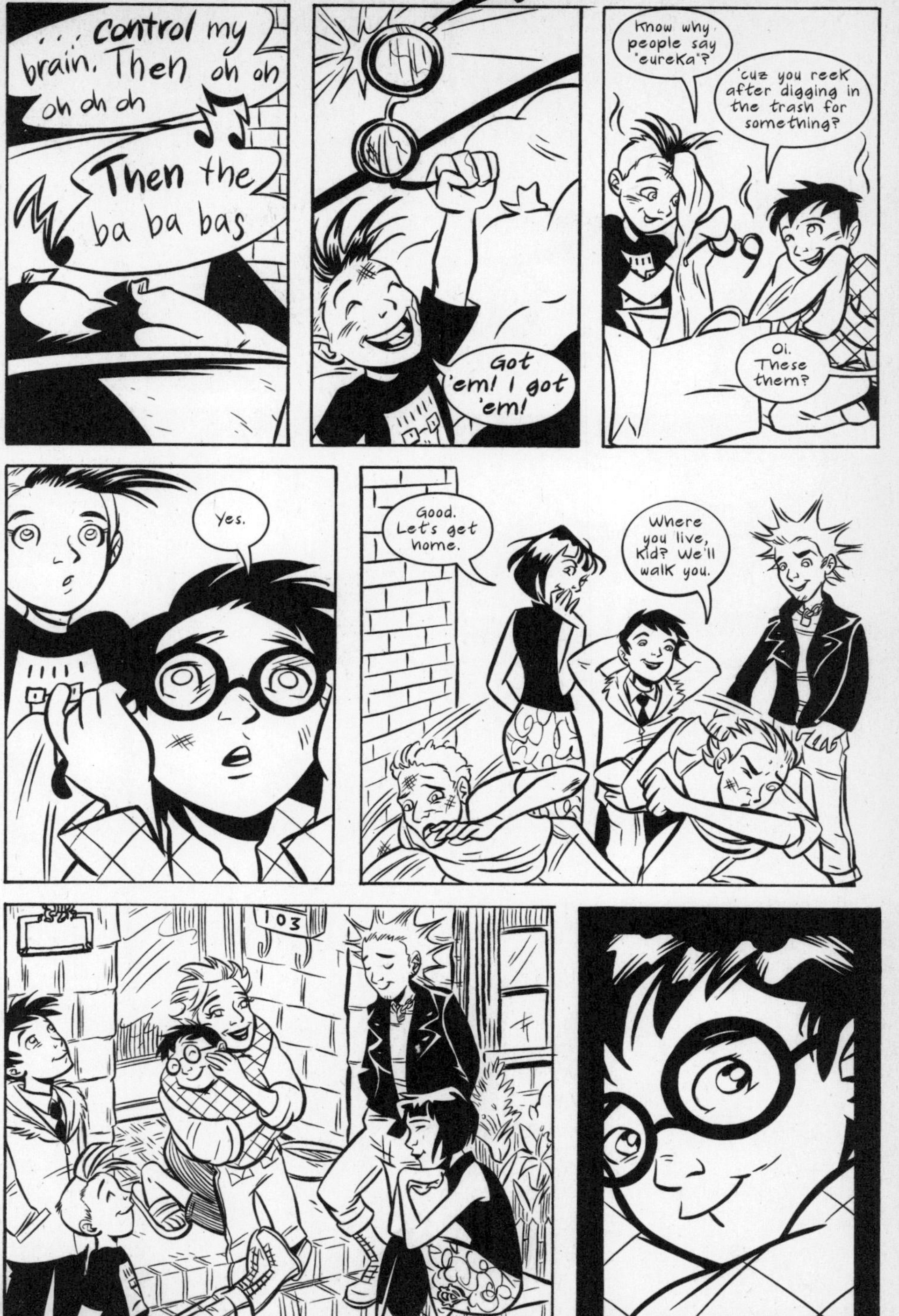

...control my brain. Then oh oh oh oh oh
Then the ba ba bas
Got 'em! I got 'em!
Know why people say "eureka"?
'cuz you reek after digging in the trash for something?
Oi. These them?
Yes.
Good. Let's get home.
Where you live, kid? We'll walk you.
103

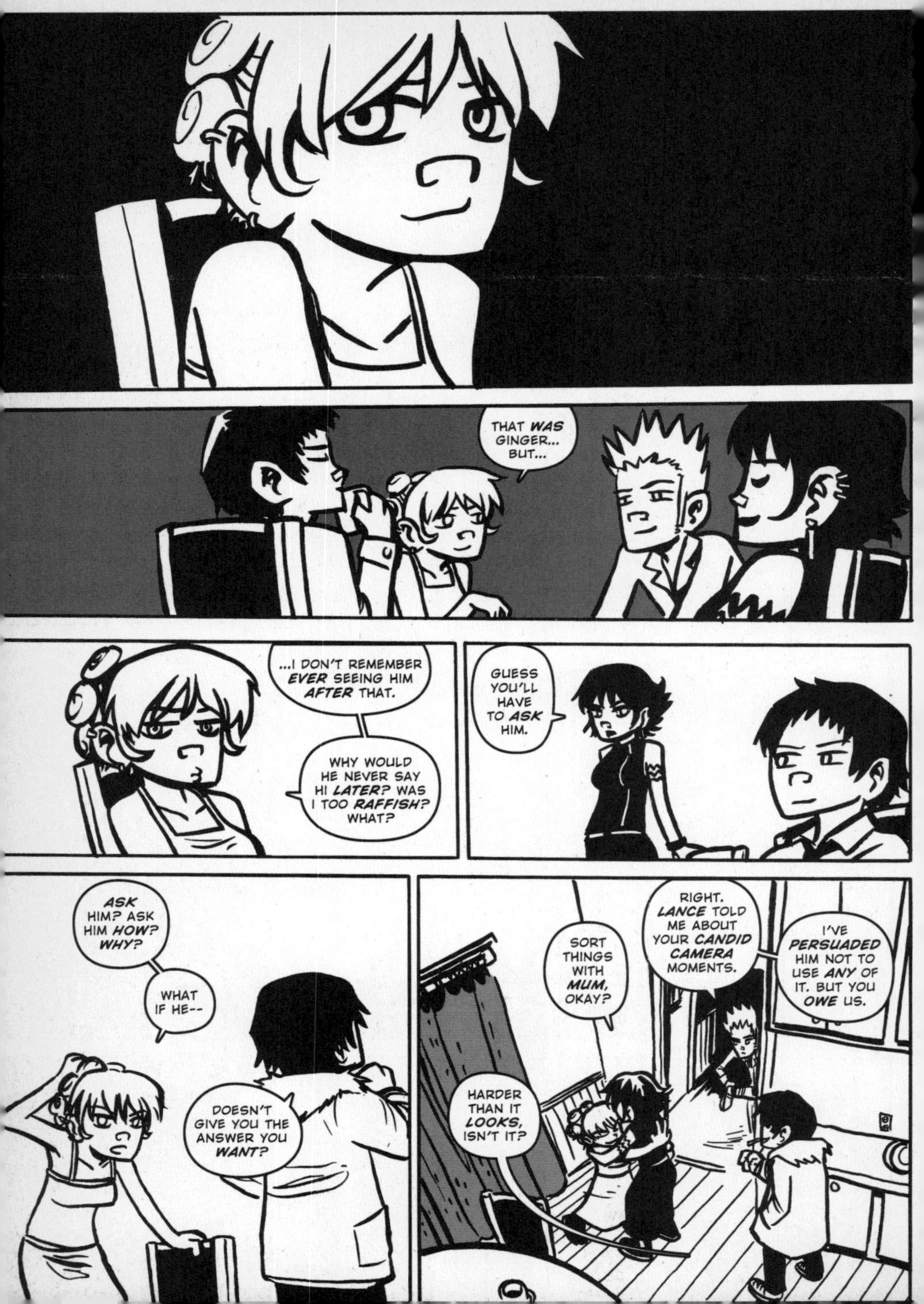
THAT WAS GINGER... BUT...
...I DON'T REMEMBER EVER SEEING HIM AFTER THAT.
WHY WOULD HE NEVER SAY HI LATER? WAS I TOO RAFFISH? WHAT?
GUESS YOU'LL HAVE TO ASK HIM.
ASK HIM? ASK HIM HOW? WHY?
WHAT IF HE--
DOESN'T GIVE YOU THE ANSWER YOU WANT?
SORT THINGS WITH MUM, OKAY?
RIGHT. LANCE TOLD ME ABOUT YOUR CANDID CAMERA MOMENTS.
I'VE PERSUADED HIM NOT TO USE ANY OF IT. BUT YOU OWE US.
HARDER THAN IT LOOKS, ISN'T IT?

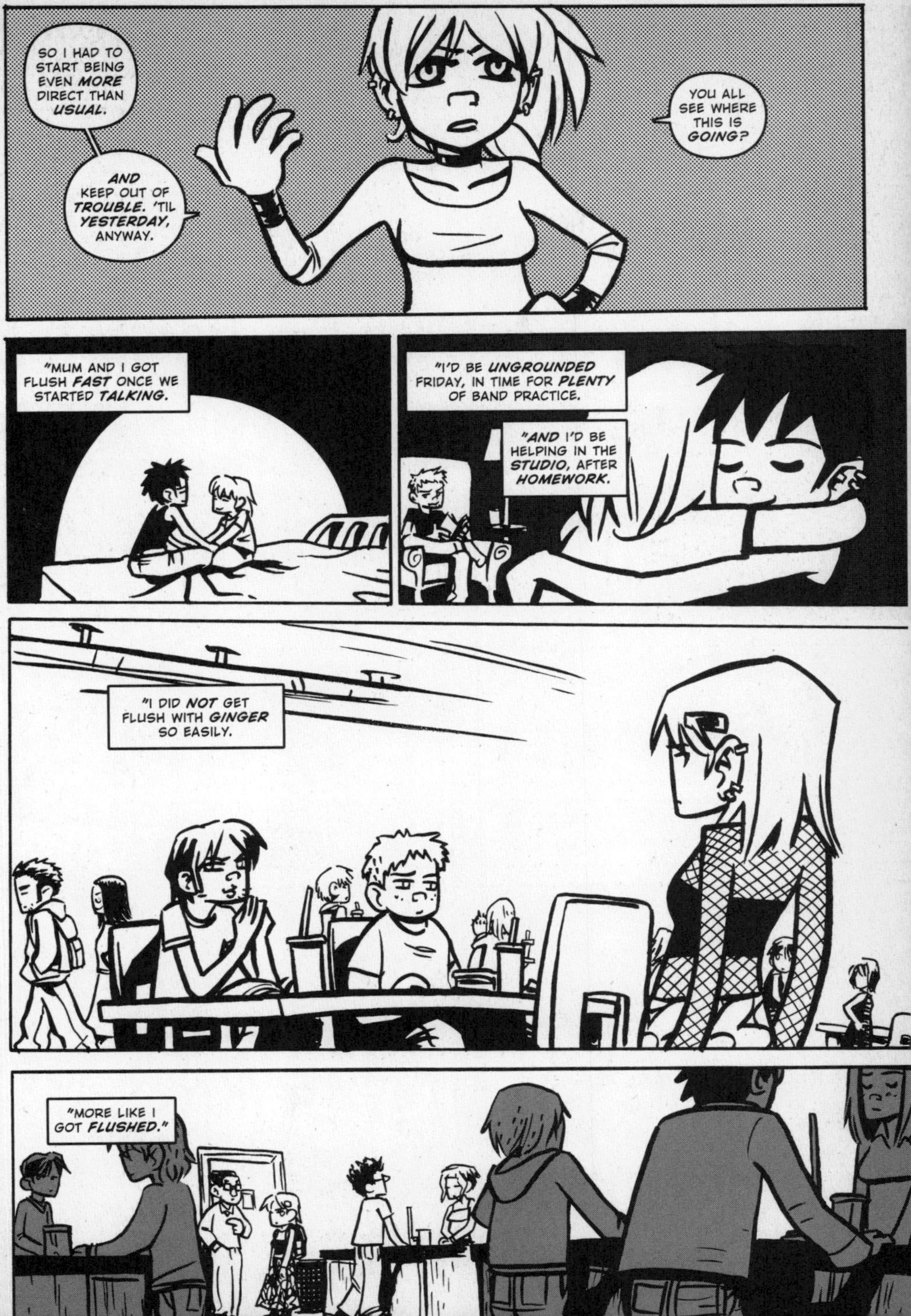
SO I HAD TO START BEING EVEN MORE DIRECT THAN USUAL.
AND KEEP OUT OF TROUBLE. 'TIL YESTERDAY, ANYWAY.
YOU ALL SEE WHERE THIS IS GOING?
"MUM AND I GOT FLUSH FAST ONCE WE STARTED TALKING.
"I'D BE UNGROUNDED FRIDAY, IN TIME FOR PLENTY OF BAND PRACTICE.
"AND I'D BE HELPING IN THE STUDIO, AFTER HOMEWORK.
"I DID NOT GET FLUSH WITH GINGER SO EASILY.
"MORE LIKE I GOT FLUSHED."

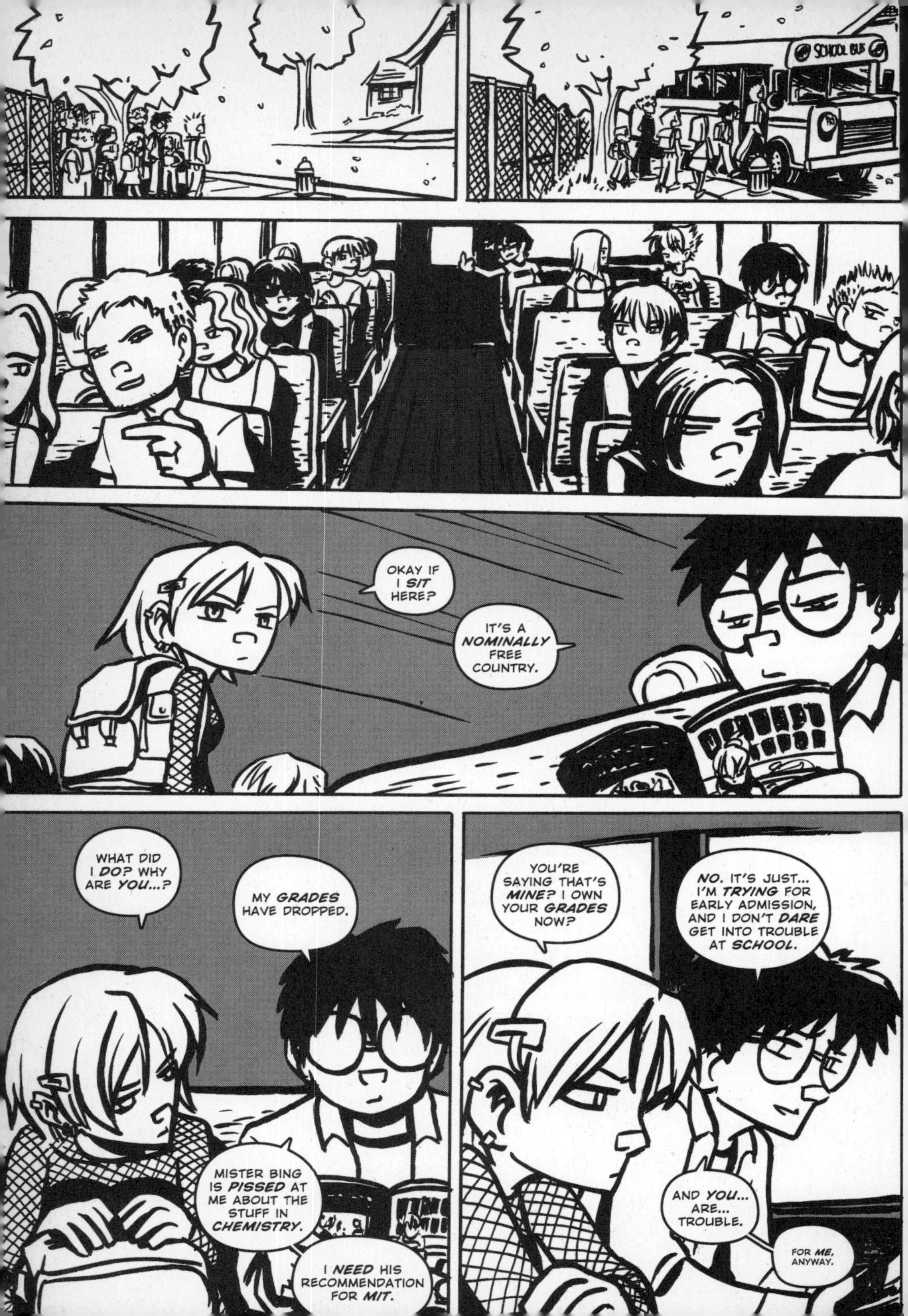
SCHOOL BUS
OKAY IF I SIT HERE?
IT'S A NOMINALLY FREE COUNTRY.
WHAT DID I DO? WHY ARE YOU...?
MY GRADES HAVE DROPPED.
MISTER BING IS PISSED AT ME ABOUT THE STUFF IN CHEMISTRY.
I NEED HIS RECOMMENDATION FOR MIT.
YOU'RE SAYING THAT'S MINE? I OWN YOUR GRADES NOW?
NO. IT'S JUST... I'M TRYING FOR EARLY ADMISSION, AND I DON'T DARE GET INTO TROUBLE AT SCHOOL.
AND YOU... ARE... TROUBLE.
FOR ME, ANYWAY.

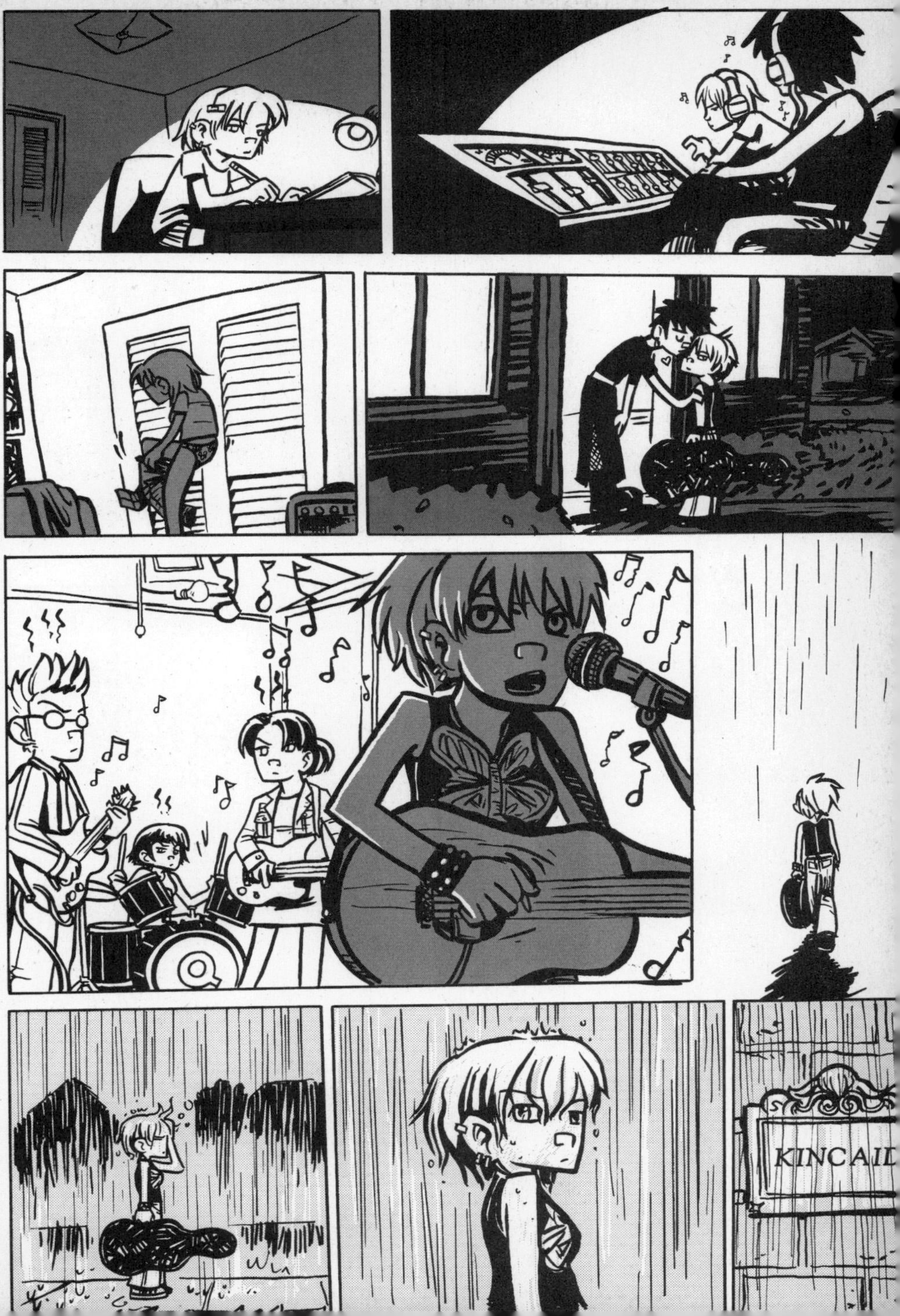
KINCAID

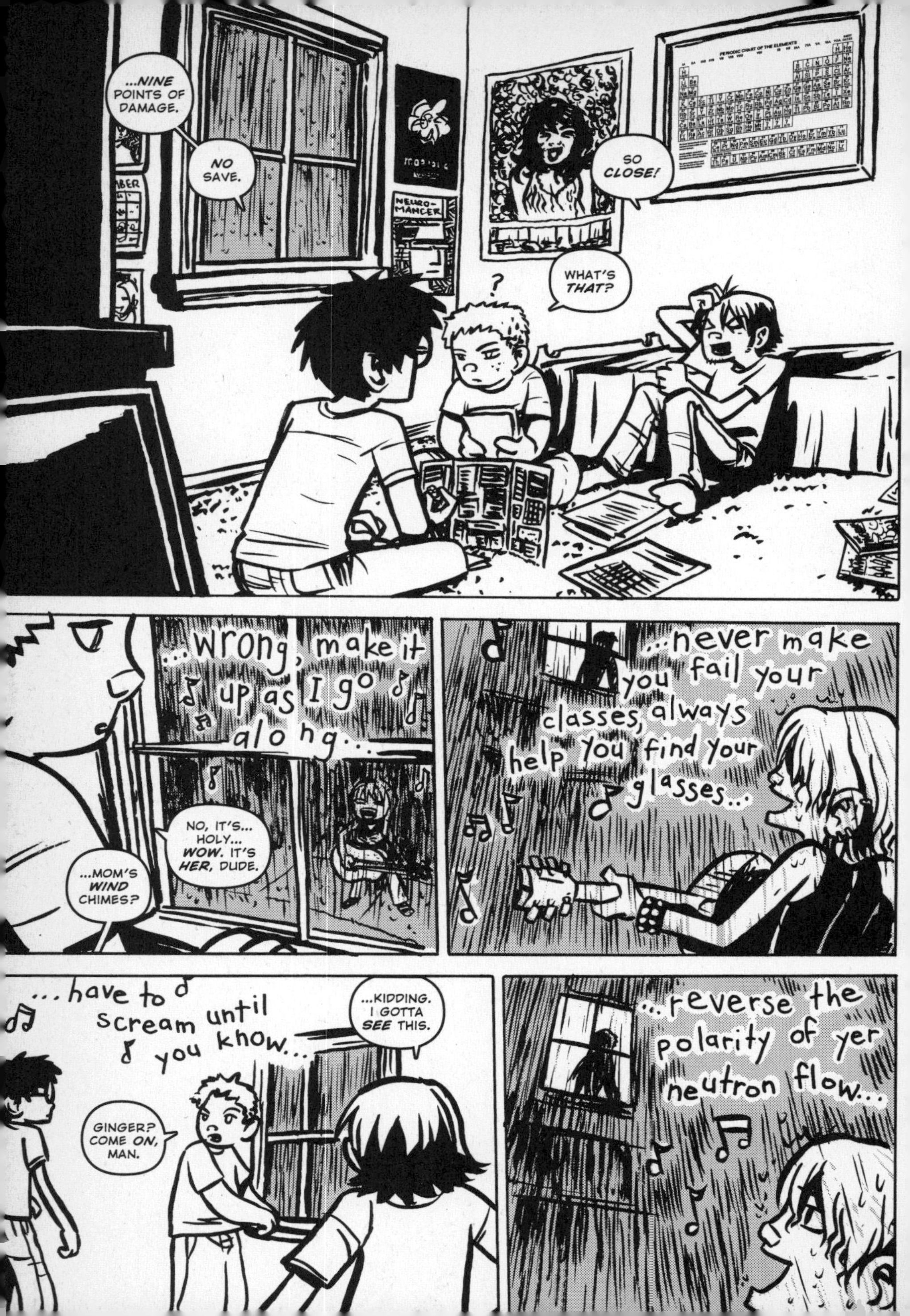
...NINE POINTS OF DAMAGE.
NO SAVE.
SO CLOSE!
WHAT'S THAT?
?
...wrong, make it up as I go along...
...MOM'S WIND CHIMES?
NO, IT'S... HOLY... WOW. IT'S HER, DUDE.
...never make you fail your classes, always help you find your glasses...
...have to scream until you know...
...KIDDING. I GOTTA SEE THIS.
GINGER? COME ON, MAN.
...reverse the polarity of yer neutron flow...

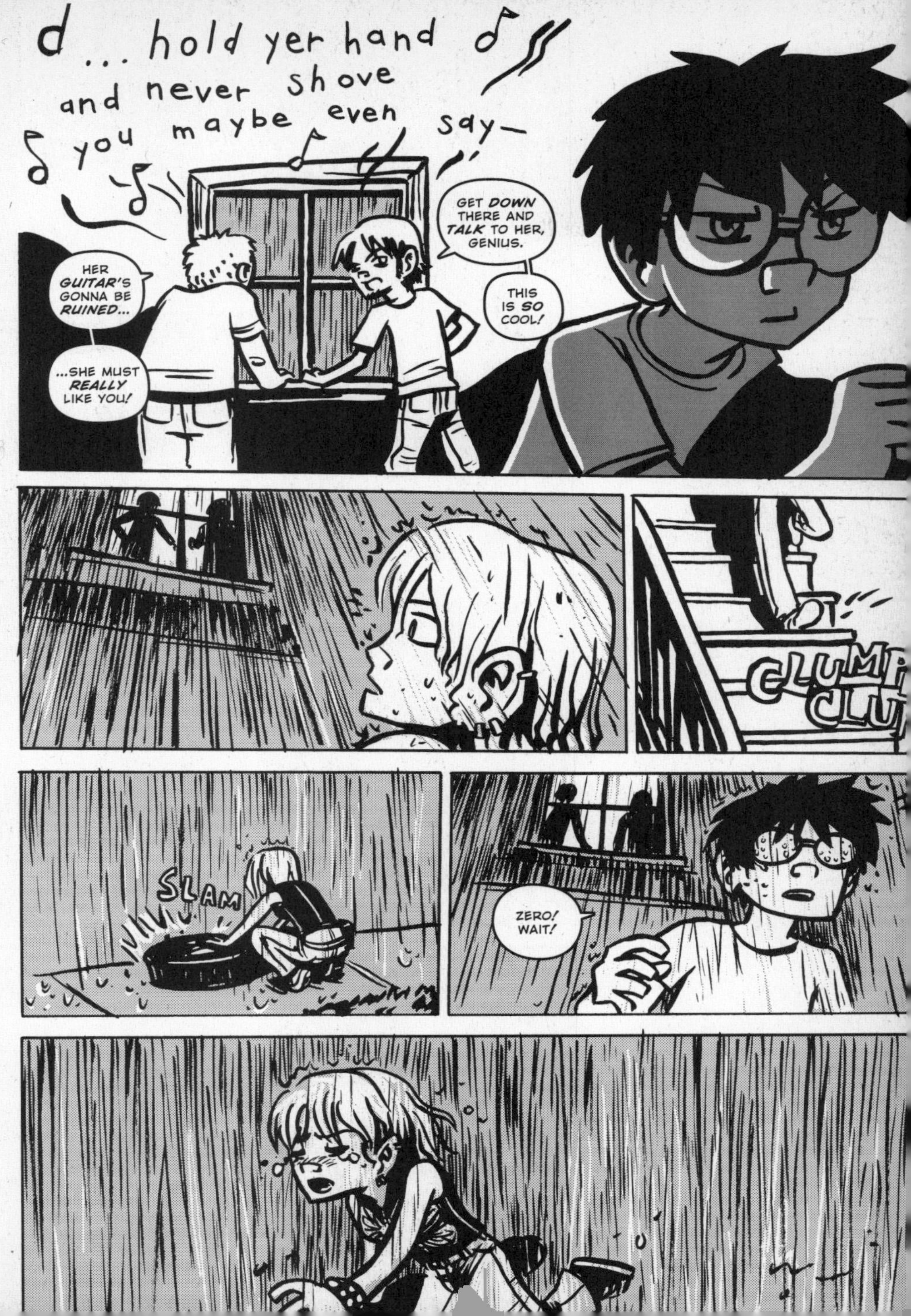
... hold yer hand and never shove you maybe even say—
HER GUITAR'S GONNA BE RUINED...
...SHE MUST REALLY LIKE YOU!
GET DOWN THERE AND TALK TO HER, GENIUS.
THIS IS SO COOL!
SLAM
ZERO! WAIT!

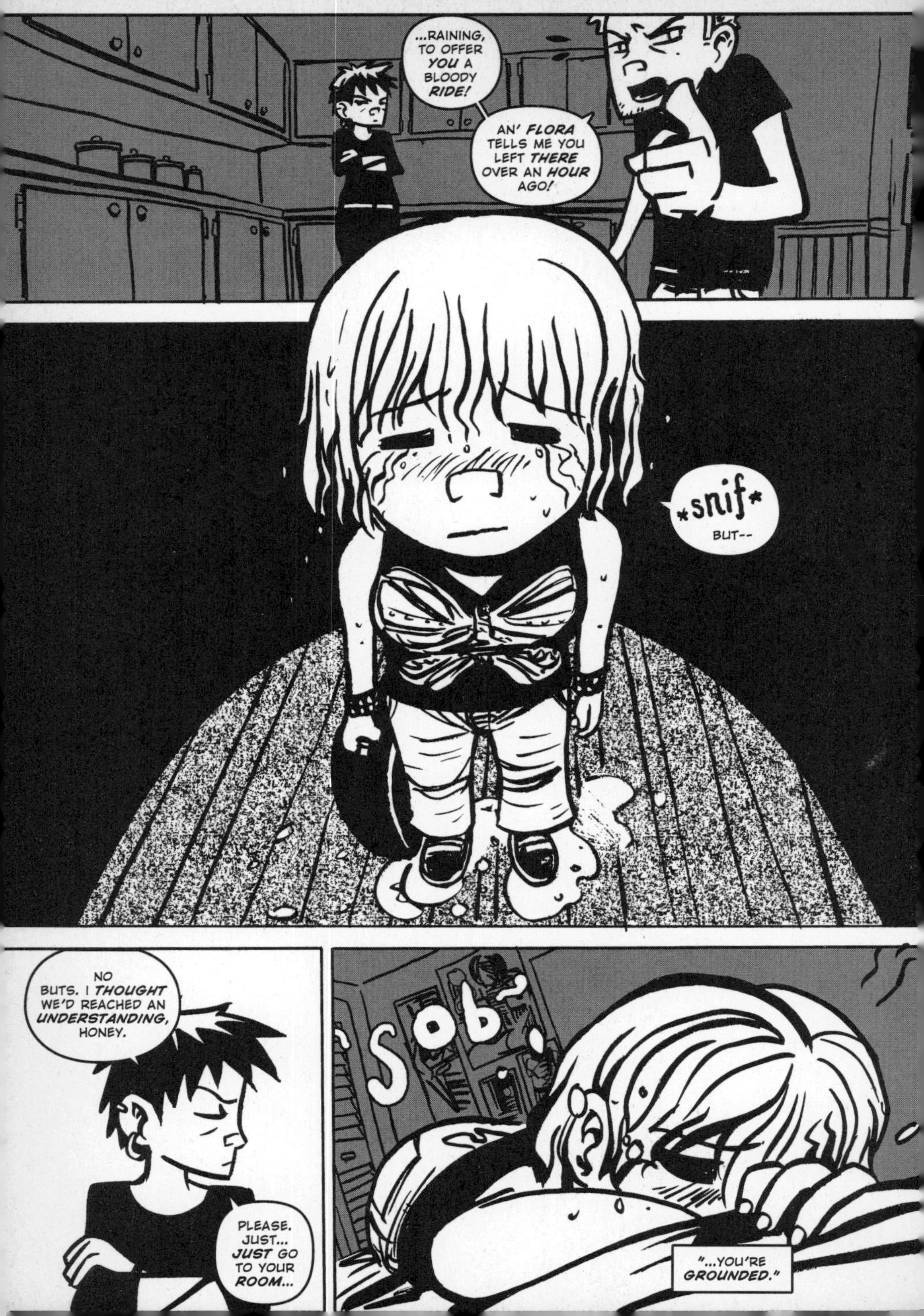
...RAINING, TO OFFER YOU A BLOODY RIDE!
AN' FLORA TELLS ME YOU LEFT THERE OVER AN HOUR AGO!
snif BUT--
NO BUTS. I THOUGHT WE'D REACHED AN UNDERSTANDING, HONEY.
PLEASE. JUST... JUST GO TO YOUR ROOM...
SOB
"...YOU'RE GROUNDED."

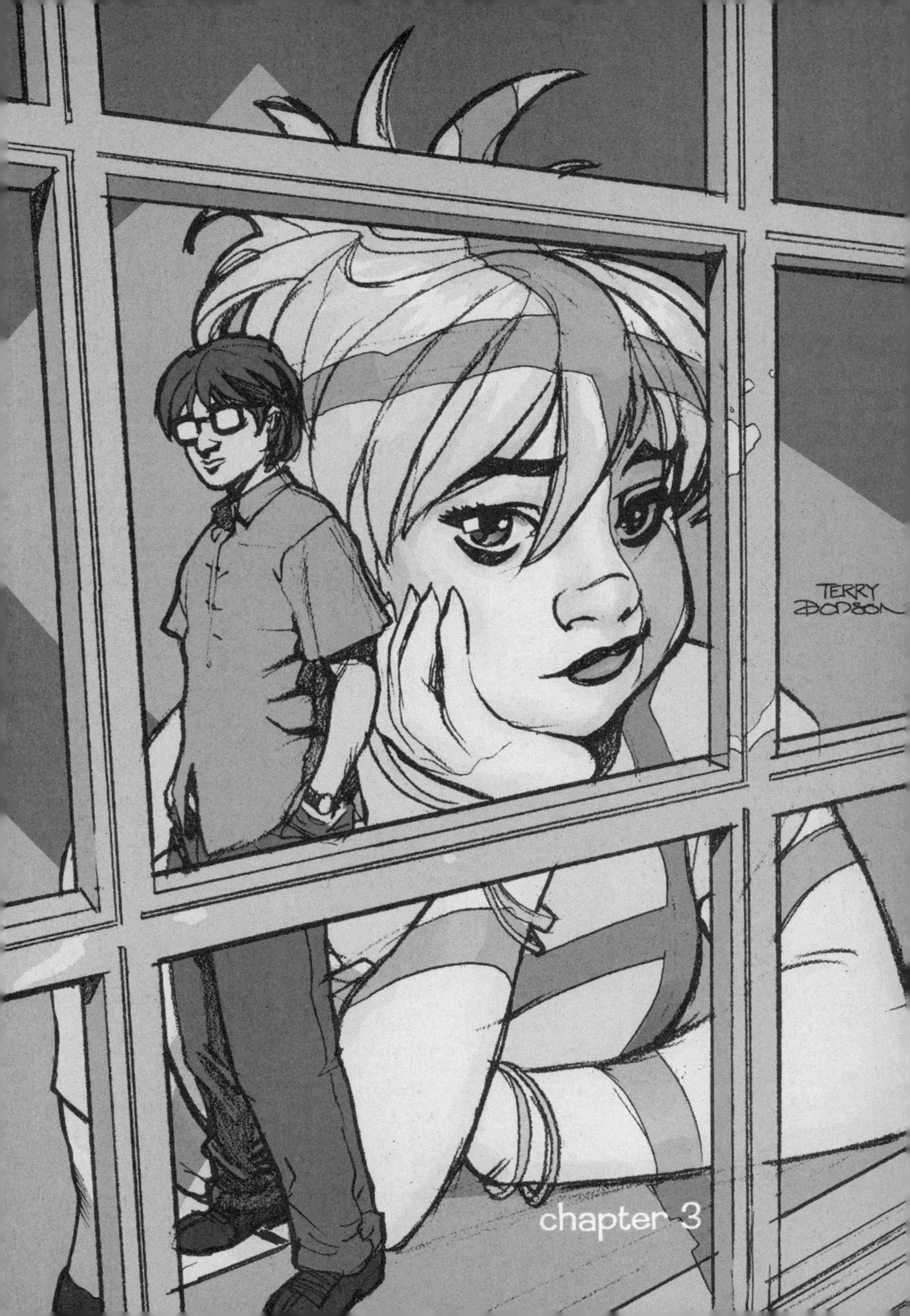
TERRY DODSON

chapter 3

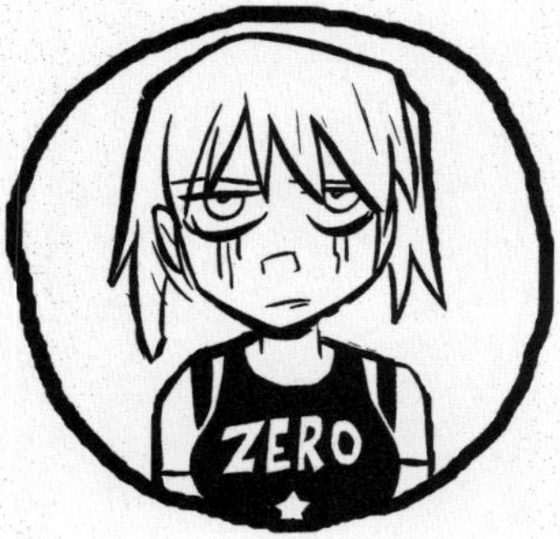
ZERO

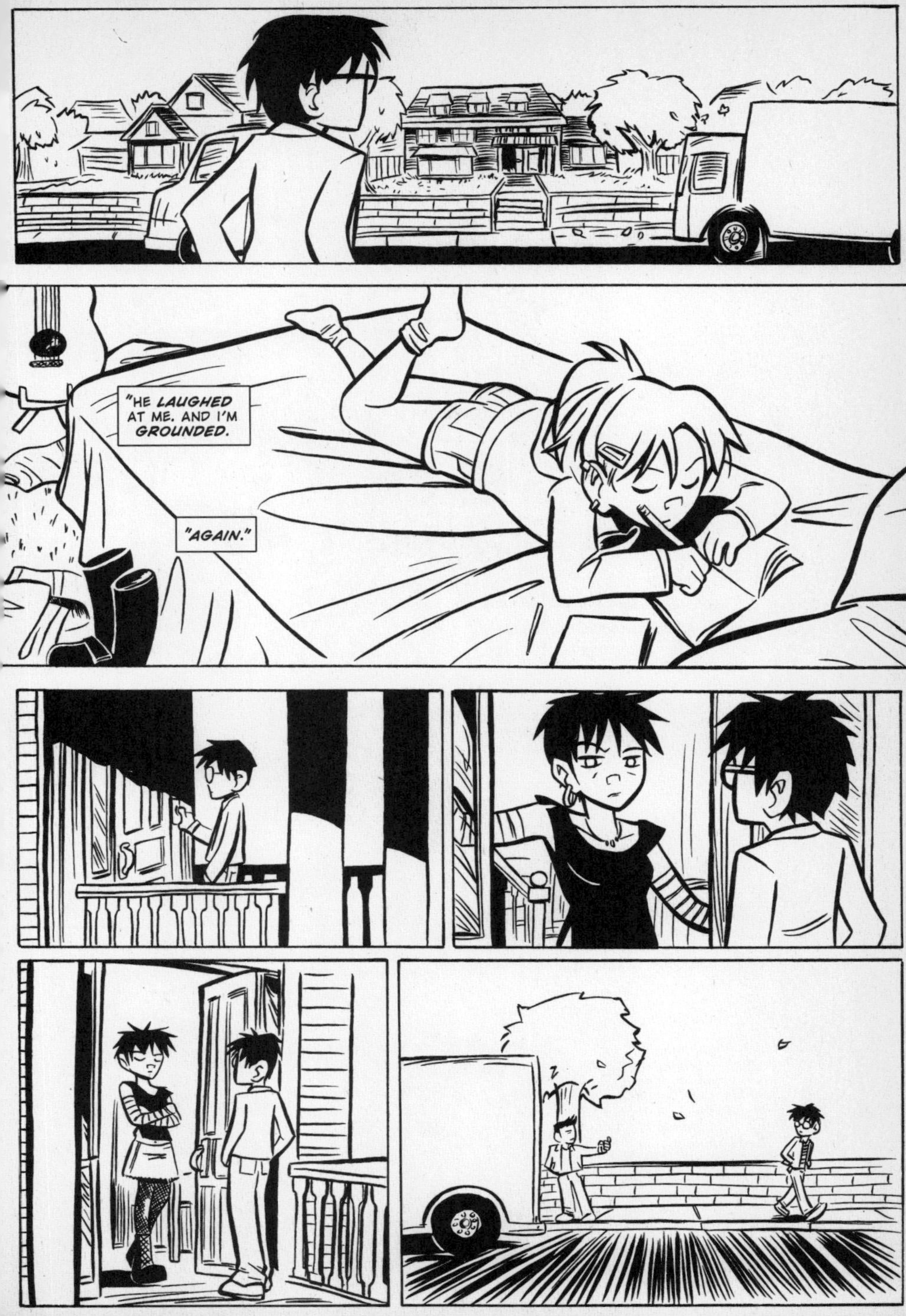
"HE LAUGHED AT ME. AND I'M GROUNDED.
"AGAIN."

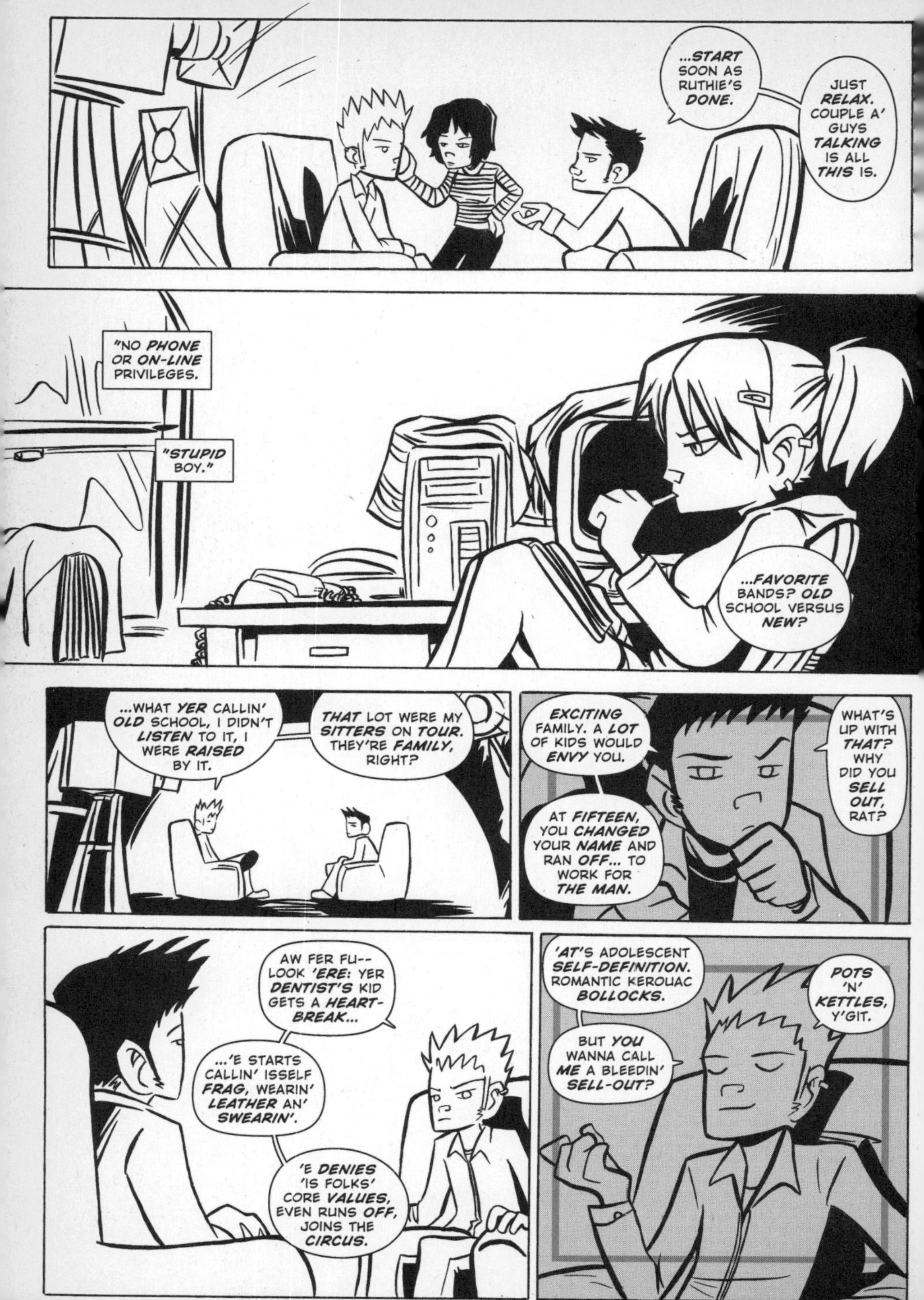

...START SOON AS RUTHIE'S DONE.
JUST RELAX. COUPLE A' GUYS TALKING IS ALL THIS IS.
"NO PHONE OR ON-LINE PRIVILEGES.
"STUPID BOY."
...FAVORITE BANDS? OLD SCHOOL VERSUS NEW?
...WHAT YER CALLIN' OLD SCHOOL, I DIDN'T LISTEN TO IT, I WERE RAISED BY IT.
THAT LOT WERE MY SITTERS ON TOUR. THEY'RE FAMILY, RIGHT?
EXCITING FAMILY. A LOT OF KIDS WOULD ENVY YOU.
AT FIFTEEN, YOU CHANGED YOUR NAME AND RAN OFF... TO WORK FOR THE MAN.
WHAT'S UP WITH THAT? WHY DID YOU SELL OUT, RAT?
AW FER FU-- LOOK 'ERE: YER DENTIST'S KID GETS A HEART-BREAK...
...'E STARTS CALLIN' ISSELF FRAG, WEARIN' LEATHER AN' SWEARIN'.
'E DENIES 'IS FOLKS' CORE VALUES, EVEN RUNS OFF, JOINS THE CIRCUS.
'AT'S ADOLESCENT SELF-DEFINITION. ROMANTIC KEROUAC BOLLOCKS.
BUT YOU WANNA CALL ME A BLEEDIN' SELL-OUT?
POTS 'N' KETTLES, Y'GIT.

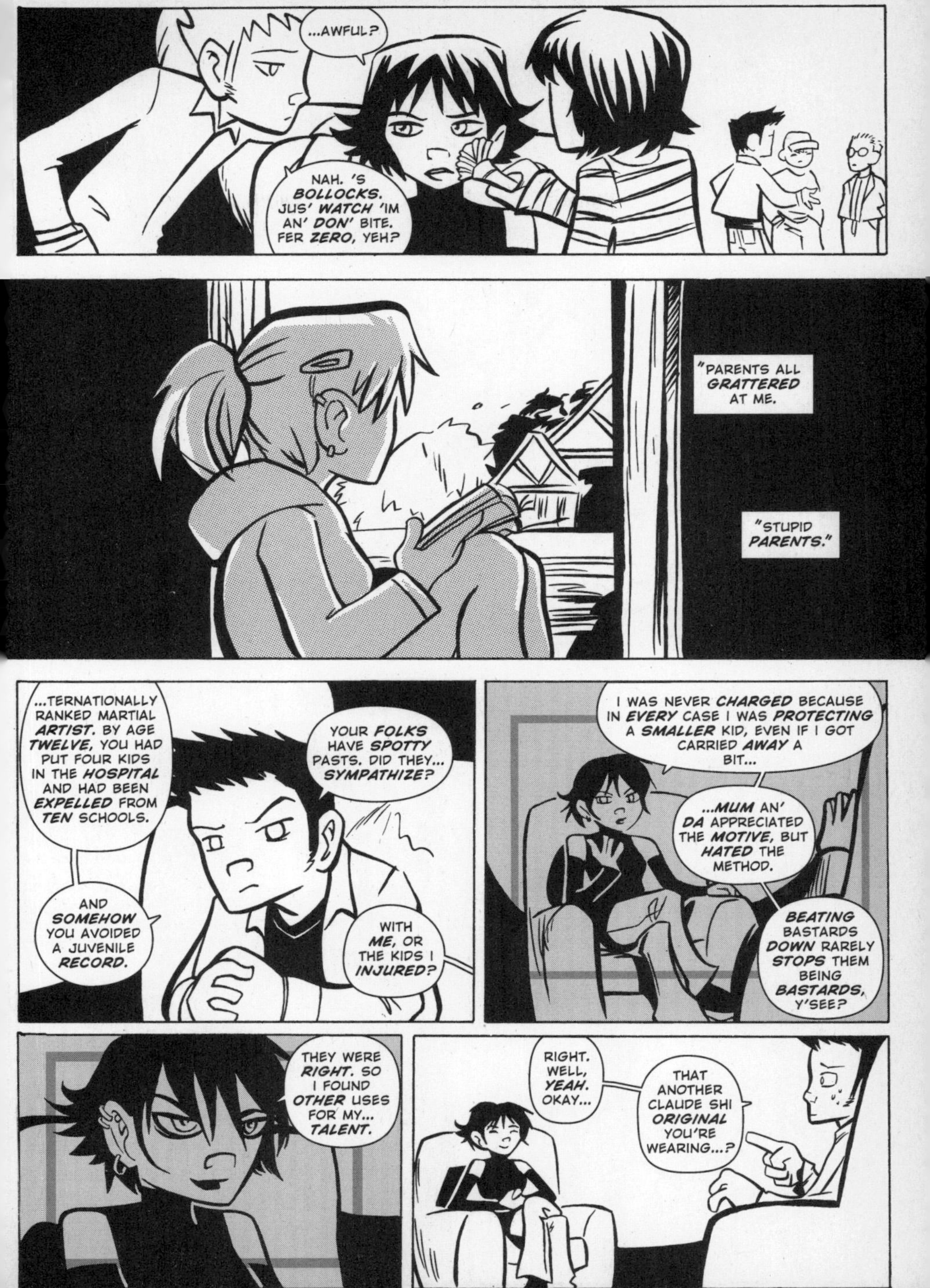
...AWFUL?
NAH. 'S BOLLOCKS. JUS' WATCH 'IM AN' DON' BITE. FER ZERO, YEH?
"PARENTS ALL GRATTERED AT ME.
"STUPID PARENTS."
...TERNATIONALLY RANKED MARTIAL ARTIST. BY AGE TWELVE, YOU HAD PUT FOUR KIDS IN THE HOSPITAL AND HAD BEEN EXPELLED FROM TEN SCHOOLS.
AND SOMEHOW YOU AVOIDED A JUVENILE RECORD.
YOUR FOLKS HAVE SPOTTY PASTS. DID THEY... SYMPATHIZE?
WITH ME, OR THE KIDS I INJURED?
I WAS NEVER CHARGED BECAUSE IN EVERY CASE I WAS PROTECTING A SMALLER KID, EVEN IF I GOT CARRIED AWAY A BIT...
...MUM AN' DA APPRECIATED THE MOTIVE, BUT HATED THE METHOD.
BEATING BASTARDS DOWN RARELY STOPS THEM BEING BASTARDS, Y'SEE?
THEY WERE RIGHT. SO I FOUND OTHER USES FOR MY... TALENT.
RIGHT. WELL, YEAH. OKAY...
THAT ANOTHER CLAUDE SHI ORIGINAL YOU'RE WEARING...?

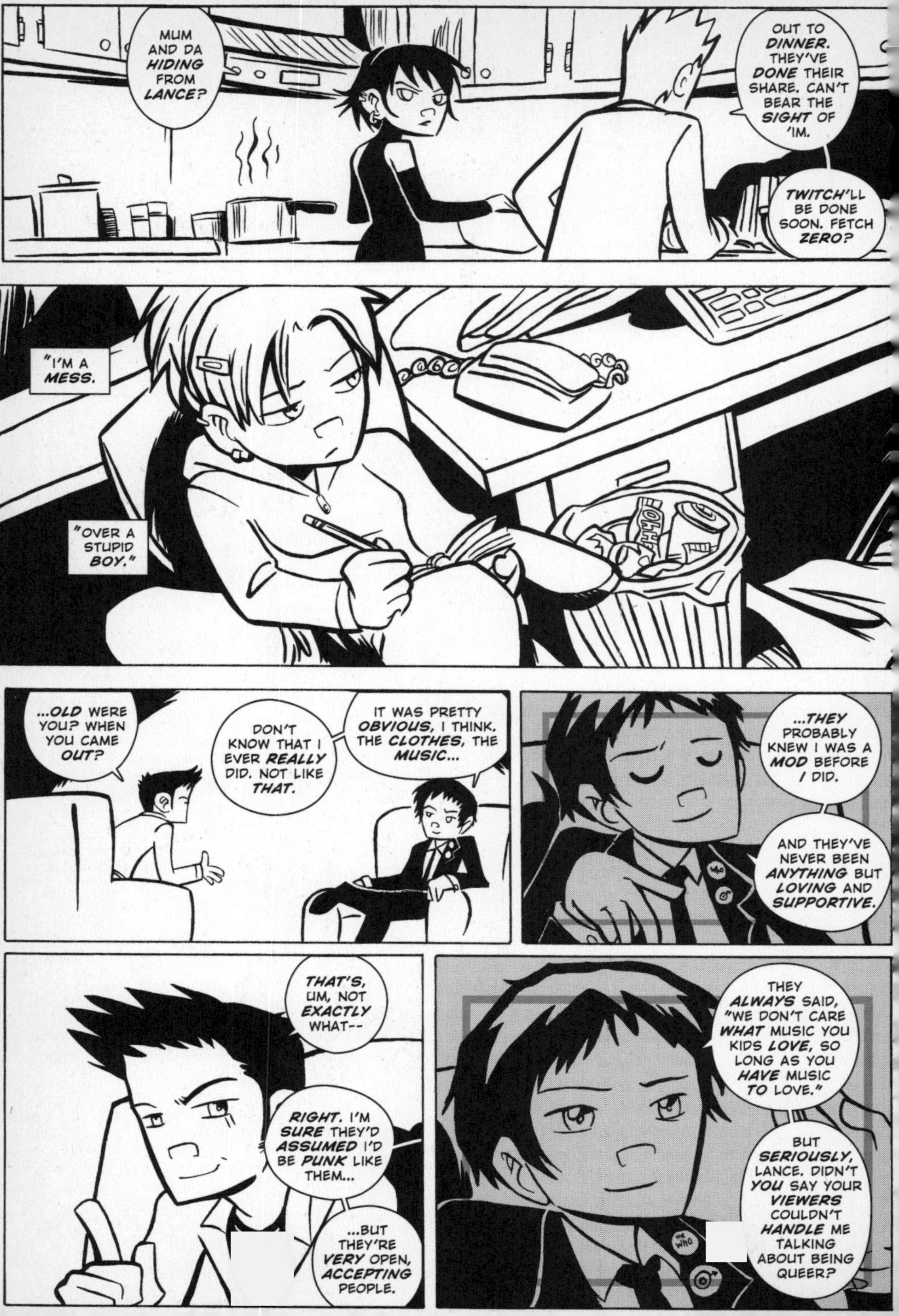
MUM AND DA HIDING FROM LANCE?
OUT TO DINNER. THEY'VE DONE THEIR SHARE. CAN'T BEAR THE SIGHT OF 'IM.
TWITCH'LL BE DONE SOON. FETCH ZERO?
"I'M A MESS.
"OVER A STUPID BOY."
...OLD WERE YOU? WHEN YOU CAME OUT?
DON'T KNOW THAT I EVER REALLY DID. NOT LIKE THAT.
IT WAS PRETTY OBVIOUS, I THINK. THE CLOTHES, THE MUSIC...
...THEY PROBABLY KNEW I WAS A MOD BEFORE I DID.
AND THEY'VE NEVER BEEN ANYTHING BUT LOVING AND SUPPORTIVE.
THAT'S, UM, NOT EXACTLY WHAT--
RIGHT. I'M SURE THEY'D ASSUMED I'D BE PUNK LIKE THEM...
...BUT THEY'RE VERY OPEN, ACCEPTING PEOPLE.
THEY ALWAYS SAID, "WE DON'T CARE WHAT MUSIC YOU KIDS LOVE, SO LONG AS YOU HAVE MUSIC TO LOVE."
BUT SERIOUSLY, LANCE. DIDN'T YOU SAY YOUR VIEWERS COULDN'T HANDLE ME TALKING ABOUT BEING QUEER?

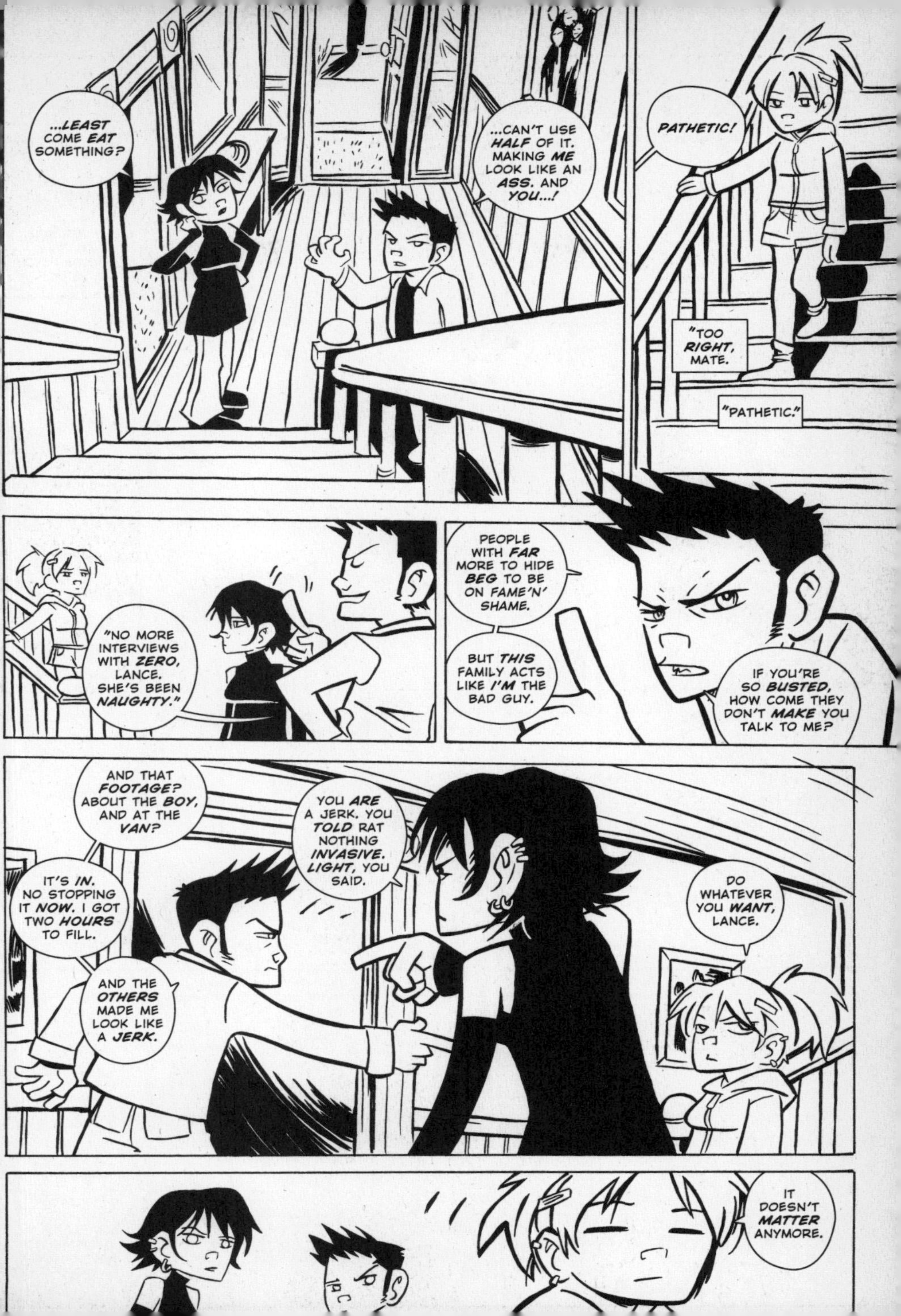
...LEAST COME EAT SOMETHING?
...CAN'T USE HALF OF IT. MAKING ME LOOK LIKE AN ASS. AND YOU...!
PATHETIC!
"TOO RIGHT, MATE.
"PATHETIC."
"NO MORE INTERVIEWS WITH ZERO, LANCE. SHE'S BEEN NAUGHTY."
PEOPLE WITH FAR MORE TO HIDE BEG TO BE ON FAME'N' SHAME.
BUT THIS FAMILY ACTS LIKE I'M THE BAD GUY.
IF YOU'RE SO BUSTED, HOW COME THEY DON'T MAKE YOU TALK TO ME?
AND THAT FOOTAGE? ABOUT THE BOY, AND AT THE VAN?
IT'S IN. NO STOPPING IT NOW. I GOT TWO HOURS TO FILL.
AND THE OTHERS MADE ME LOOK LIKE A JERK.
YOU ARE A JERK. YOU TOLD RAT NOTHING INVASIVE. LIGHT, YOU SAID.
DO WHATEVER YOU WANT, LANCE.
IT DOESN'T MATTER ANYMORE.

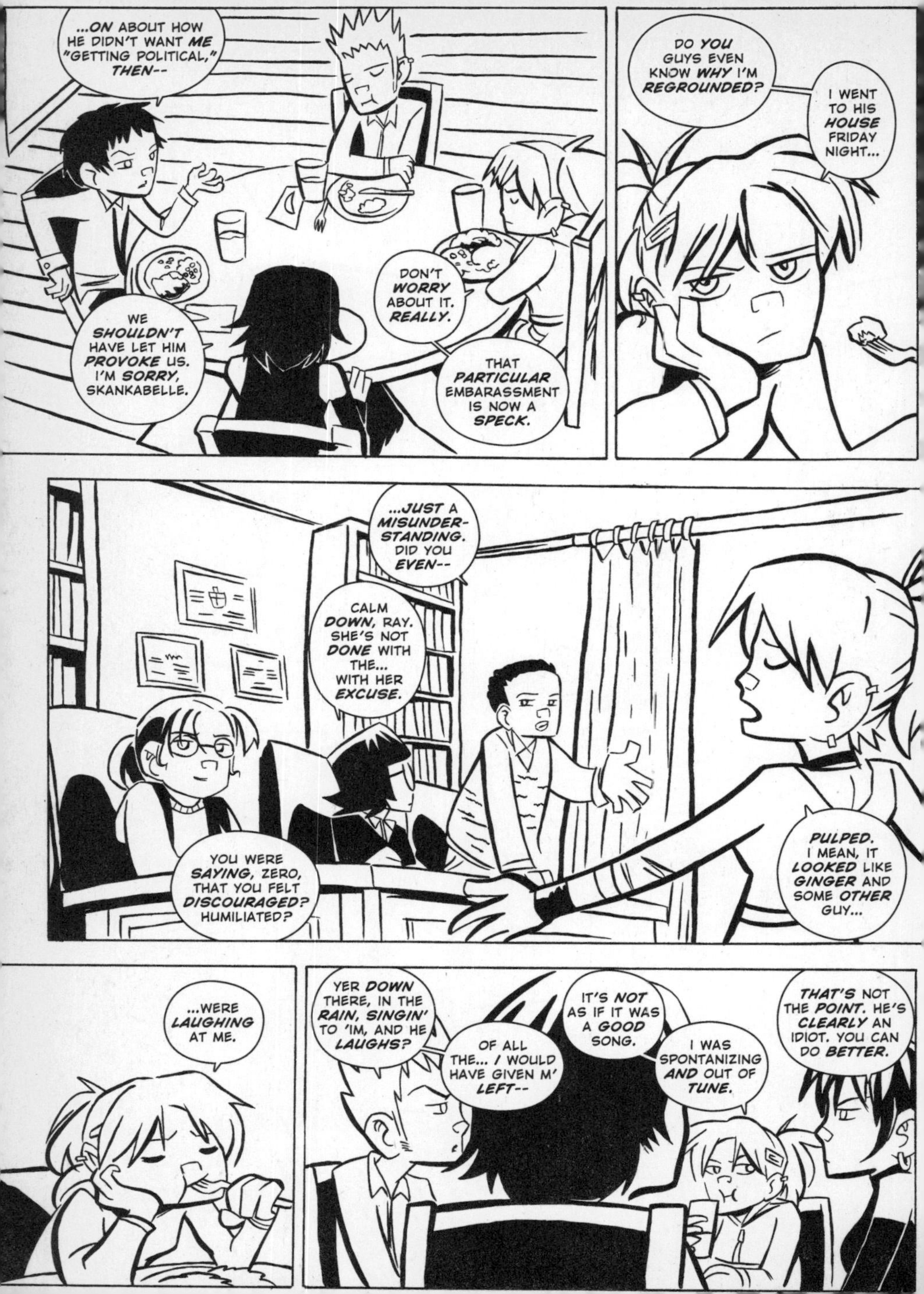
...ON ABOUT HOW HE DIDN'T WANT ME "GETTING POLITICAL," THEN--
WE SHOULDN'T HAVE LET HIM PROVOKE US. I'M SORRY, SKANKABELLE.
DON'T WORRY ABOUT IT. REALLY.
THAT PARTICULAR EMBARASSMENT IS NOW A SPECK.
DO YOU GUYS EVEN KNOW WHY I'M REGROUNDED?
I WENT TO HIS HOUSE FRIDAY NIGHT...
...JUST A MISUNDER-STANDING. DID YOU EVEN--
CALM DOWN, RAY. SHE'S NOT DONE WITH THE... WITH HER EXCUSE.
YOU WERE SAYING, ZERO, THAT YOU FELT DISCOURAGED? HUMILIATED?
PULPED. I MEAN, IT LOOKED LIKE GINGER AND SOME OTHER GUY...
...WERE LAUGHING AT ME.
YER DOWN THERE, IN THE RAIN, SINGIN' TO 'IM, AND HE LAUGHS?
OF ALL THE... I WOULD HAVE GIVEN M' LEFT--
IT'S NOT AS IF IT WAS A GOOD SONG.
I WAS SPONTANIZING AND OUT OF TUNE.
THAT'S NOT THE POINT. HE'S CLEARLY AN IDIOT. YOU CAN DO BETTER.

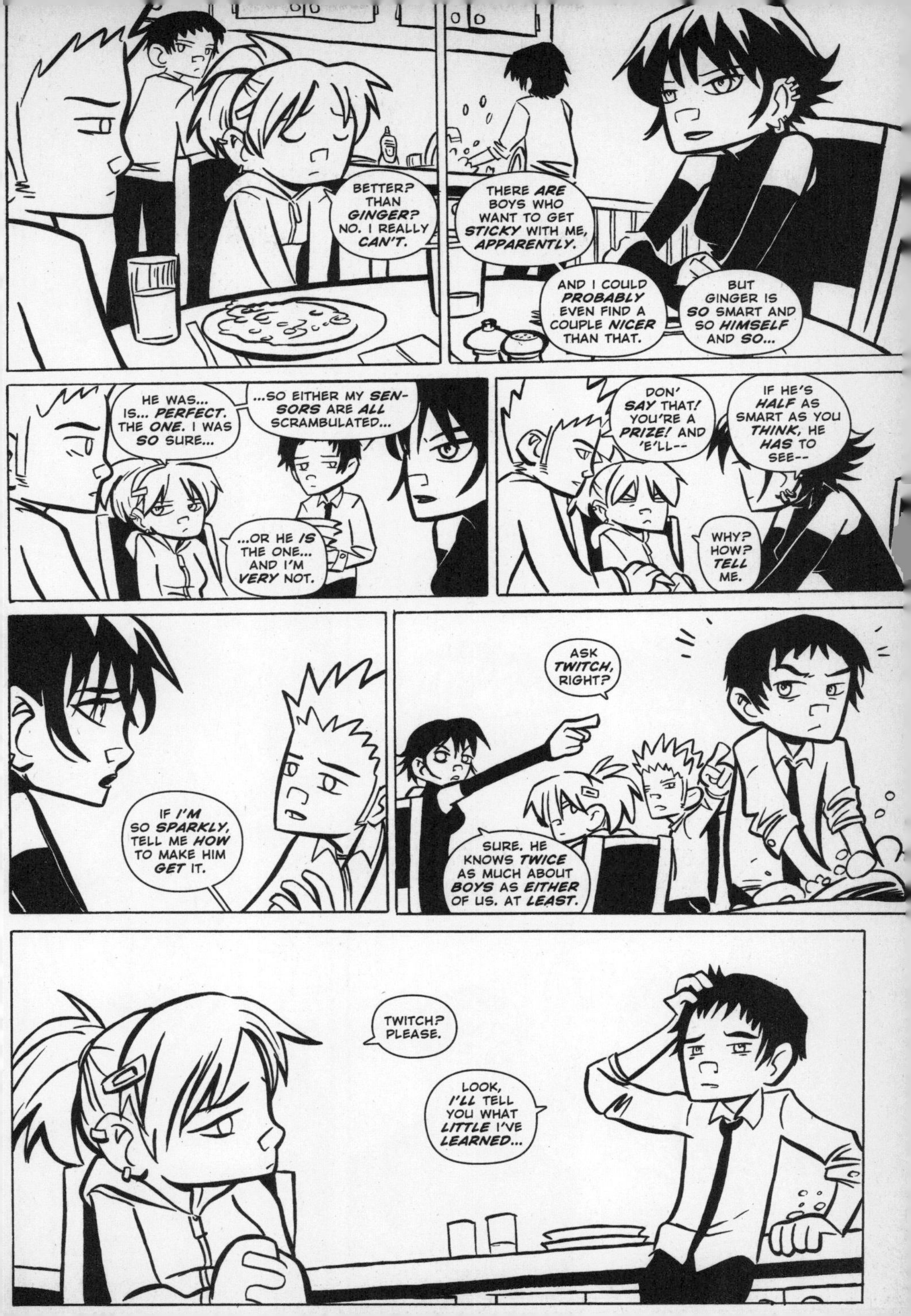
BETTER? THAN GINGER? NO. I REALLY CAN'T.
THERE ARE BOYS WHO WANT TO GET STICKY WITH ME, APPARENTLY.
AND I COULD PROBABLY EVEN FIND A COUPLE NICER THAN THAT.
BUT GINGER IS SO SMART AND SO HIMSELF AND SO...
HE WAS... IS... PERFECT. THE ONE. I WAS SO SURE...
...SO EITHER MY SEN-SORS ARE ALL SCRAMBULATED...
...OR HE IS THE ONE... AND I'M VERY NOT.
DON' SAY THAT! YOU'RE A PRIZE! AND 'E'LL--
IF HE'S HALF AS SMART AS YOU THINK, HE HAS TO SEE--
WHY? HOW? TELL ME.
IF I'M SO SPARKLY, TELL ME HOW TO MAKE HIM GET IT.
ASK TWITCH, RIGHT?
SURE. HE KNOWS TWICE AS MUCH ABOUT BOYS AS EITHER OF US. AT LEAST.
TWITCH? PLEASE.
LOOK, I'LL TELL YOU WHAT LITTLE I'VE LEARNED...

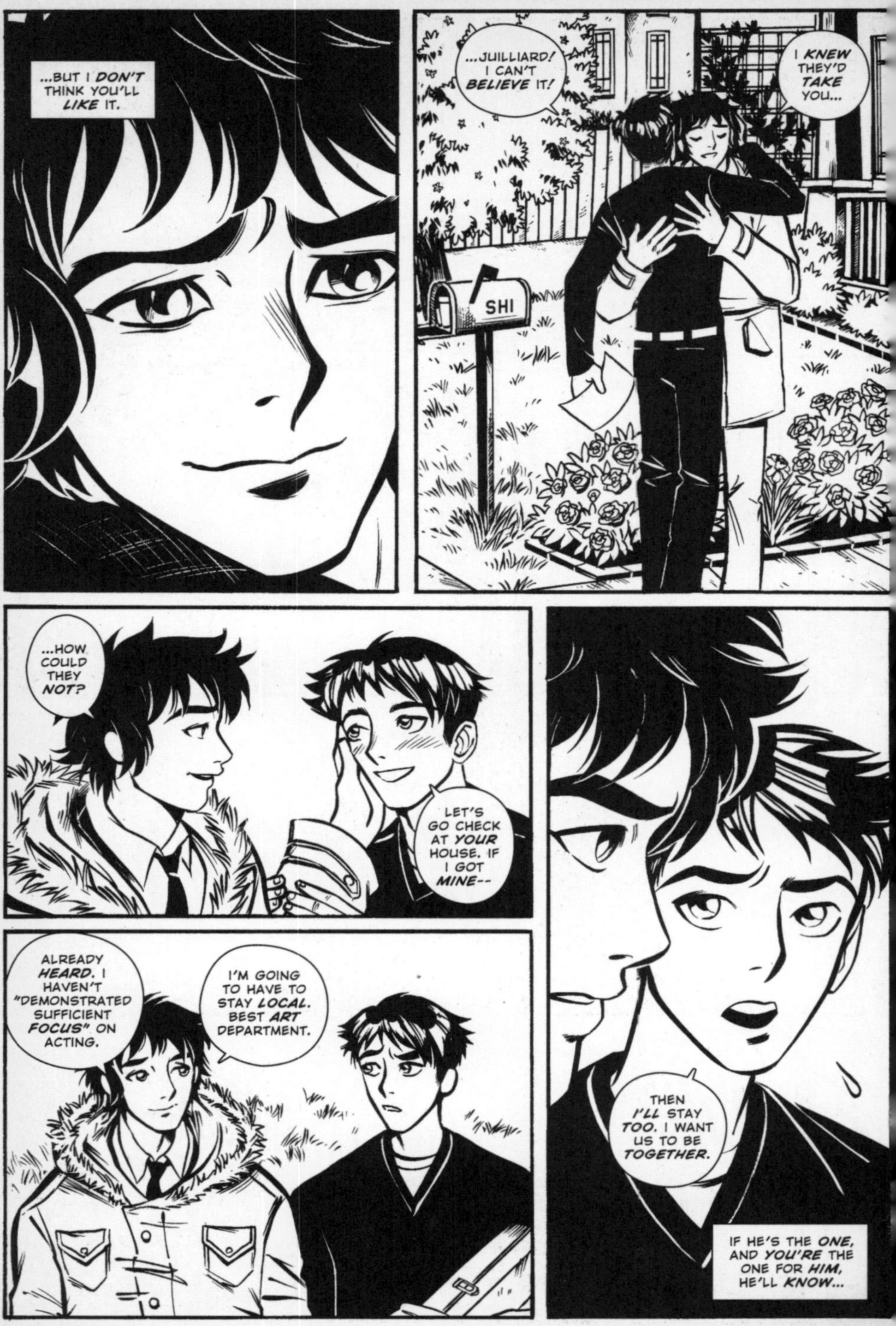
...BUT I DON'T THINK YOU'LL LIKE IT.
...JUILLIARD! I CAN'T BELIEVE IT!
I KNEW THEY'D TAKE YOU...
SHI
...HOW COULD THEY NOT?
LET'S GO CHECK AT YOUR HOUSE. IF I GOT MINE--
ALREADY HEARD. I HAVEN'T "DEMONSTRATED SUFFICIENT FOCUS" ON ACTING.
I'M GOING TO HAVE TO STAY LOCAL. BEST ART DEPARTMENT.
THEN I'LL STAY TOO. I WANT US TO BE TOGETHER.
IF HE'S THE ONE, AND YOU'RE THE ONE FOR HIM, HE'LL KNOW...

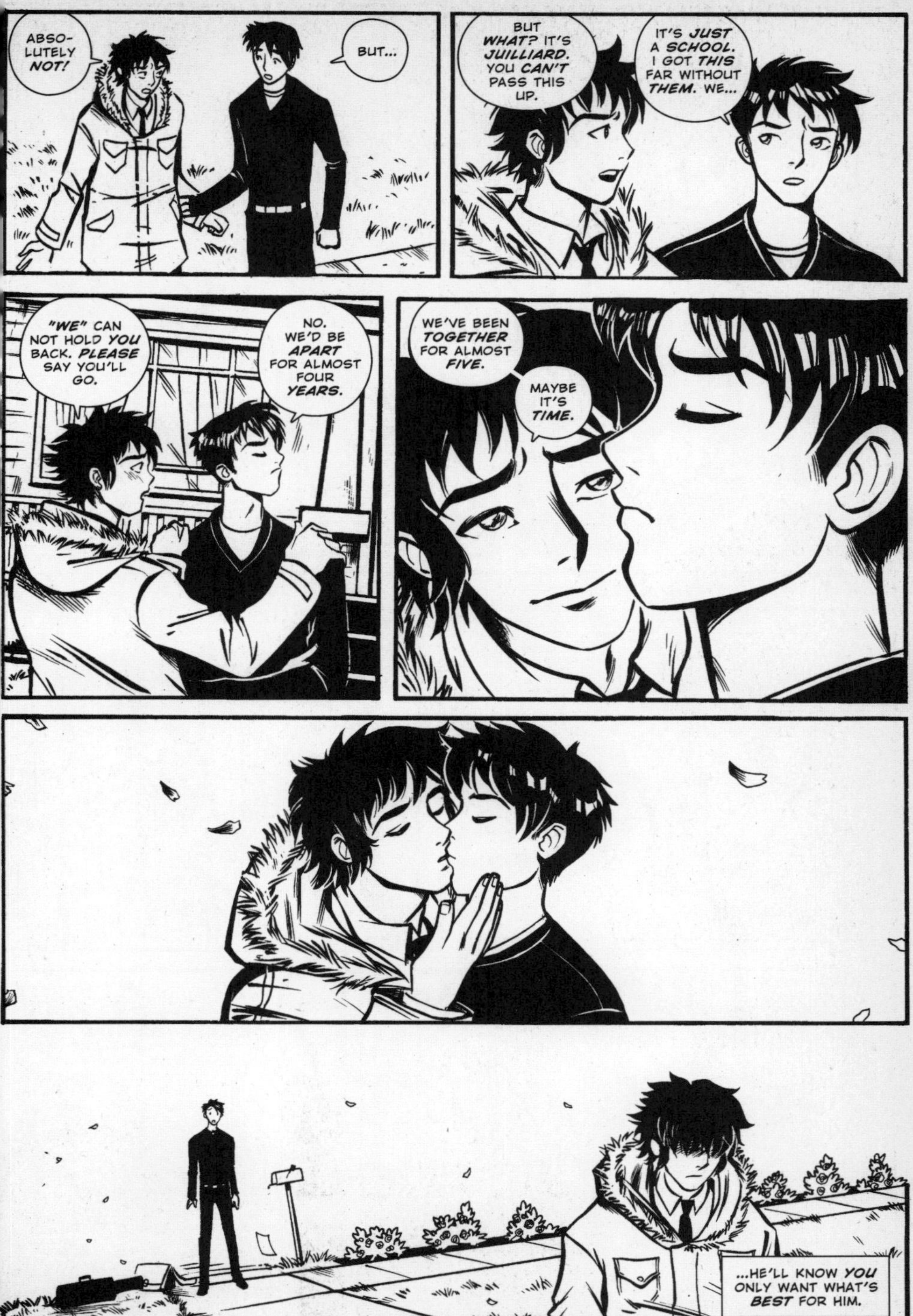
ABSOLUTELY NOT!
BUT...
BUT WHAT? IT'S JUILLIARD. YOU CAN'T PASS THIS UP.
IT'S JUST A SCHOOL. I GOT THIS FAR WITHOUT THEM. WE...
"WE" CAN NOT HOLD YOU BACK. PLEASE SAY YOU'LL GO.
NO. WE'D BE APART FOR ALMOST FOUR YEARS.
WE'VE BEEN TOGETHER FOR ALMOST FIVE.
MAYBE IT'S TIME.
...HE'LL KNOW YOU ONLY WANT WHAT'S BEST FOR HIM.

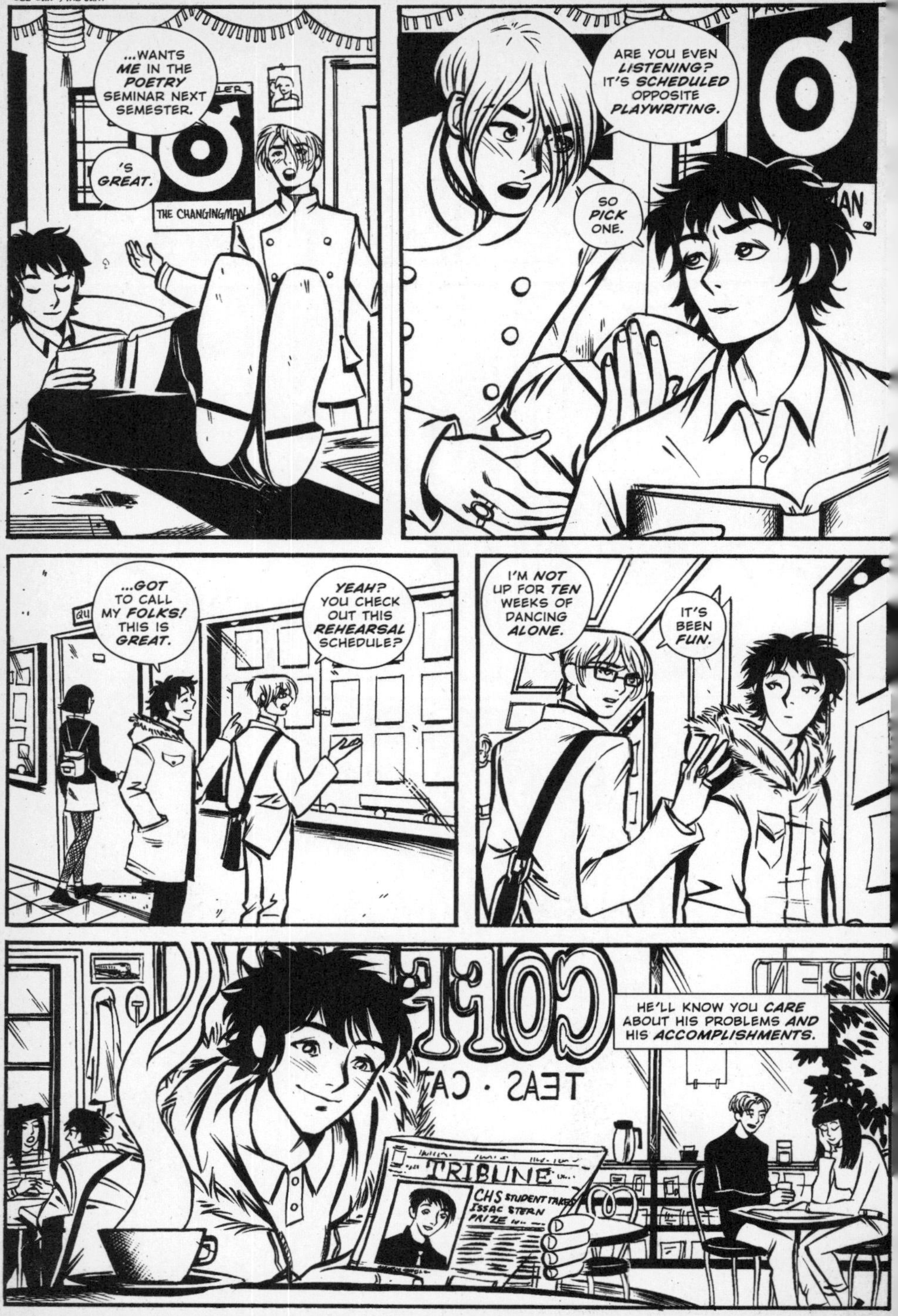
...WANTS *ME* IN THE *POETRY* SEMINAR NEXT SEMESTER.
'S *GREAT.*
THE CHANGINGMAN
ARE YOU EVEN *LISTENING?* IT'S *SCHEDULED* OPPOSITE *PLAYWRITING.*
SO *PICK* ONE.
...*GOT* TO CALL MY *FOLKS!* THIS IS *GREAT.*
YEAH? YOU CHECK OUT THIS *REHEARSAL* SCHEDULE?
I'M *NOT* UP FOR *TEN* WEEKS OF DANCING *ALONE.*
IT'S BEEN *FUN.*
HE'LL KNOW YOU *CARE* ABOUT HIS PROBLEMS *AND* HIS *ACCOMPLISHMENTS.*
TRIBUNE
CHS STUDENT TAKES ISSAC STERN PRIZE

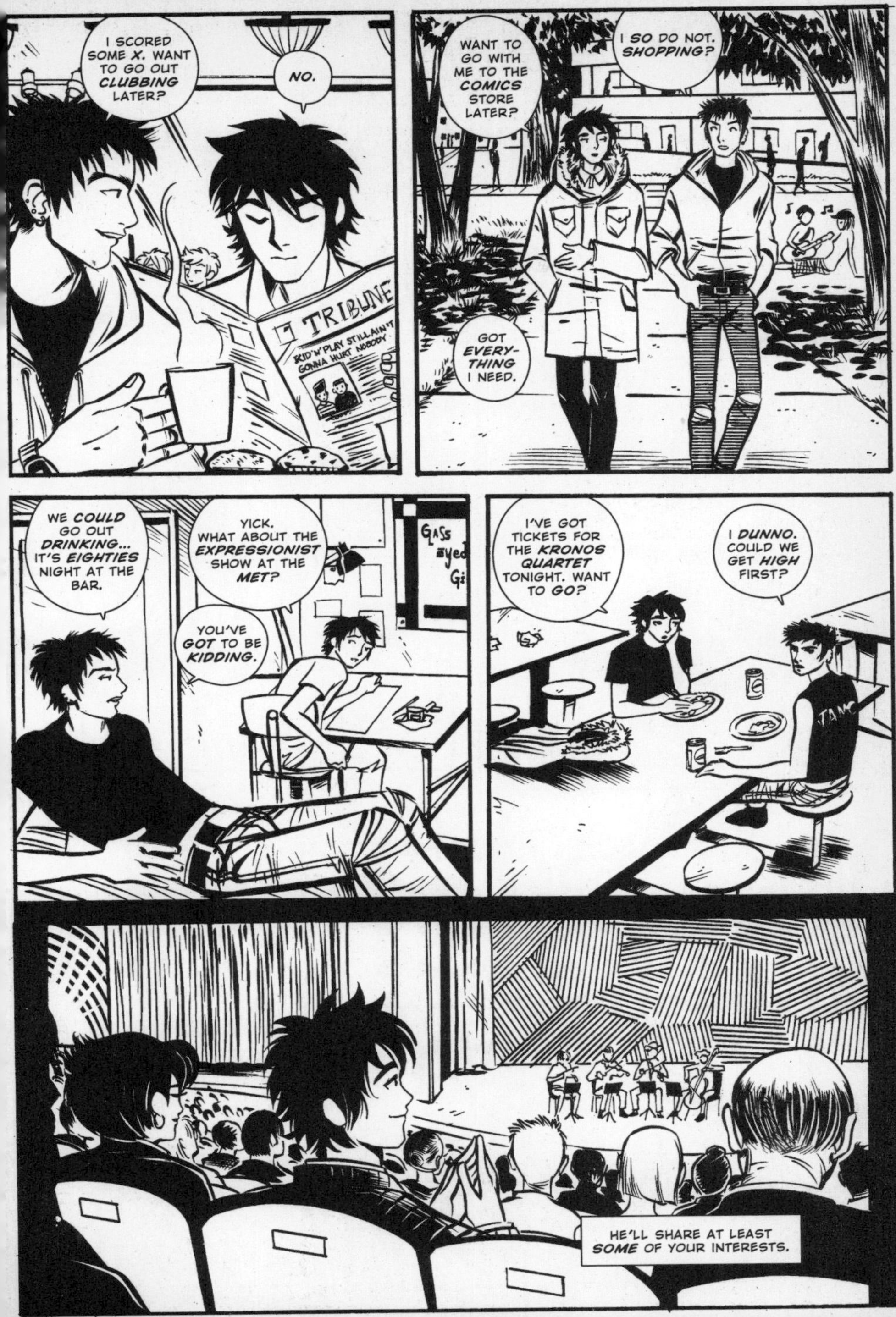
I SCORED SOME *X*. WANT TO GO OUT *CLUBBING* LATER?
NO.
TRIBUNE
KID'N'PLAY STILL AIN'T GONNA HURT NOBODY
WANT TO GO WITH ME TO THE *COMICS* STORE LATER?
I *SO* DO NOT. *SHOPPING?*
GOT *EVERYTHING* I NEED.
WE *COULD* GO OUT *DRINKING*... IT'S *EIGHTIES* NIGHT AT THE BAR.
YICK. WHAT ABOUT THE *EXPRESSIONIST* SHOW AT THE *MET?*
YOU'VE *GOT* TO BE *KIDDING.*
I'VE GOT TICKETS FOR THE *KRONOS QUARTET* TONIGHT. WANT TO *GO?*
I *DUNNO.* COULD WE GET *HIGH* FIRST?
HE'LL SHARE AT LEAST *SOME* OF YOUR INTERESTS.

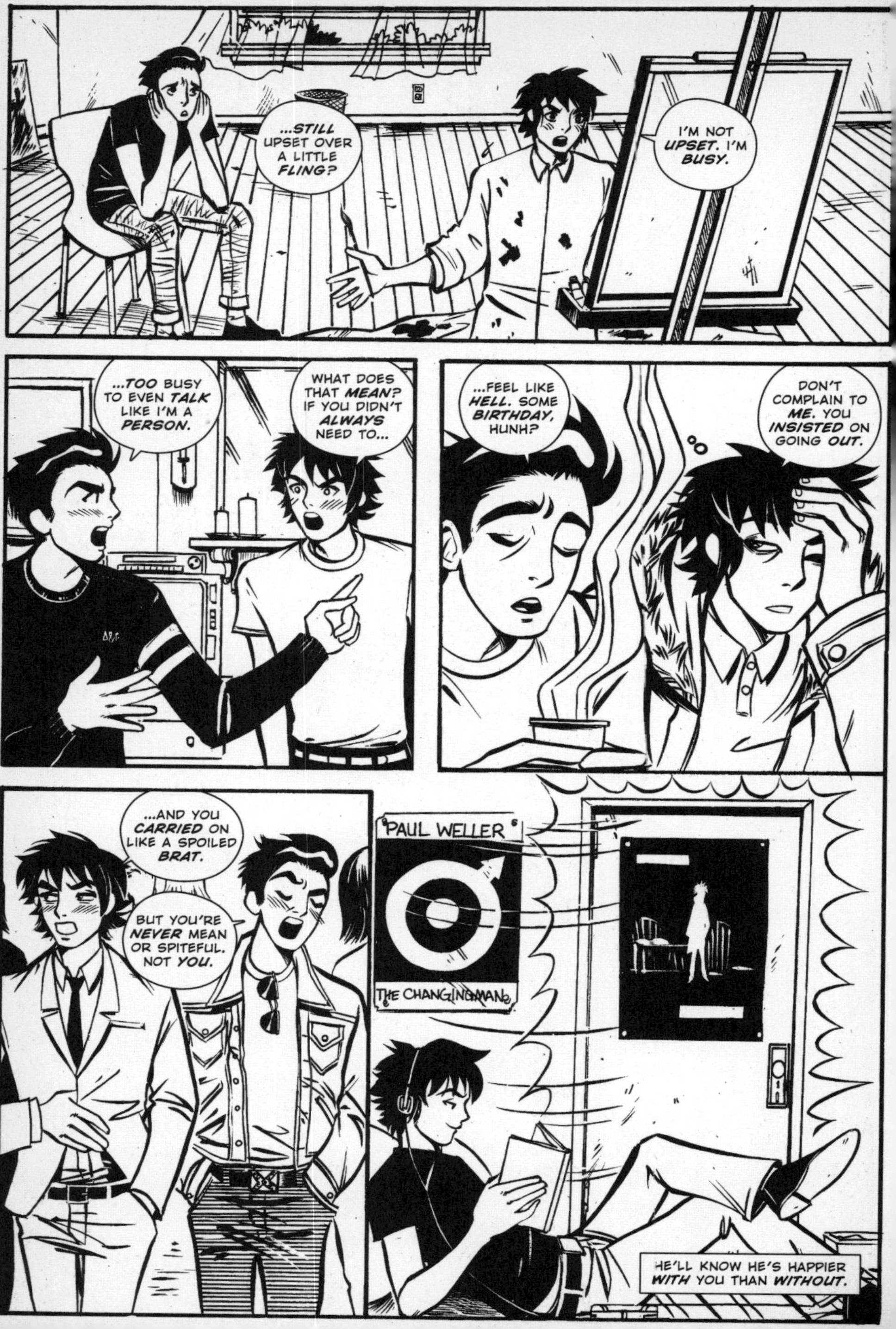

...STILL UPSET OVER A LITTLE FLING?
I'M NOT UPSET. I'M BUSY.
...TOO BUSY TO EVEN TALK LIKE I'M A PERSON.
WHAT DOES THAT MEAN? IF YOU DIDN'T ALWAYS NEED TO...
...FEEL LIKE HELL. SOME BIRTHDAY, HUNH?
DON'T COMPLAIN TO ME. YOU INSISTED ON GOING OUT.
...AND YOU CARRIED ON LIKE A SPOILED BRAT.
BUT YOU'RE NEVER MEAN OR SPITEFUL. NOT YOU.
PAUL WELLER
THE CHANGINGMAN
HE'LL KNOW HE'S HAPPIER WITH YOU THAN WITHOUT.

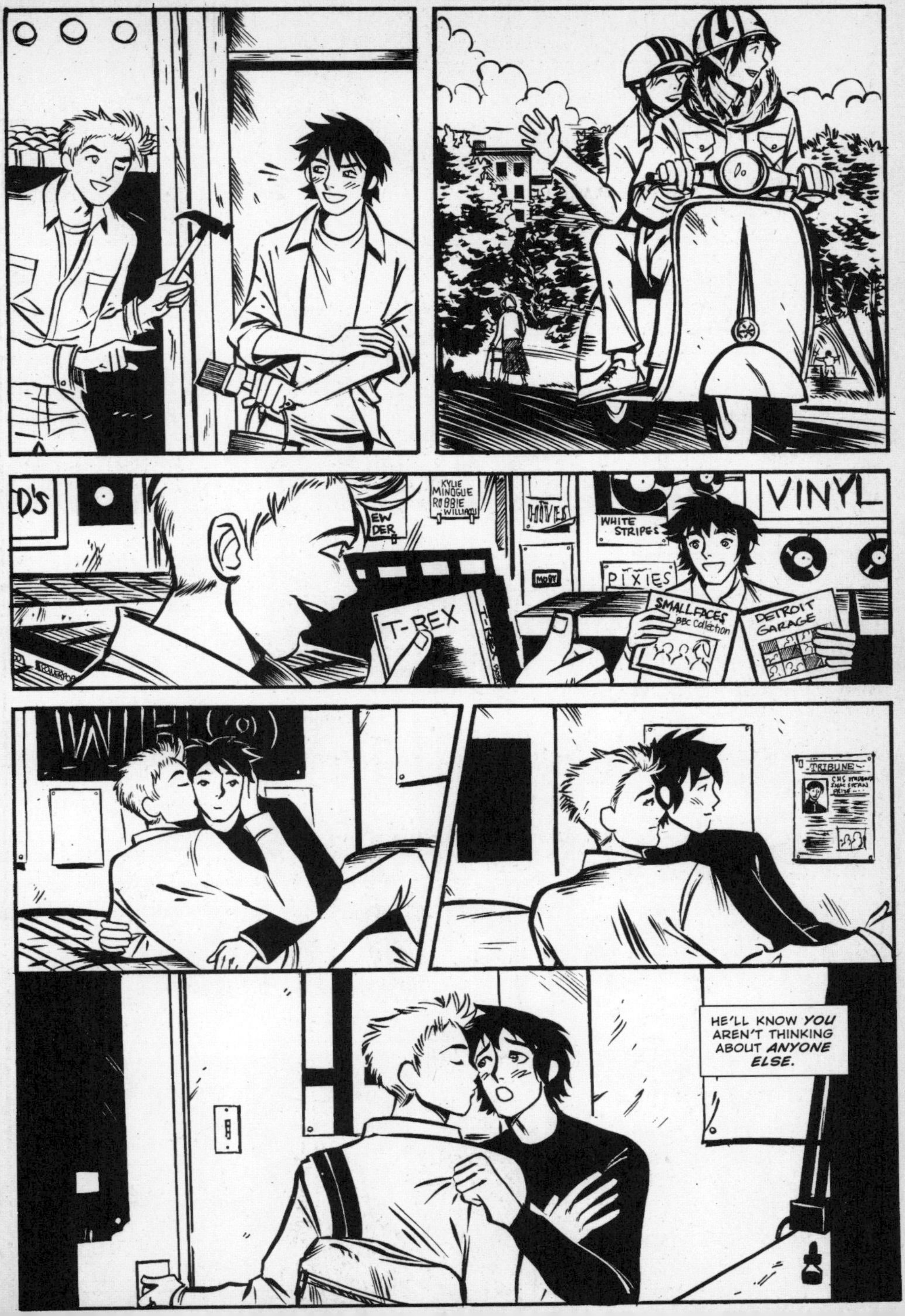
KYLIE MINOGUE
ROBBIE WILLIAMS
HIVES
WHITE STRIPES
VINYL
PIXIES
T-REX
SMALLFACES
BBC Collection
DETROIT GARAGE
TRIBUNE
HE'LL KNOW *YOU* AREN'T THINKING ABOUT *ANYONE ELSE*.

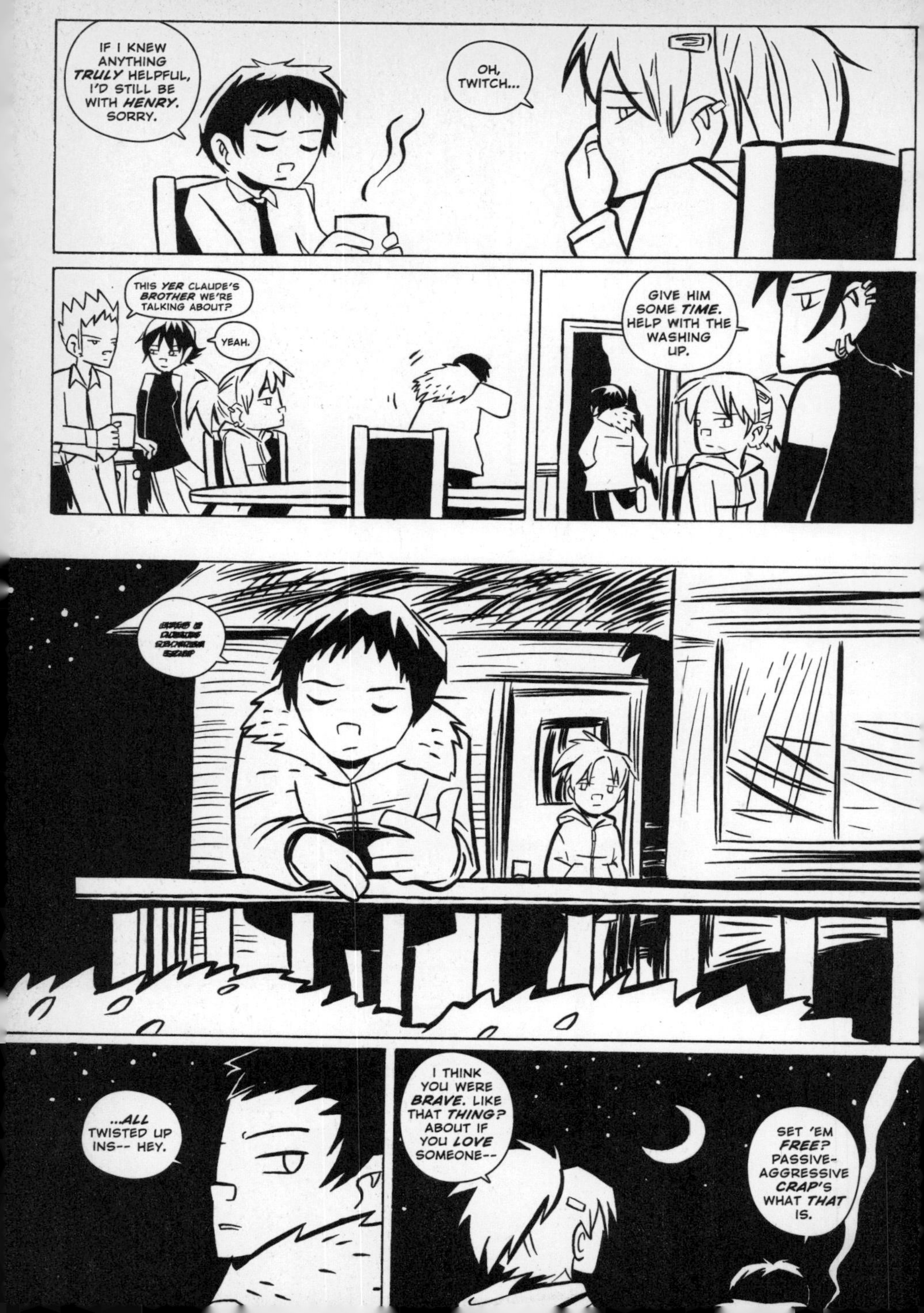
IF I KNEW ANYTHING TRULY HELPFUL, I'D STILL BE WITH HENRY. SORRY.
OH, TWITCH...
THIS YER CLAUDE'S BROTHER WE'RE TALKING ABOUT?
YEAH.
GIVE HIM SOME TIME. HELP WITH THE WASHING UP.
...ALL TWISTED UP INS-- HEY.
I THINK YOU WERE BRAVE. LIKE THAT THING? ABOUT IF YOU LOVE SOMEONE--
SET 'EM FREE? PASSIVE-AGGRESSIVE CRAP'S WHAT THAT IS.

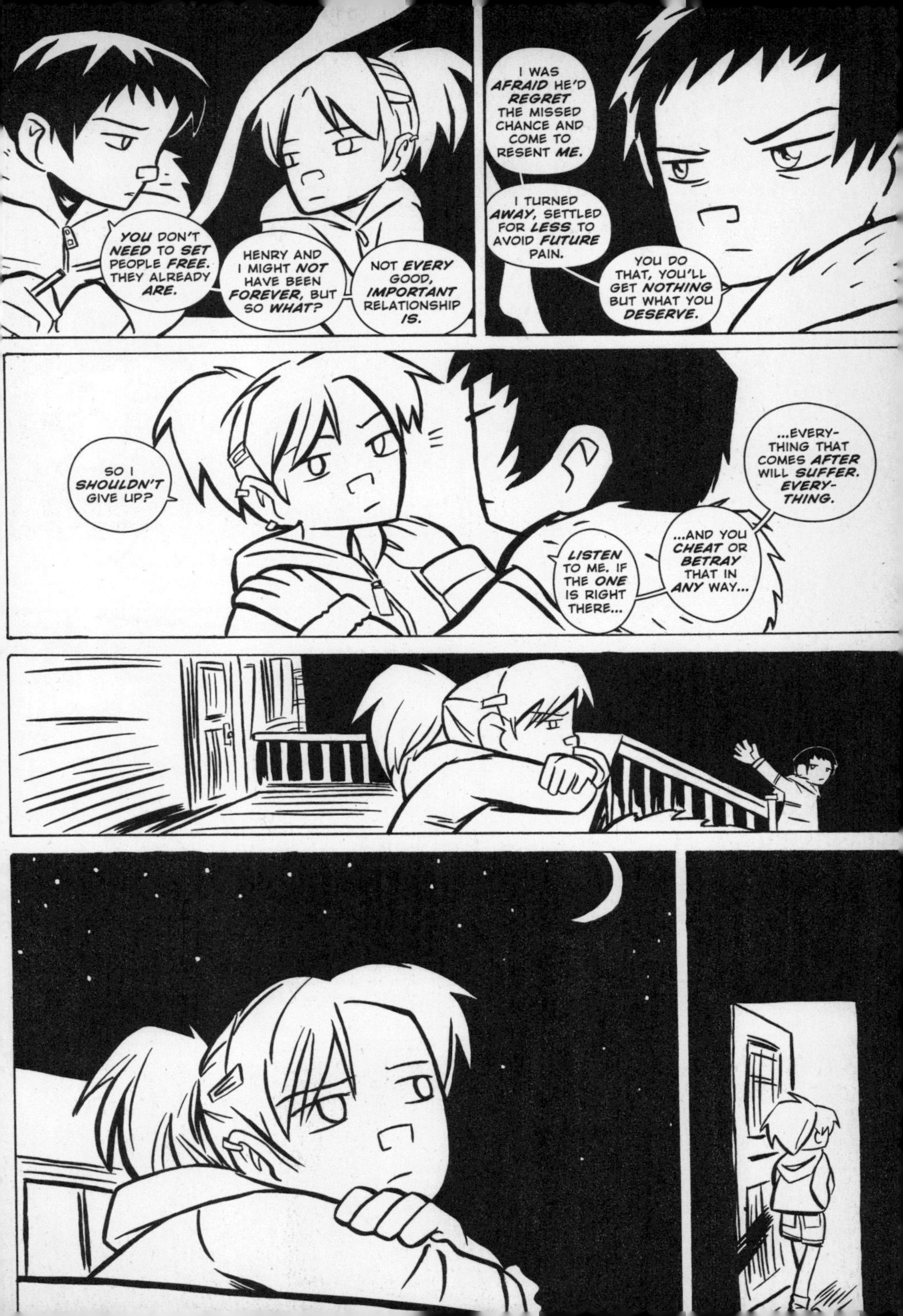
YOU DON'T NEED TO SET PEOPLE FREE. THEY ALREADY ARE.
HENRY AND I MIGHT NOT HAVE BEEN FOREVER, BUT SO WHAT?
NOT EVERY GOOD, IMPORTANT RELATIONSHIP IS.
I WAS AFRAID HE'D REGRET THE MISSED CHANCE AND COME TO RESENT ME.
I TURNED AWAY, SETTLED FOR LESS TO AVOID FUTURE PAIN.
YOU DO THAT, YOU'LL GET NOTHING BUT WHAT YOU DESERVE.
SO I SHOULDN'T GIVE UP?
LISTEN TO ME. IF THE ONE IS RIGHT THERE...
...AND YOU CHEAT OR BETRAY THAT IN ANY WAY...
...EVERY-THING THAT COMES AFTER WILL SUFFER. EVERY-THING.

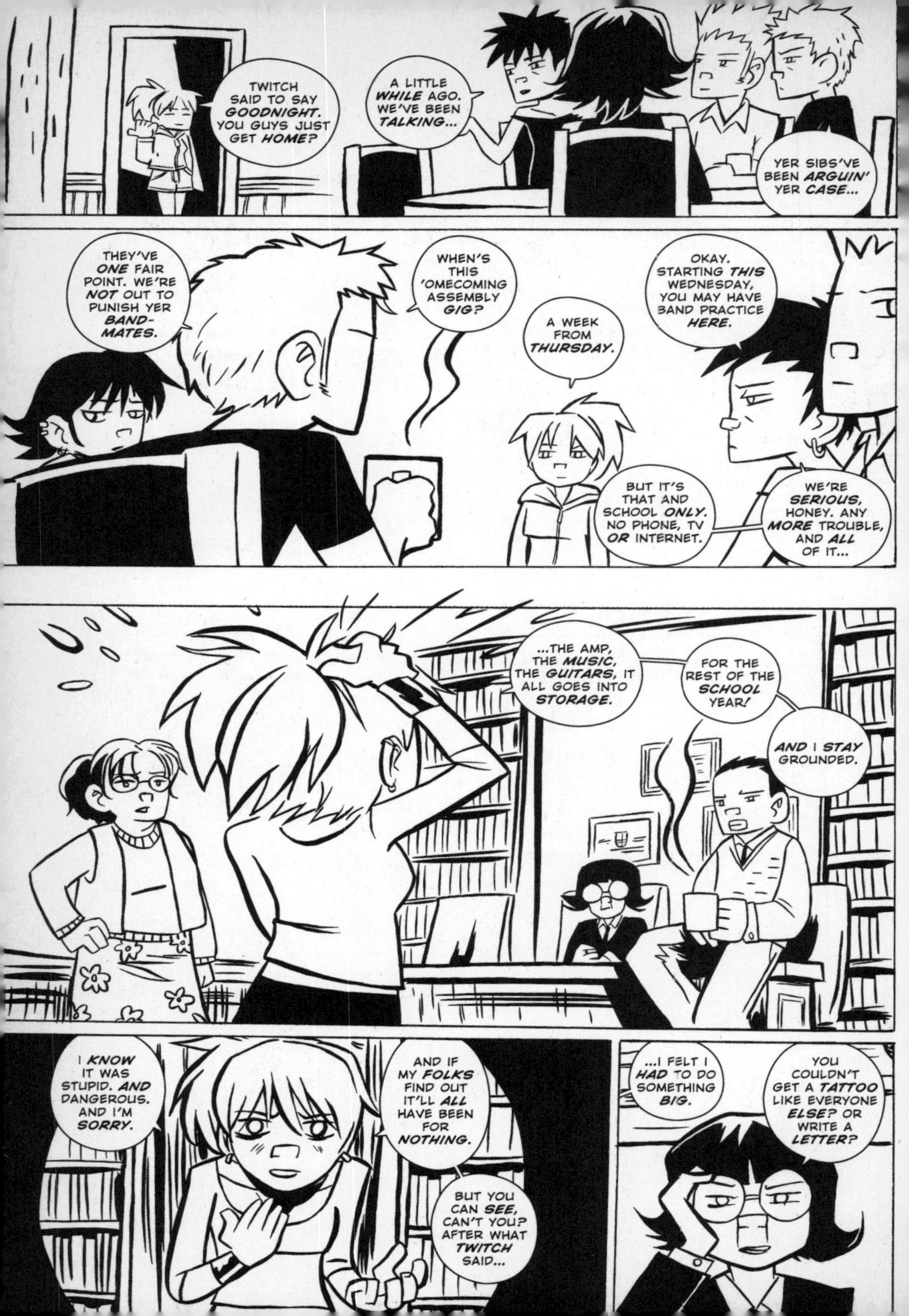
TWITCH SAID TO SAY GOODNIGHT. YOU GUYS JUST GET HOME?
A LITTLE WHILE AGO. WE'VE BEEN TALKING...
YER SIBS'VE BEEN ARGUIN' YER CASE...
THEY'VE ONE FAIR POINT. WE'RE NOT OUT TO PUNISH YER BAND-MATES.
WHEN'S THIS 'OMECOMING ASSEMBLY GIG?
A WEEK FROM THURSDAY.
OKAY. STARTING THIS WEDNESDAY, YOU MAY HAVE BAND PRACTICE HERE.
BUT IT'S THAT AND SCHOOL ONLY. NO PHONE, TV OR INTERNET.
WE'RE SERIOUS, HONEY. ANY MORE TROUBLE, AND ALL OF IT...
...THE AMP, THE MUSIC, THE GUITARS, IT ALL GOES INTO STORAGE.
FOR THE REST OF THE SCHOOL YEAR!
AND I STAY GROUNDED.
I KNOW IT WAS STUPID. AND DANGEROUS. AND I'M SORRY.
AND IF MY FOLKS FIND OUT IT'LL ALL HAVE BEEN FOR NOTHING.
BUT YOU CAN SEE, CAN'T YOU? AFTER WHAT TWITCH SAID...
...I FELT I HAD TO DO SOMETHING BIG.
YOU COULDN'T GET A TATTOO LIKE EVERYONE ELSE? OR WRITE A LETTER?

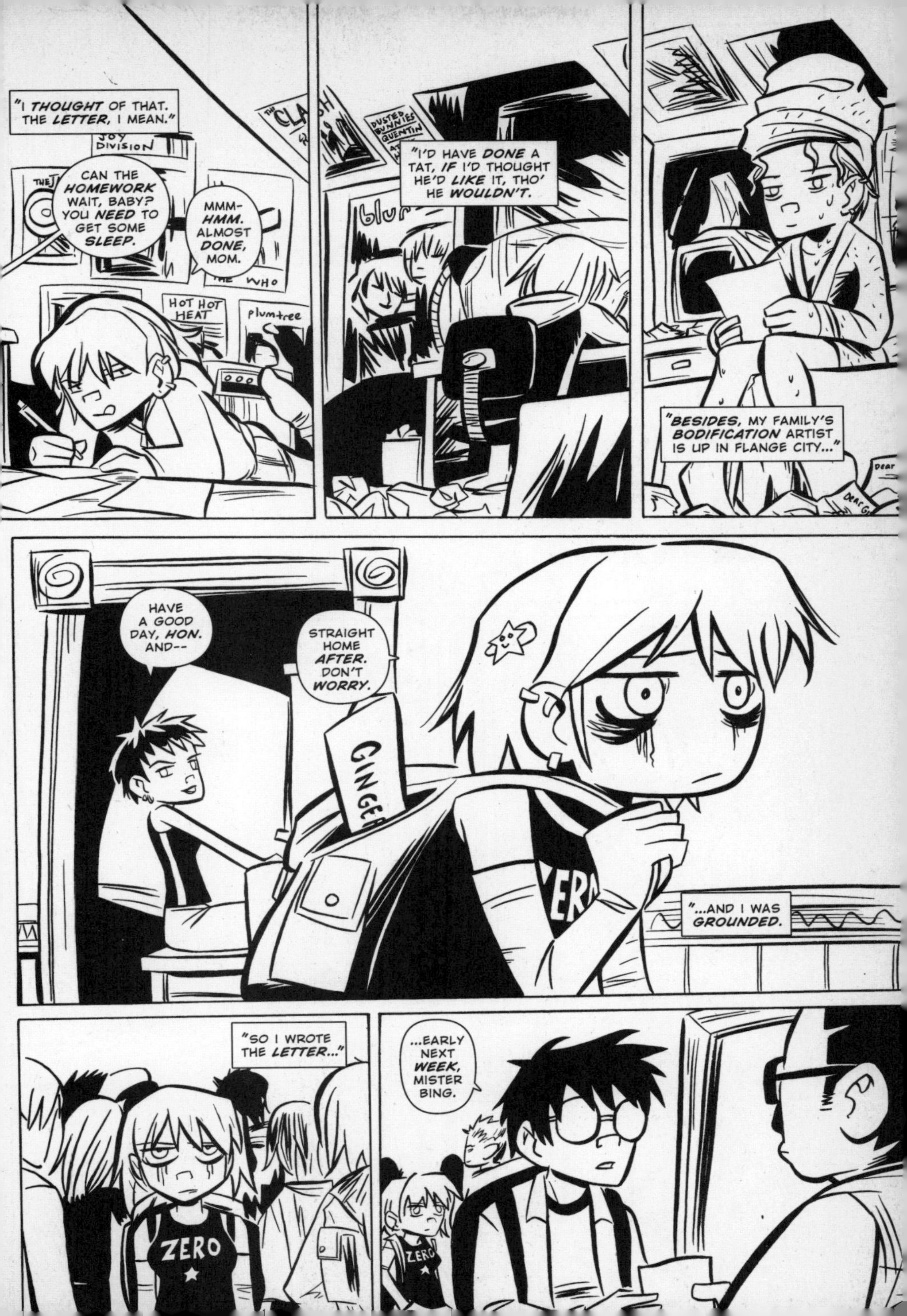
"I THOUGHT OF THAT. THE LETTER, I MEAN."
JOY DIVISION
CAN THE HOMEWORK WAIT, BABY? YOU NEED TO GET SOME SLEEP.
MMM-HMM. ALMOST DONE, MOM.
THE WHO
HOT HOT HEAT
plumtree
THE CLASH
DUSTED BUNNIES
QUENTIN
blur
"I'D HAVE DONE A TAT, IF I'D THOUGHT HE'D LIKE IT, THO' HE WOULDN'T.
"BESIDES, MY FAMILY'S BODIFICATION ARTIST IS UP IN FLANGE CITY..."
HAVE A GOOD DAY, HON. AND--
STRAIGHT HOME AFTER. DON'T WORRY.
GINGE
ZERO
"...AND I WAS GROUNDED.
"SO I WROTE THE LETTER..."
ZERO
...EARLY NEXT WEEK, MISTER BING.
ZERO

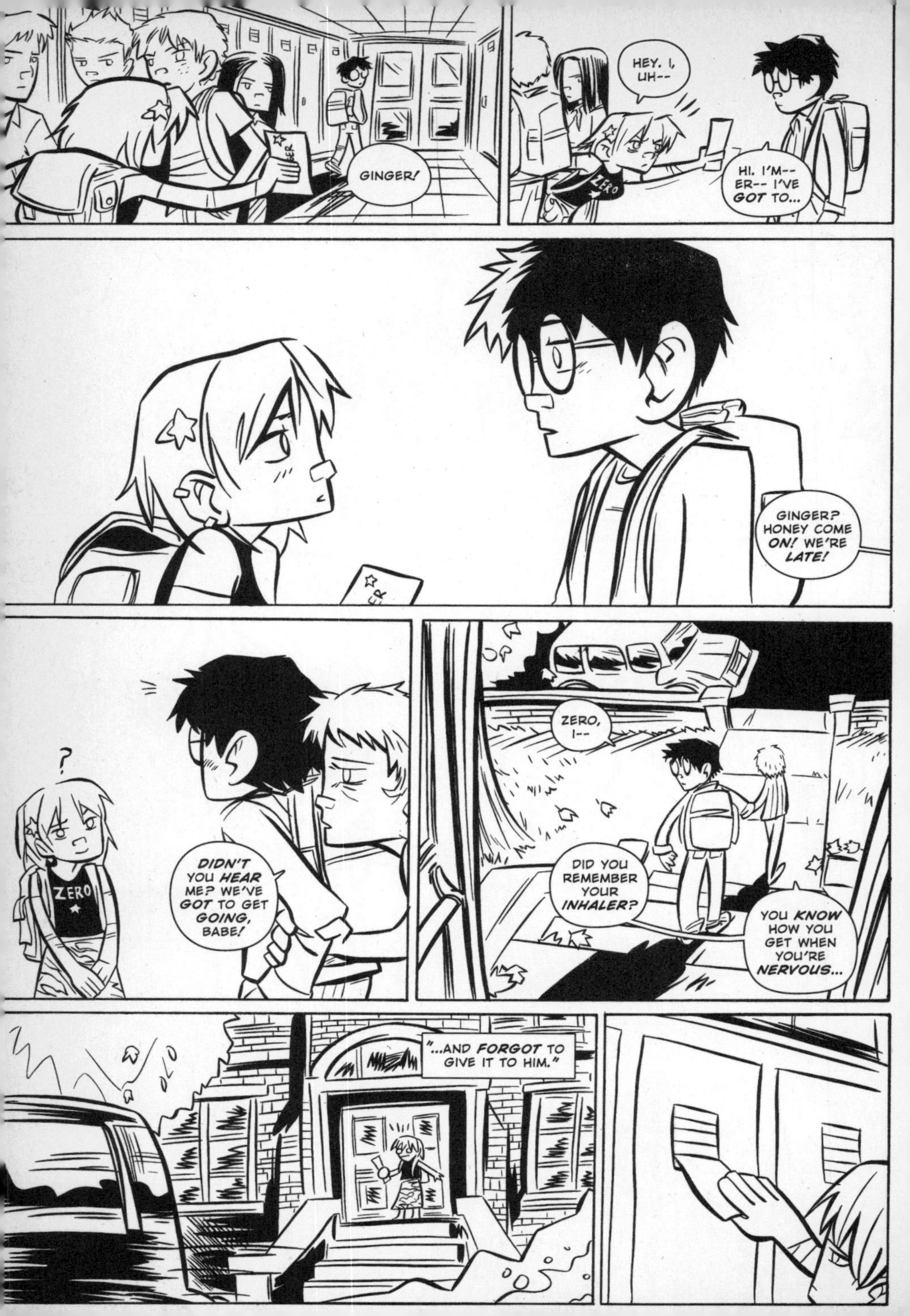
GER
GINGER!
HEY. I, UH--
HI. I'M-- ER-- I'VE GOT TO...
ZERO
GINGER? HONEY COME ON! WE'RE LATE!
?
DIDN'T YOU HEAR ME? WE'VE GOT TO GET GOING, BABE!
ZERO
ZERO, I--
DID YOU REMEMBER YOUR INHALER?
YOU KNOW HOW YOU GET WHEN YOU'RE NERVOUS...
"...AND FORGOT TO GIVE IT TO HIM."

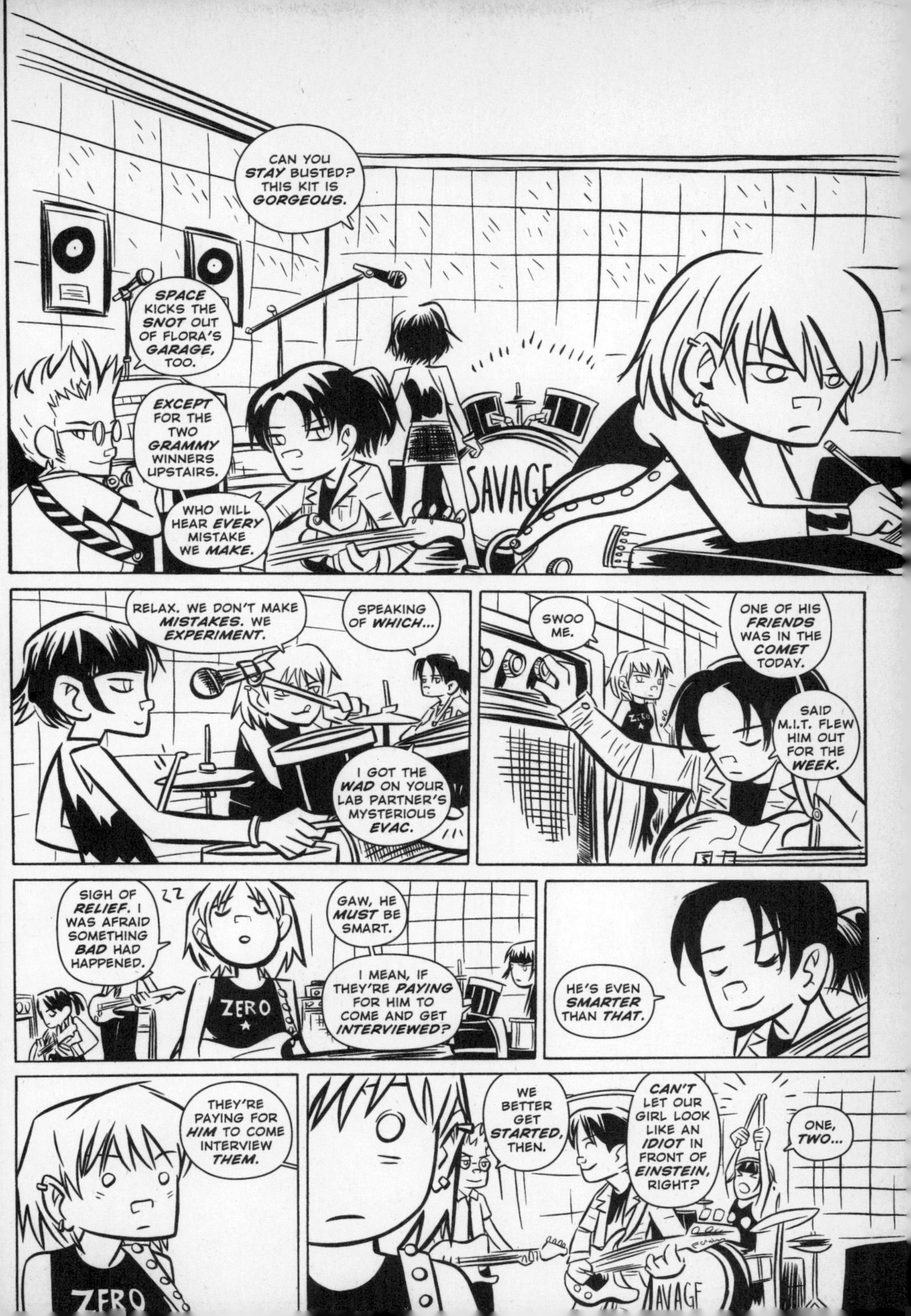
CAN YOU STAY BUSTED? THIS KIT IS GORGEOUS.
SPACE KICKS THE SNOT OUT OF FLORA'S GARAGE, TOO.
EXCEPT FOR THE TWO GRAMMY WINNERS UPSTAIRS.
WHO WILL HEAR EVERY MISTAKE WE MAKE.
SAVAGE
RELAX. WE DON'T MAKE MISTAKES. WE EXPERIMENT.
SPEAKING OF WHICH...
I GOT THE WAD ON YOUR LAB PARTNER'S MYSTERIOUS EVAC.
SWOO ME.
ONE OF HIS FRIENDS WAS IN THE COMET TODAY.
SAID M.I.T. FLEW HIM OUT FOR THE WEEK.
SIGH OF RELIEF. I WAS AFRAID SOMETHING BAD HAD HAPPENED.
GAW, HE MUST BE SMART.
ZERO
I MEAN, IF THEY'RE PAYING FOR HIM TO COME AND GET INTERVIEWED?
HE'S EVEN SMARTER THAN THAT.
THEY'RE PAYING FOR HIM TO COME INTERVIEW THEM.
WE BETTER GET STARTED, THEN.
CAN'T LET OUR GIRL LOOK LIKE AN IDIOT IN FRONT OF EINSTEIN, RIGHT?
ONE, TWO...
ZERO

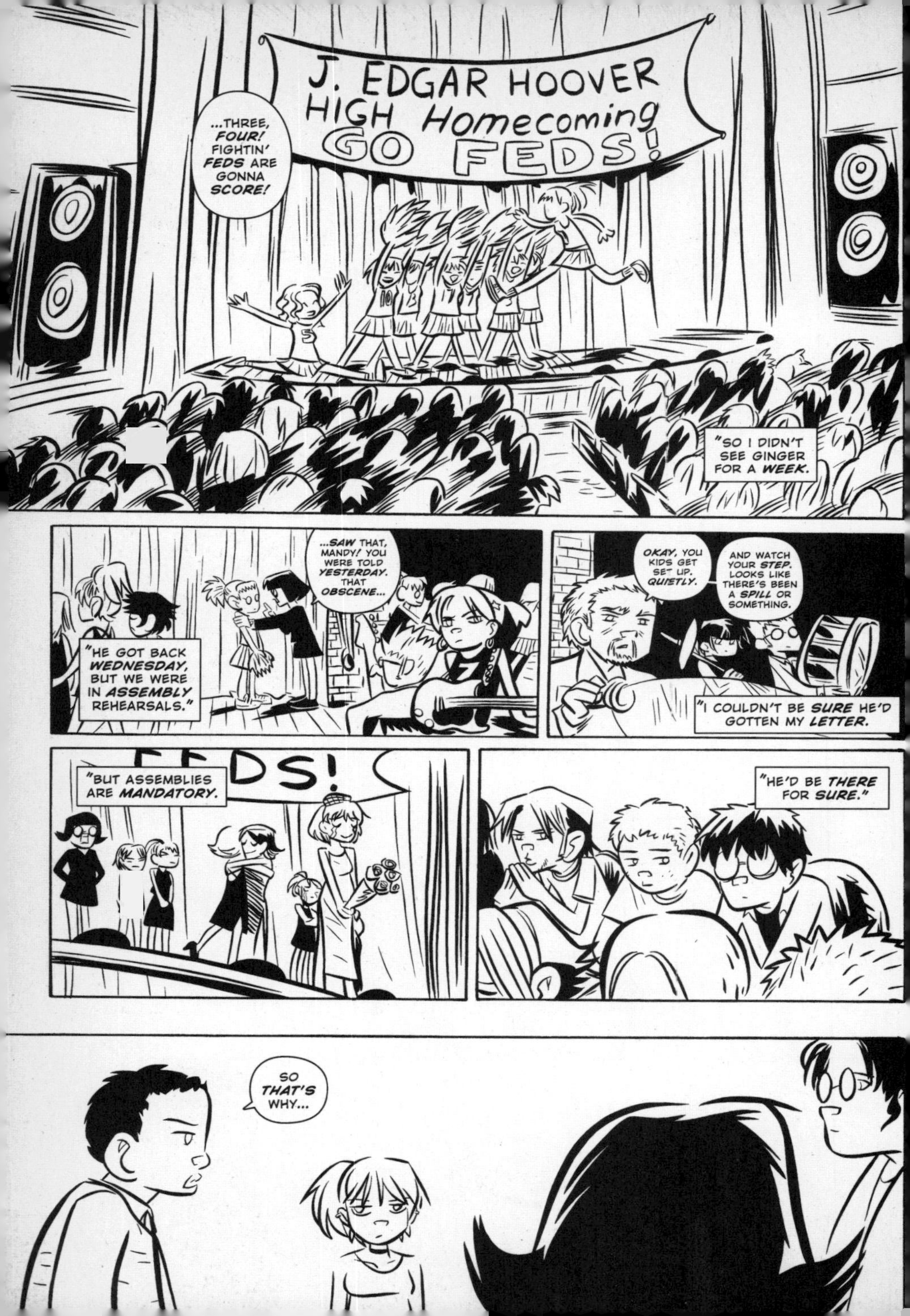
J. EDGAR HOOVER HIGH Homecoming GO FEDS!
...THREE, FOUR! FIGHTIN' FEDS ARE GONNA SCORE!
"SO I DIDN'T SEE GINGER FOR A WEEK.
"HE GOT BACK WEDNESDAY, BUT WE WERE IN ASSEMBLY REHEARSALS."
...SAW THAT, MANDY! YOU WERE TOLD YESTERDAY. THAT OBSCENE...
OKAY, YOU KIDS GET SET UP. QUIETLY.
AND WATCH YOUR STEP. LOOKS LIKE THERE'S BEEN A SPILL OR SOMETHING.
"I COULDN'T BE SURE HE'D GOTTEN MY LETTER.
"BUT ASSEMBLIES ARE MANDATORY.
DS!
"HE'D BE THERE FOR SURE."
SO THAT'S WHY...

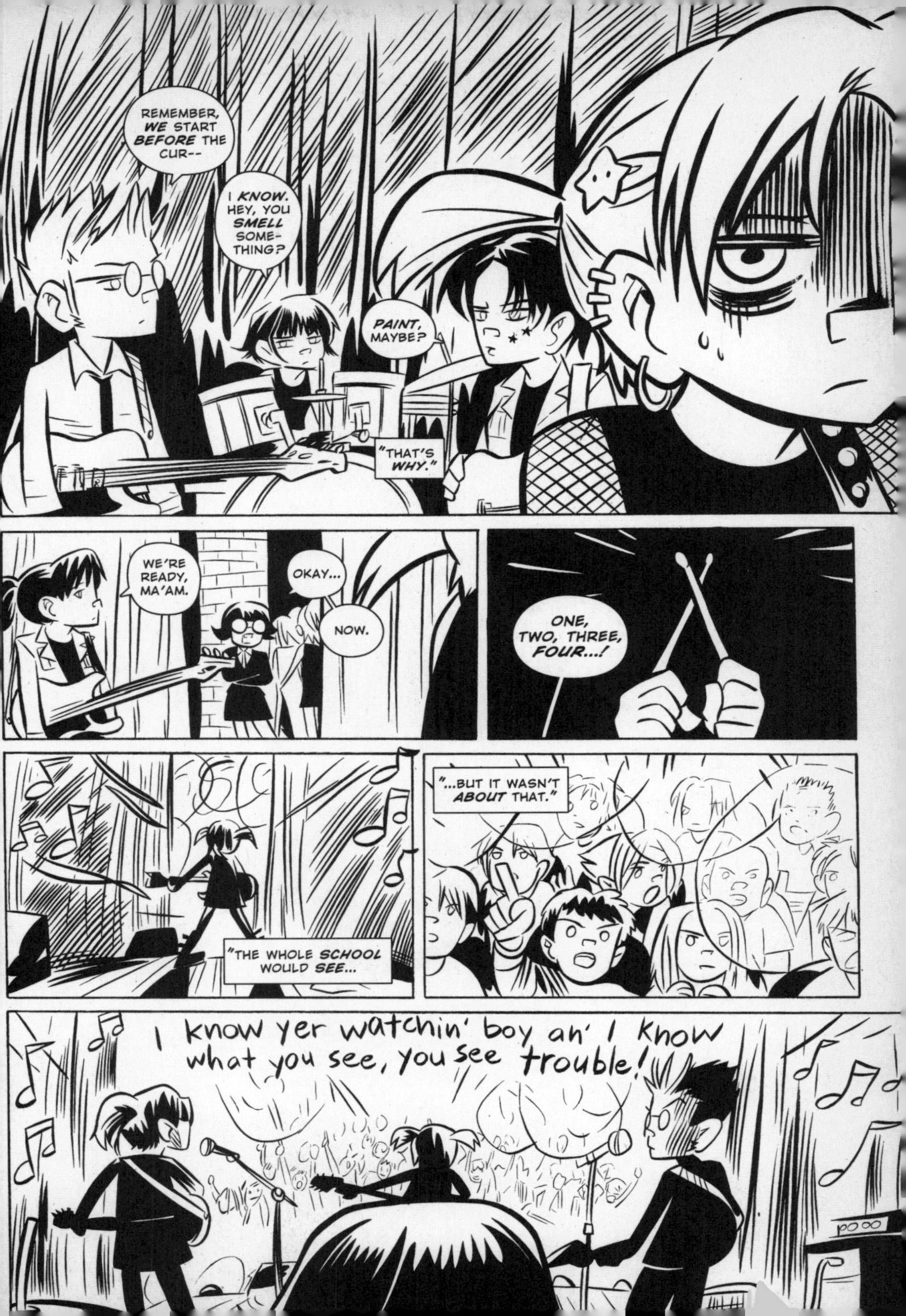

REMEMBER, WE START BEFORE THE CUR--
I KNOW. HEY, YOU SMELL SOMETHING?
PAINT, MAYBE?
"THAT'S WHY."
WE'RE READY, MA'AM.
OKAY...
NOW.
ONE, TWO, THREE, FOUR...!
"THE WHOLE SCHOOL WOULD SEE...
"...BUT IT WASN'T ABOUT THAT."
I know yer watchin' boy an' I know what you see, you see trouble!

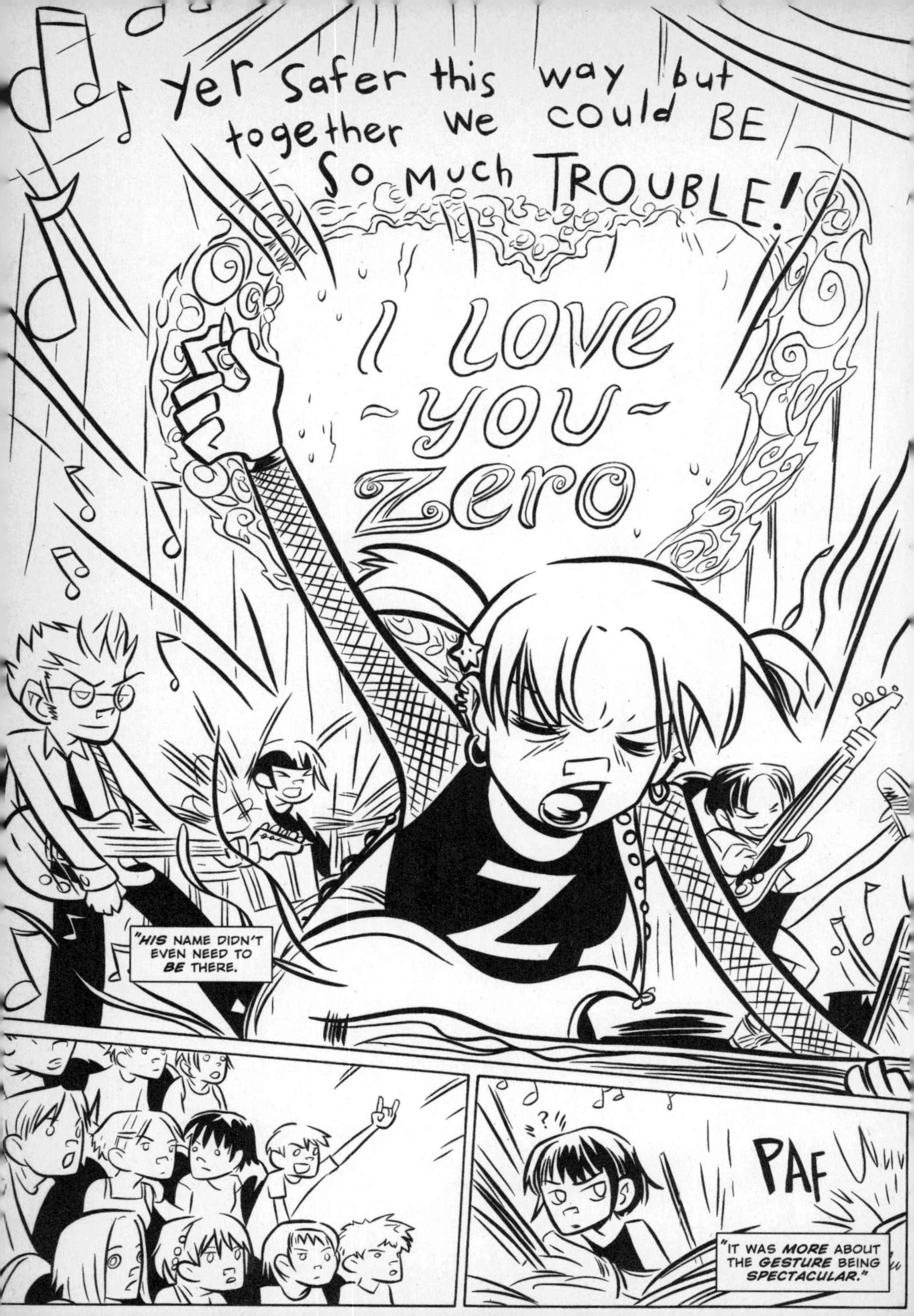
yer Safer this way but together we could BE So much TROUBLE!
I LOVE ~YOU~ ZERO
"HIS NAME DIDN'T EVEN NEED TO BE THERE.
?!
PAF
"IT WAS MORE ABOUT THE GESTURE BEING SPECTACULAR."

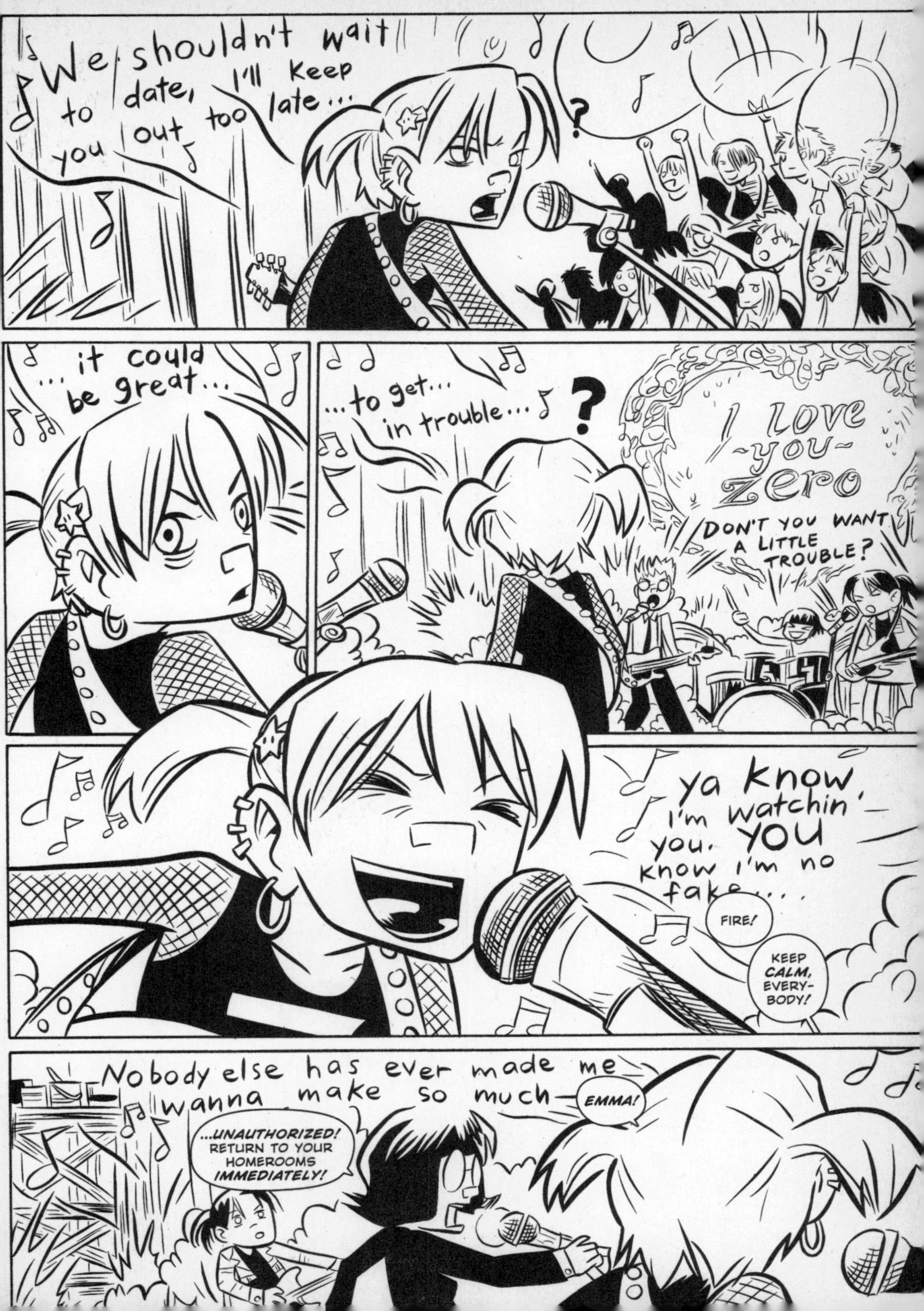

We shouldn't wait to date, I'll keep you out too late...
?
...it could be great...
...to get... in trouble...
?
I love you zero
DON'T YOU WANT A LITTLE TROUBLE?
ya know, I'm watchin' you. YOU know I'm no fake...
FIRE!
KEEP CALM, EVERYBODY!
Nobody else has ever made me wanna make so much—
EMMA!
...UNAUTHORIZED! RETURN TO YOUR HOMEROOMS IMMEDIATELY!

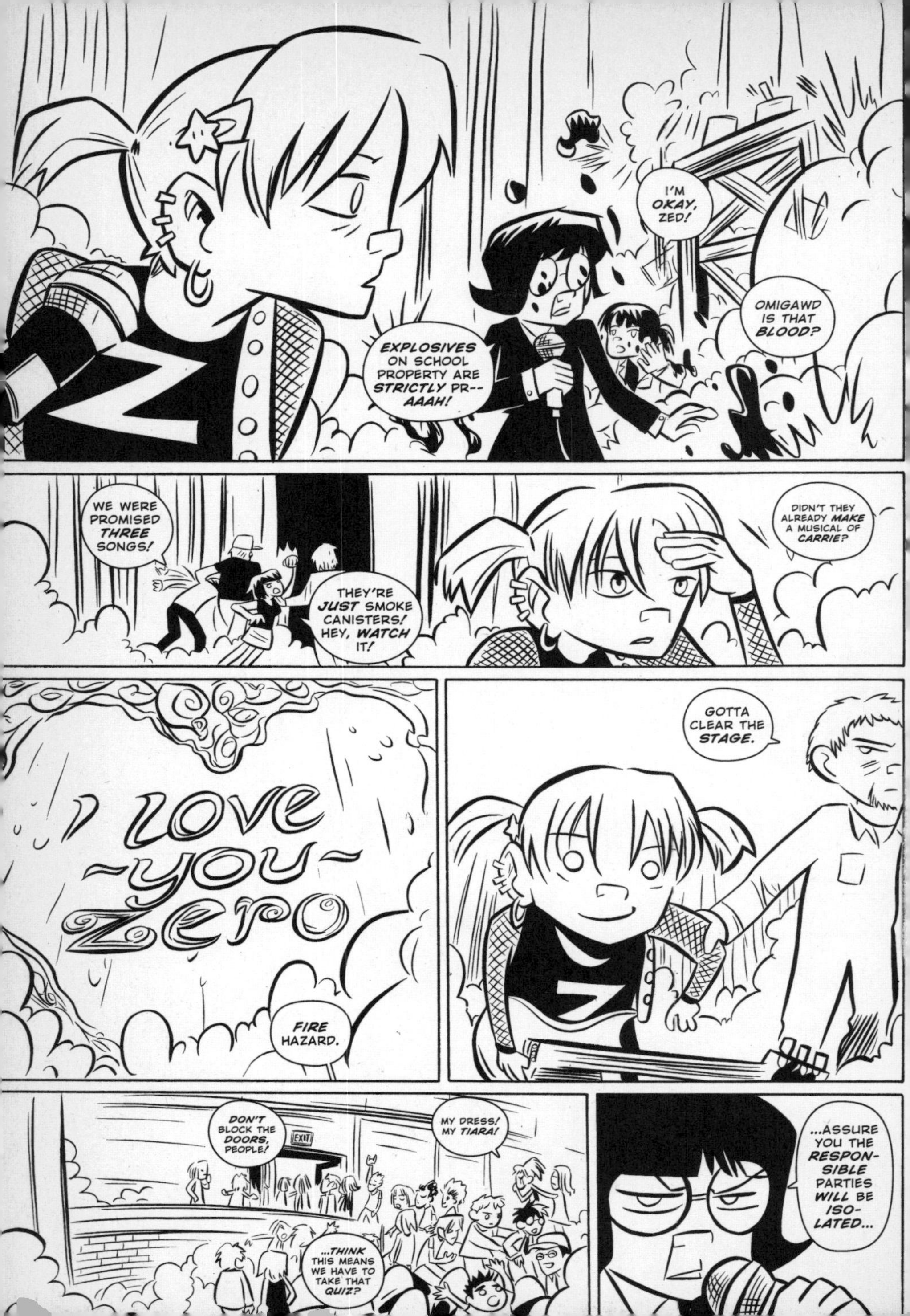

I'M OKAY, ZED!
OMIGAWD IS THAT BLOOD?
EXPLOSIVES ON SCHOOL PROPERTY ARE STRICTLY PR-- AAAH!
WE WERE PROMISED THREE SONGS!
THEY'RE JUST SMOKE CANISTERS! HEY, WATCH IT!
DIDN'T THEY ALREADY MAKE A MUSICAL OF CARRIE?
I LOVE -YOU- ZERO
FIRE HAZARD.
GOTTA CLEAR THE STAGE.
DON'T BLOCK THE DOORS, PEOPLE!
EXIT
MY DRESS! MY TIARA!
...THINK THIS MEANS WE HAVE TO TAKE THAT QUIZ?
...ASSURE YOU THE RESPONSIBLE PARTIES WILL BE ISOLATED...

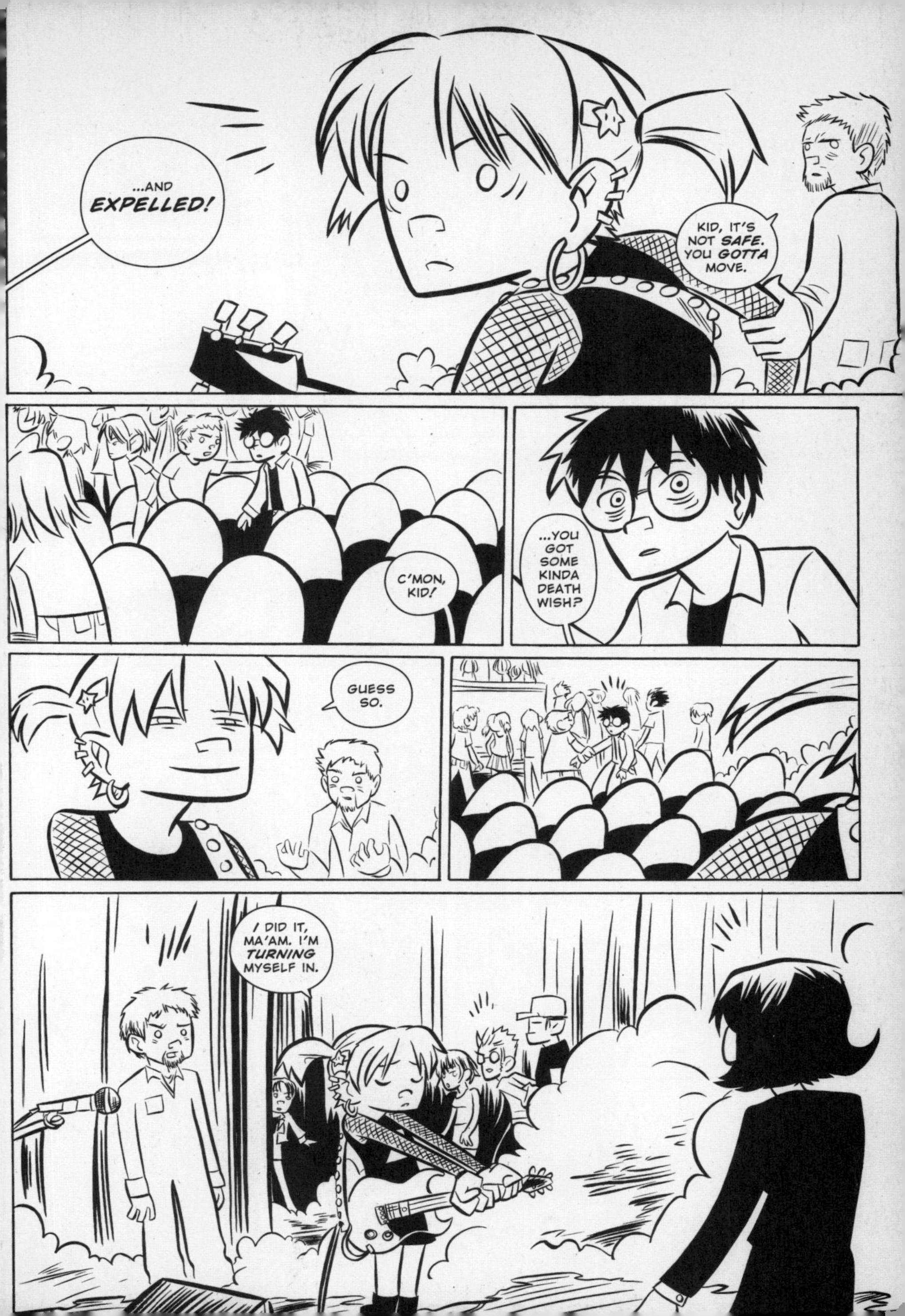
...AND EXPELLED!
KID, IT'S NOT SAFE. YOU GOTTA MOVE.
C'MON, KID!
...YOU GOT SOME KINDA DEATH WISH?
GUESS SO.
I DID IT, MA'AM. I'M TURNING MYSELF IN.

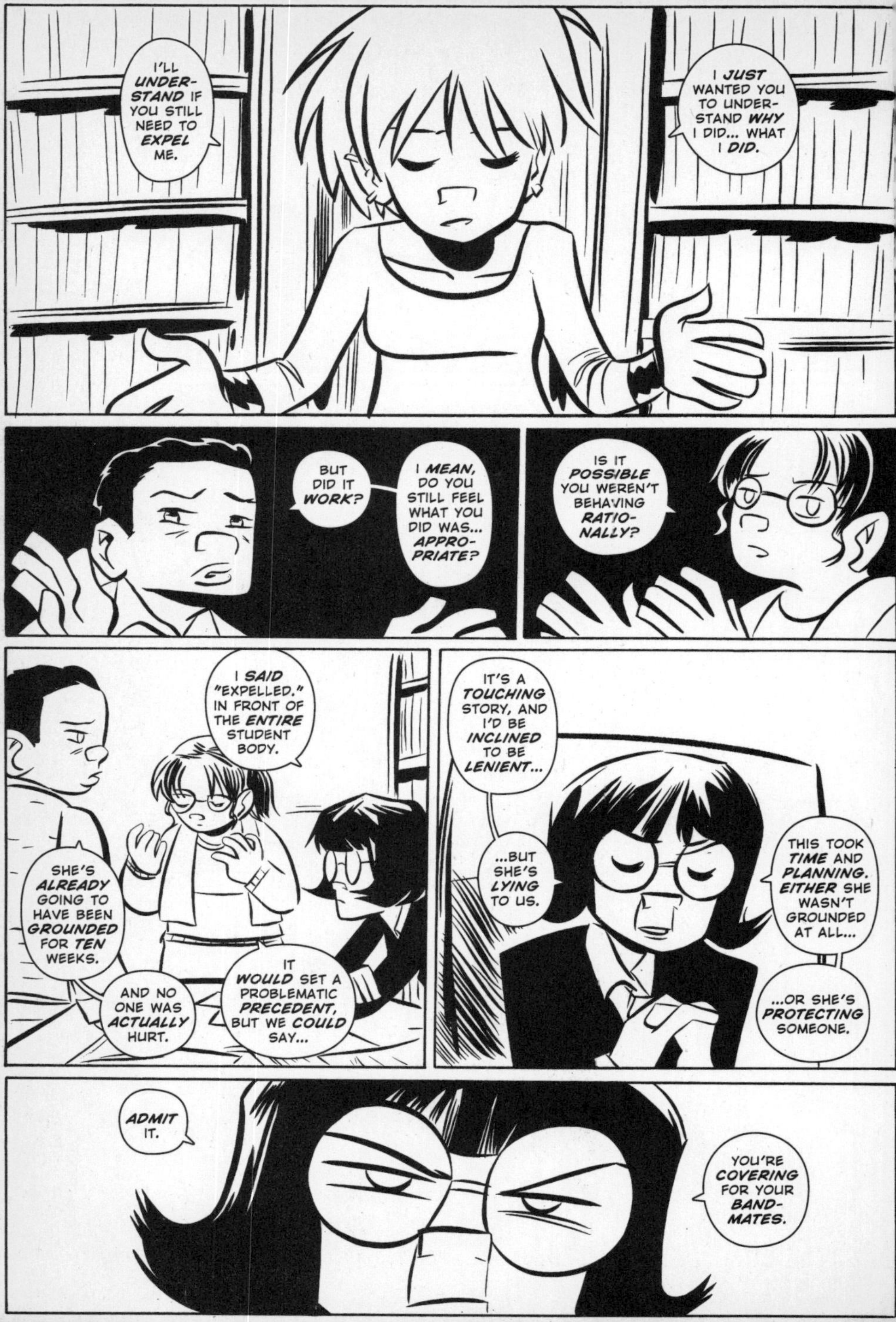
I'LL UNDERSTAND IF YOU STILL NEED TO EXPEL ME.
I JUST WANTED YOU TO UNDERSTAND WHY I DID... WHAT I DID.
BUT DID IT WORK?
I MEAN, DO YOU STILL FEEL WHAT YOU DID WAS... APPROPRIATE?
IS IT POSSIBLE YOU WEREN'T BEHAVING RATIONALLY?
I SAID "EXPELLED." IN FRONT OF THE ENTIRE STUDENT BODY.
SHE'S ALREADY GOING TO HAVE BEEN GROUNDED FOR TEN WEEKS.
AND NO ONE WAS ACTUALLY HURT.
IT WOULD SET A PROBLEMATIC PRECEDENT, BUT WE COULD SAY...
IT'S A TOUCHING STORY, AND I'D BE INCLINED TO BE LENIENT...
...BUT SHE'S LYING TO US.
THIS TOOK TIME AND PLANNING. EITHER SHE WASN'T GROUNDED AT ALL...
...OR SHE'S PROTECTING SOMEONE.
ADMIT IT.
YOU'RE COVERING FOR YOUR BANDMATES.

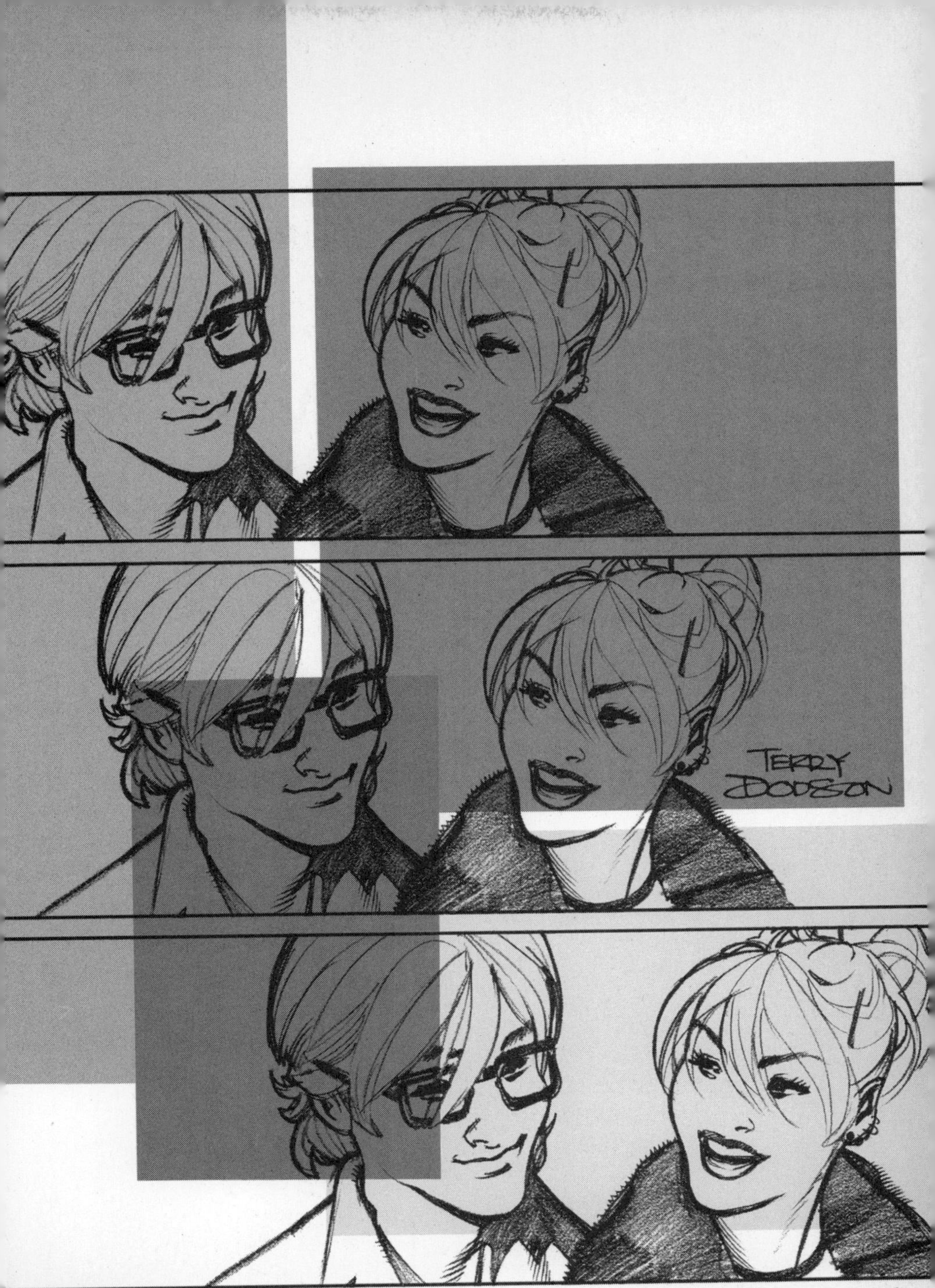
TERRY DODSON

chapter 4

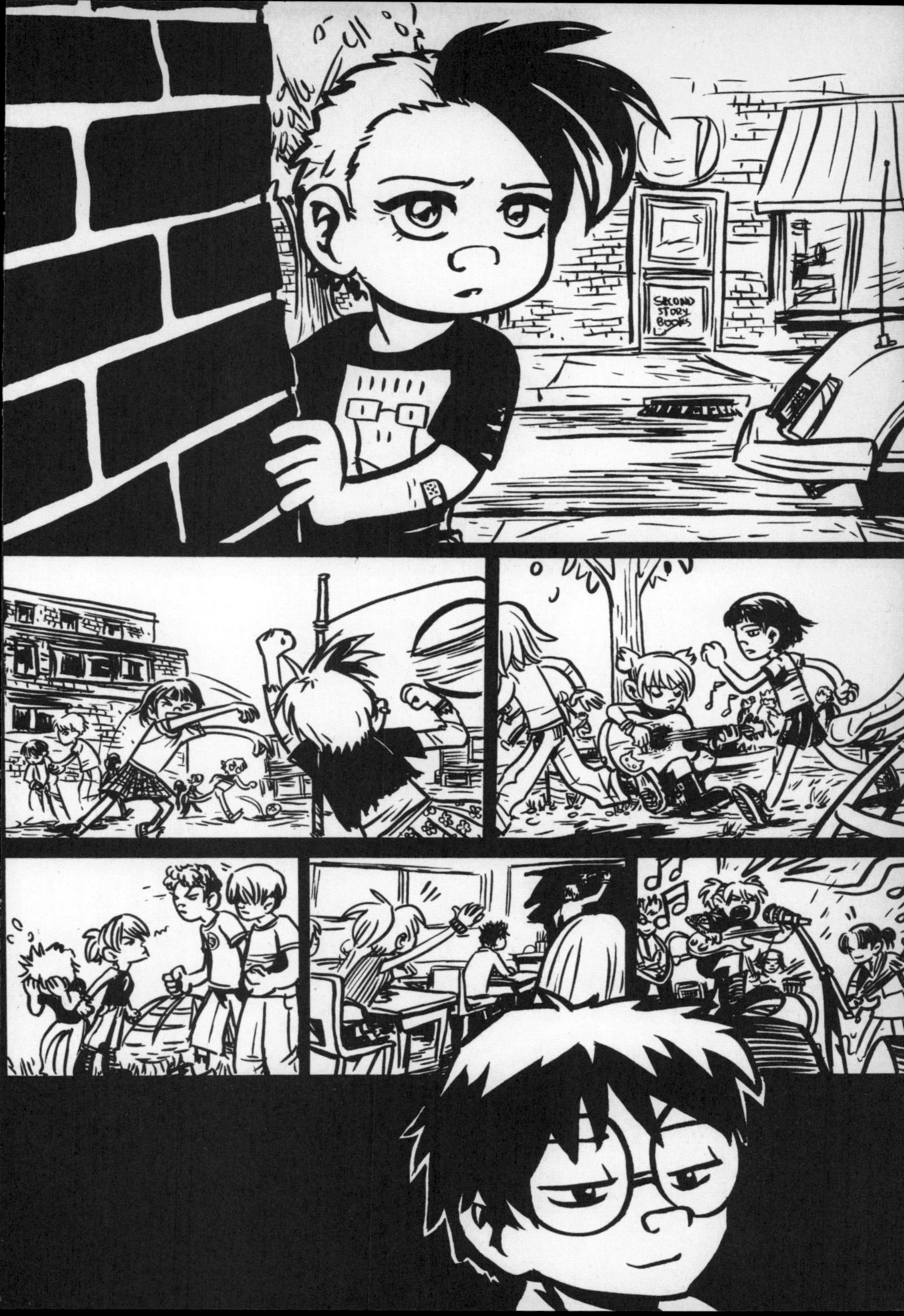
SECOND STORY BOOKS

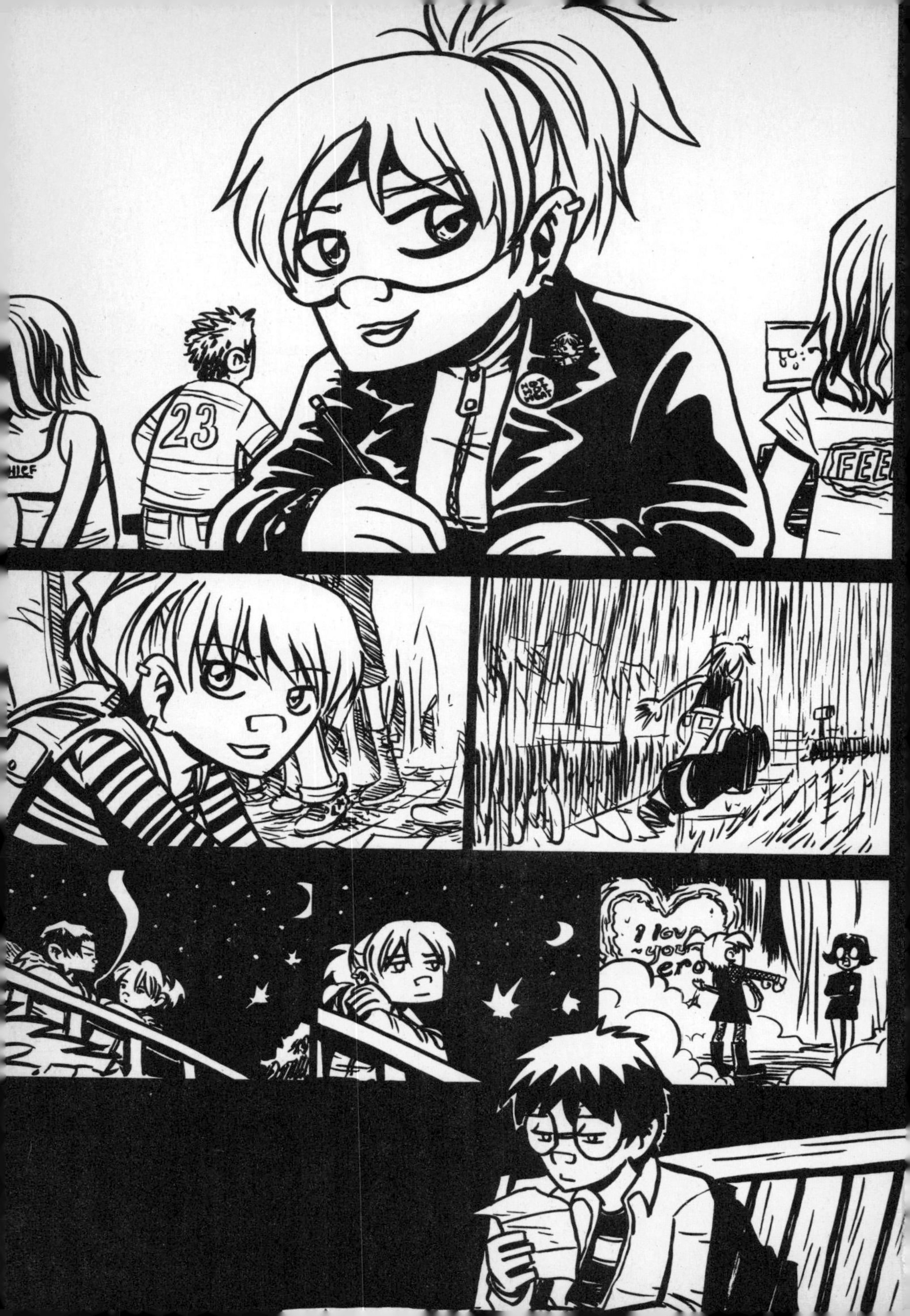
23
FEE
I love
~you
ero

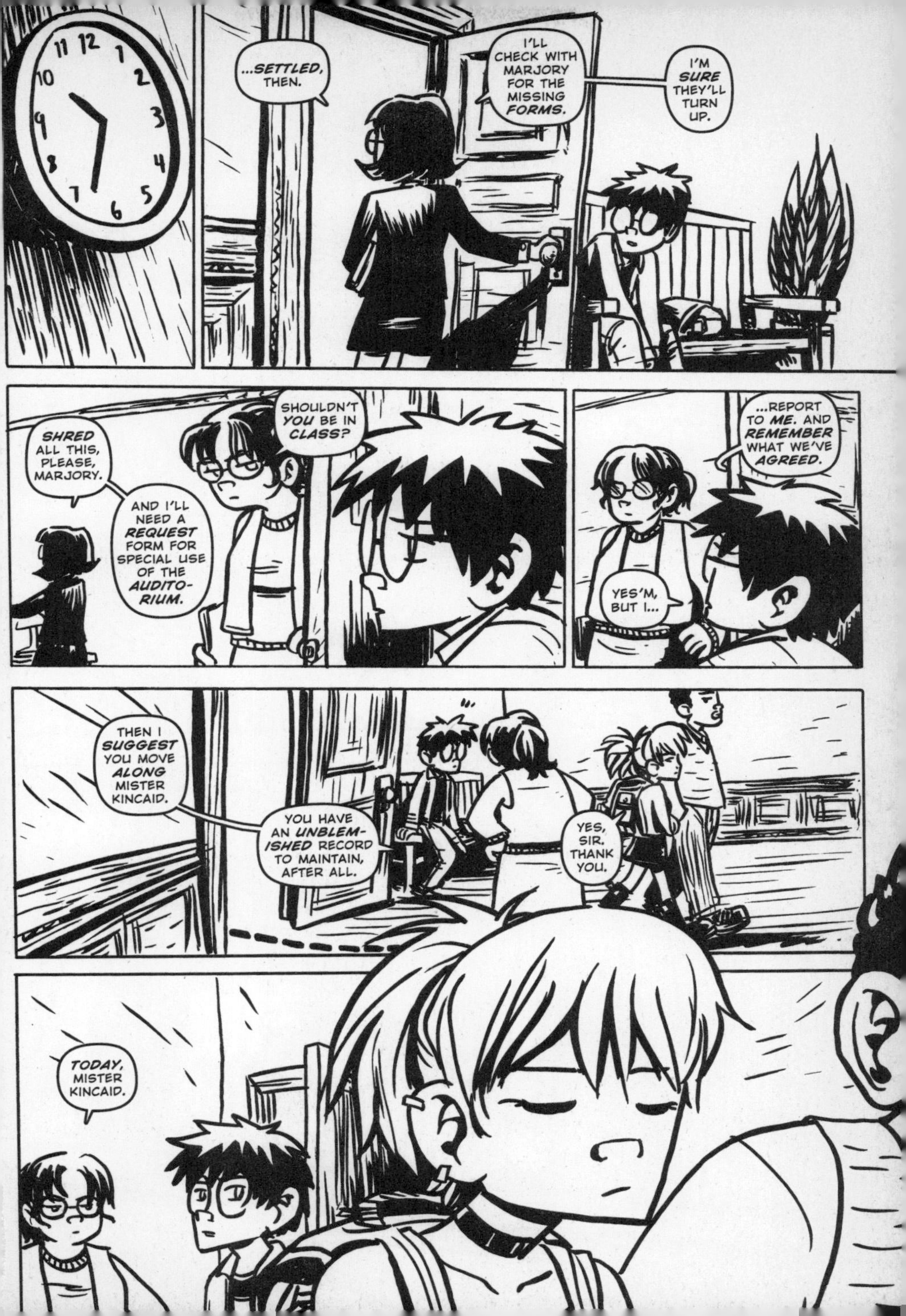
...SETTLED, THEN.
I'LL CHECK WITH MARJORY FOR THE MISSING FORMS.
I'M SURE THEY'LL TURN UP.
SHRED ALL THIS, PLEASE, MARJORY.
AND I'LL NEED A REQUEST FORM FOR SPECIAL USE OF THE AUDITORIUM.
SHOULDN'T YOU BE IN CLASS?
...REPORT TO ME. AND REMEMBER WHAT WE'VE AGREED.
YES'M, BUT I...
THEN I SUGGEST YOU MOVE ALONG MISTER KINCAID.
YOU HAVE AN UNBLEMISHED RECORD TO MAINTAIN, AFTER ALL.
YES, SIR. THANK YOU.
TODAY, MISTER KINCAID.

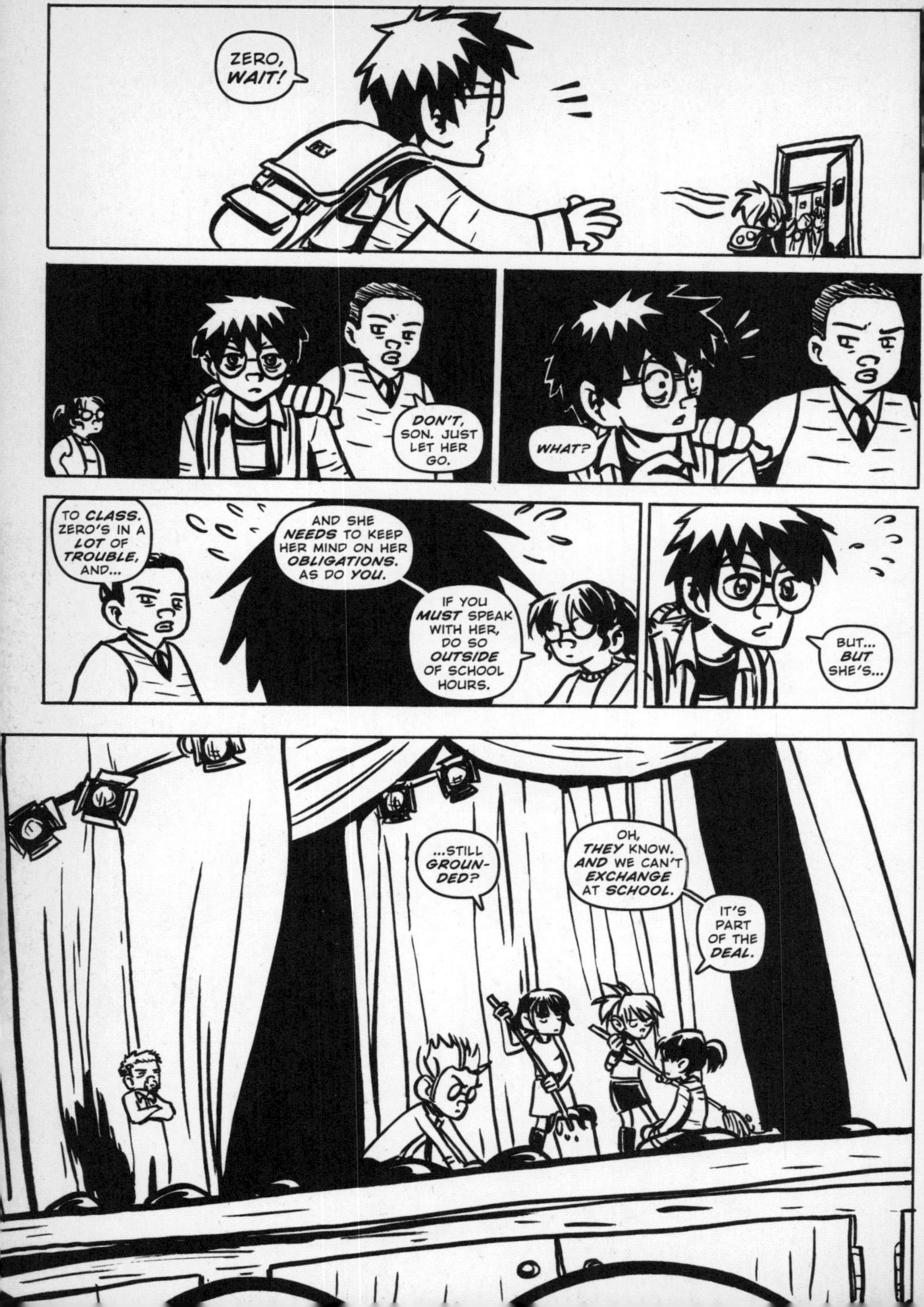

ZERO, WAIT!
DON'T, SON. JUST LET HER GO.
WHAT?
TO CLASS. ZERO'S IN A LOT OF TROUBLE, AND...
AND SHE NEEDS TO KEEP HER MIND ON HER OBLIGATIONS. AS DO YOU.
IF YOU MUST SPEAK WITH HER, DO SO OUTSIDE OF SCHOOL HOURS.
BUT... BUT SHE'S...
...STILL GROUNDED?
OH, THEY KNOW. AND WE CAN'T EXCHANGE AT SCHOOL.
IT'S PART OF THE DEAL.

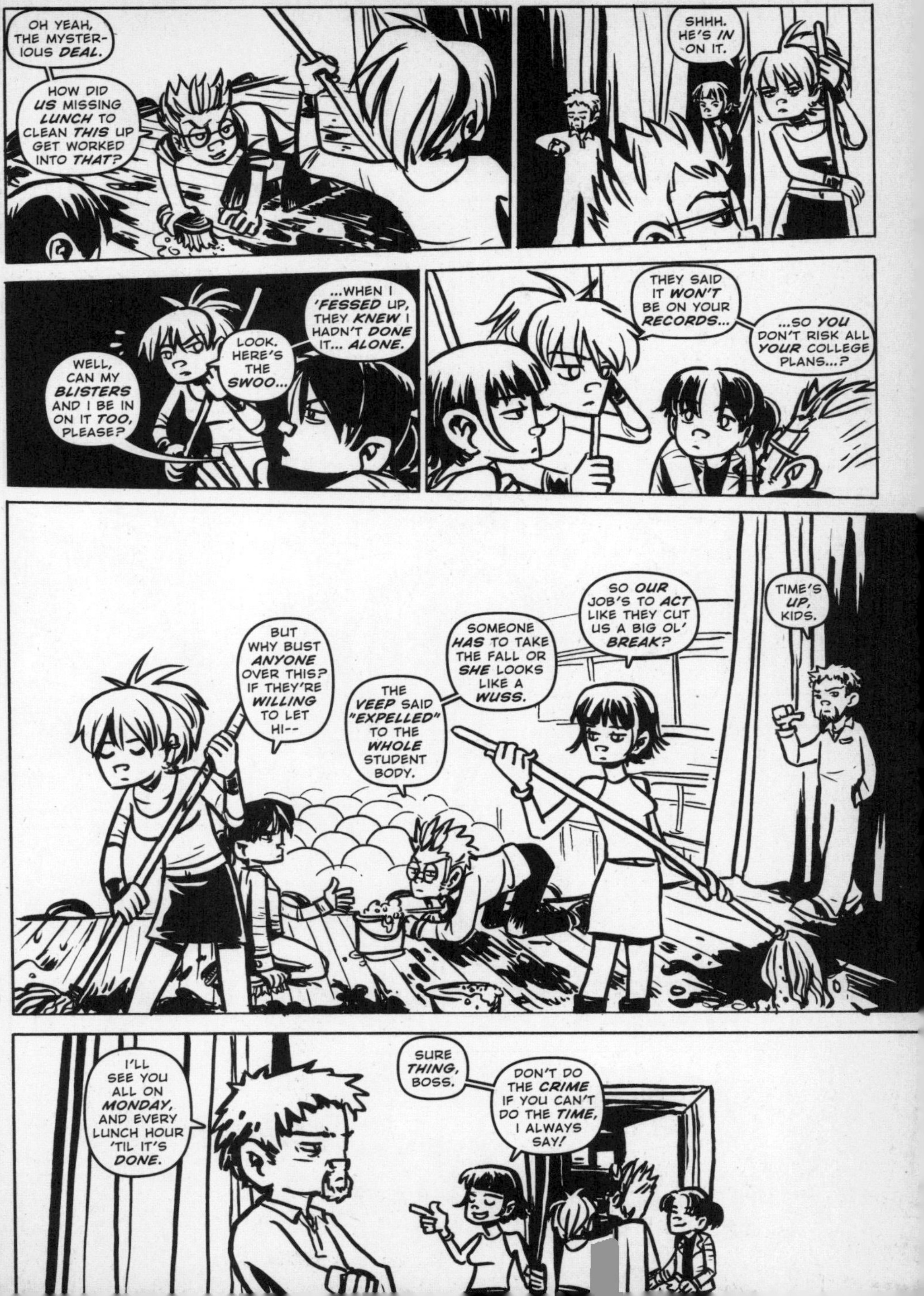

OH YEAH, THE MYSTERIOUS DEAL.
HOW DID US MISSING LUNCH TO CLEAN THIS UP GET WORKED INTO THAT?
SHHH. HE'S IN ON IT.
WELL, CAN MY BLISTERS AND I BE IN ON IT TOO, PLEASE?
LOOK. HERE'S THE SWOO...
...WHEN I 'FESSED UP, THEY KNEW I HADN'T DONE IT... ALONE.
THEY SAID IT WON'T BE ON YOUR RECORDS...
...SO YOU DON'T RISK ALL YOUR COLLEGE PLANS...?
BUT WHY BUST ANYONE OVER THIS? IF THEY'RE WILLING TO LET HI--
THE VEEP SAID "EXPELLED" TO THE WHOLE STUDENT BODY.
SOMEONE HAS TO TAKE THE FALL OR SHE LOOKS LIKE A WUSS.
SO OUR JOB'S TO ACT LIKE THEY CUT US A BIG OL' BREAK?
TIME'S UP, KIDS.
I'LL SEE YOU ALL ON MONDAY, AND EVERY LUNCH HOUR 'TIL IT'S DONE.
SURE THING, BOSS.
DON'T DO THE CRIME IF YOU CAN'T DO THE TIME, I ALWAYS SAY!

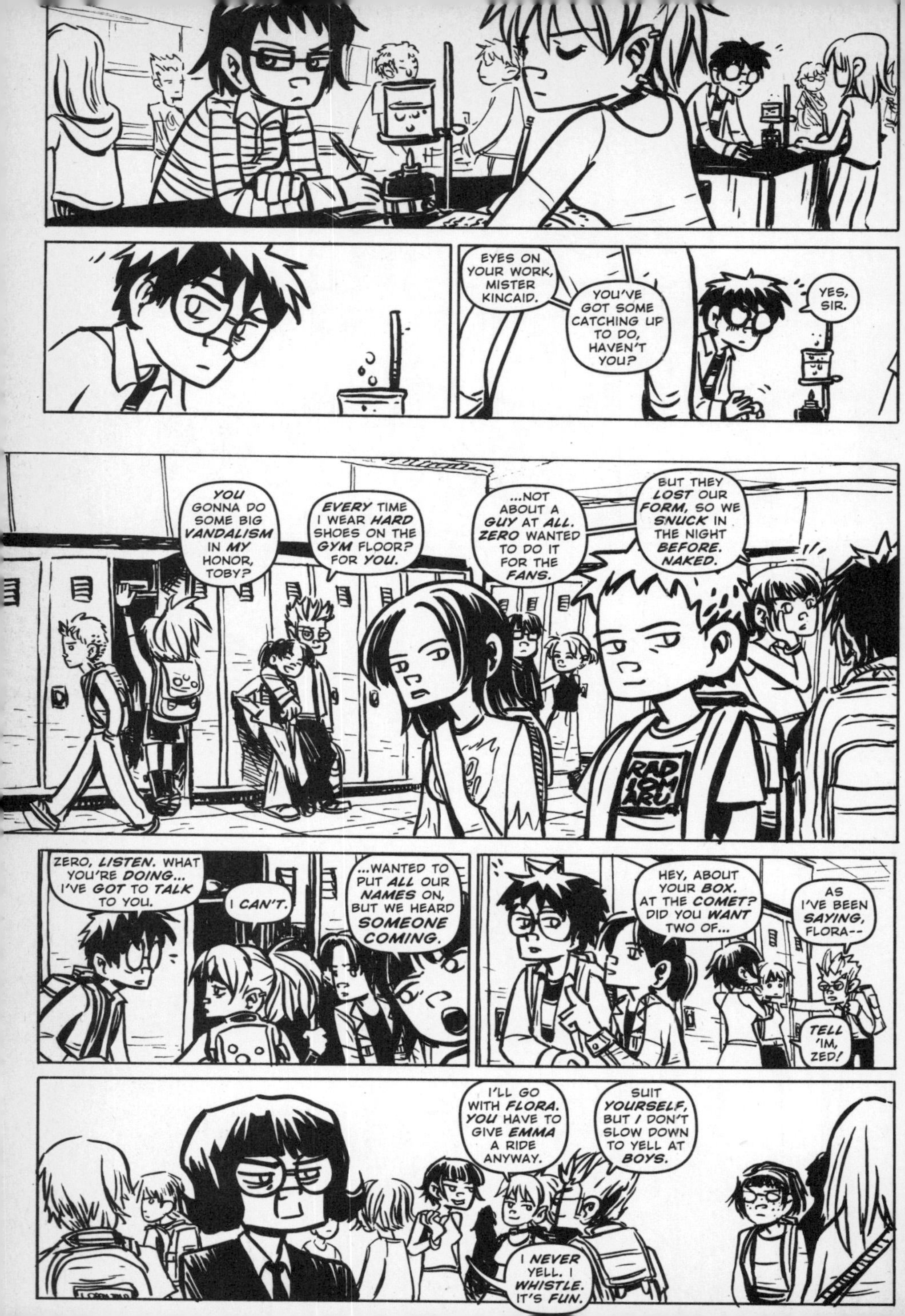

EYES ON YOUR WORK, MISTER KINCAID.
YOU'VE GOT SOME CATCHING UP TO DO, HAVEN'T YOU?
YES, SIR.
YOU GONNA DO SOME BIG VANDALISM IN MY HONOR, TOBY?
EVERY TIME I WEAR HARD SHOES ON THE GYM FLOOR? FOR YOU.
...NOT ABOUT A GUY AT ALL. ZERO WANTED TO DO IT FOR THE FANS.
BUT THEY LOST OUR FORM, SO WE SNUCK IN THE NIGHT BEFORE. NAKED.
RAD IOM ARU
ZERO, LISTEN. WHAT YOU'RE DOING... I'VE GOT TO TALK TO YOU.
I CAN'T.
...WANTED TO PUT ALL OUR NAMES ON, BUT WE HEARD SOMEONE COMING.
HEY, ABOUT YOUR BOX. AT THE COMET? DID YOU WANT TWO OF...
AS I'VE BEEN SAYING, FLORA--
TELL 'IM, ZED!
I'LL GO WITH FLORA. YOU HAVE TO GIVE EMMA A RIDE ANYWAY.
SUIT YOURSELF, BUT I DON'T SLOW DOWN TO YELL AT BOYS.
I NEVER YELL. I WHISTLE. IT'S FUN.

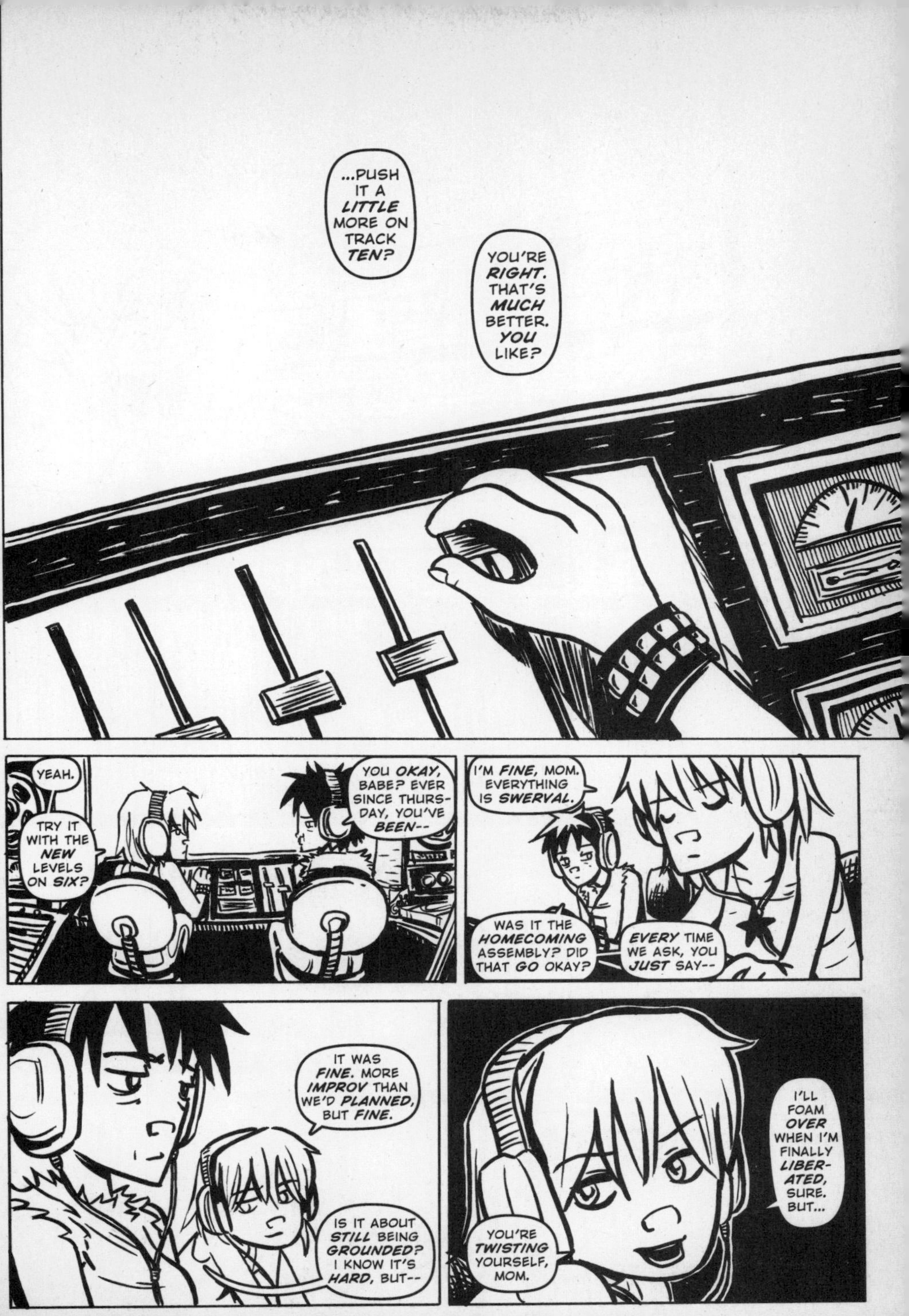
...PUSH IT A LITTLE MORE ON TRACK TEN?
YOU'RE RIGHT. THAT'S MUCH BETTER. YOU LIKE?
YEAH.
TRY IT WITH THE NEW LEVELS ON SIX?
YOU OKAY, BABE? EVER SINCE THURS-DAY, YOU'VE BEEN--
I'M FINE, MOM. EVERYTHING IS SWERVAL.
WAS IT THE HOMECOMING ASSEMBLY? DID THAT GO OKAY?
EVERY TIME WE ASK, YOU JUST SAY--
IT WAS FINE. MORE IMPROV THAN WE'D PLANNED, BUT FINE.
IS IT ABOUT STILL BEING GROUNDED? I KNOW IT'S HARD, BUT--
I'LL FOAM OVER WHEN I'M FINALLY LIBER-ATED, SURE. BUT...
YOU'RE TWISTING YOURSELF, MOM.

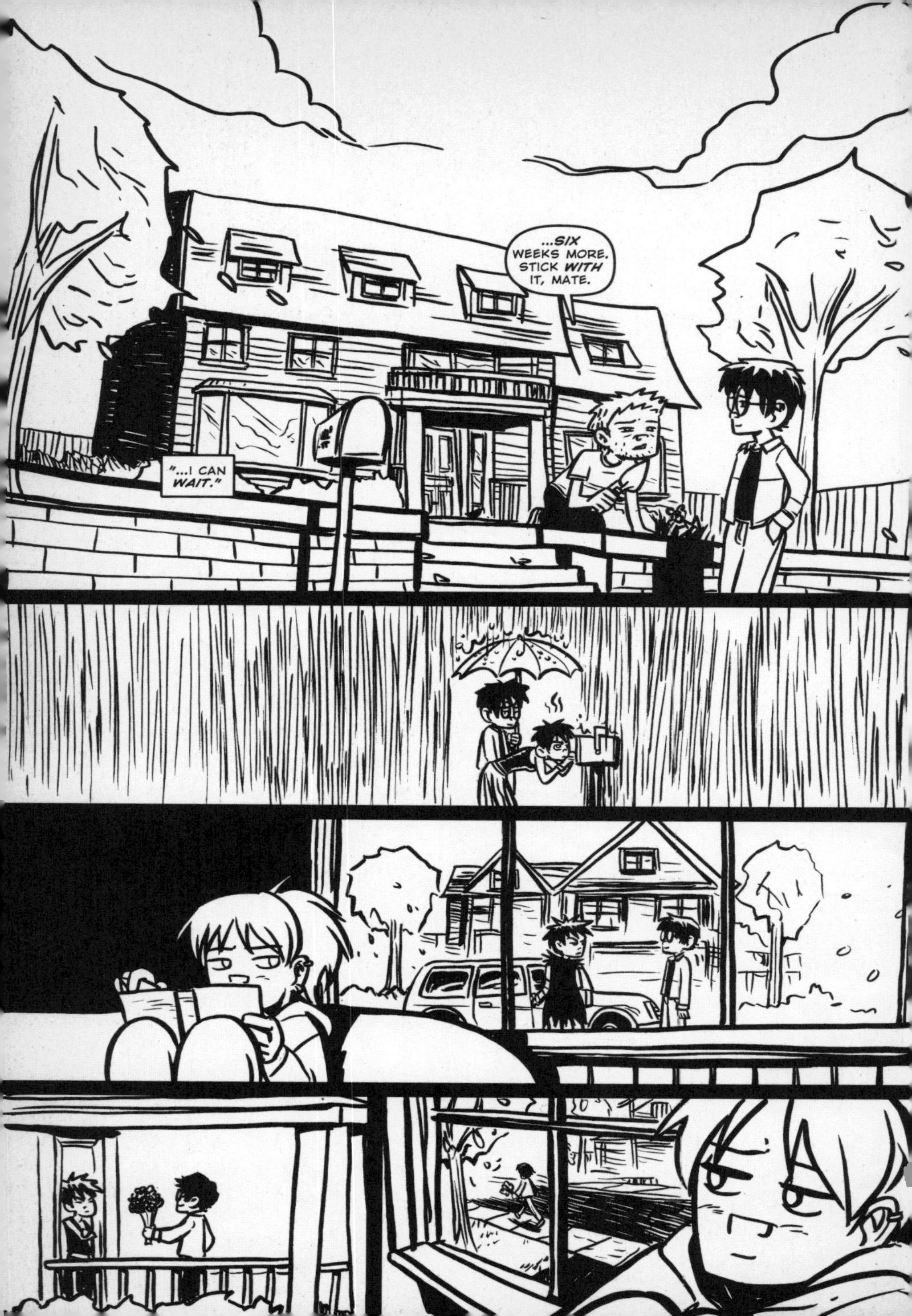
...SIX WEEKS MORE. STICK WITH IT, MATE.
"...I CAN WAIT."

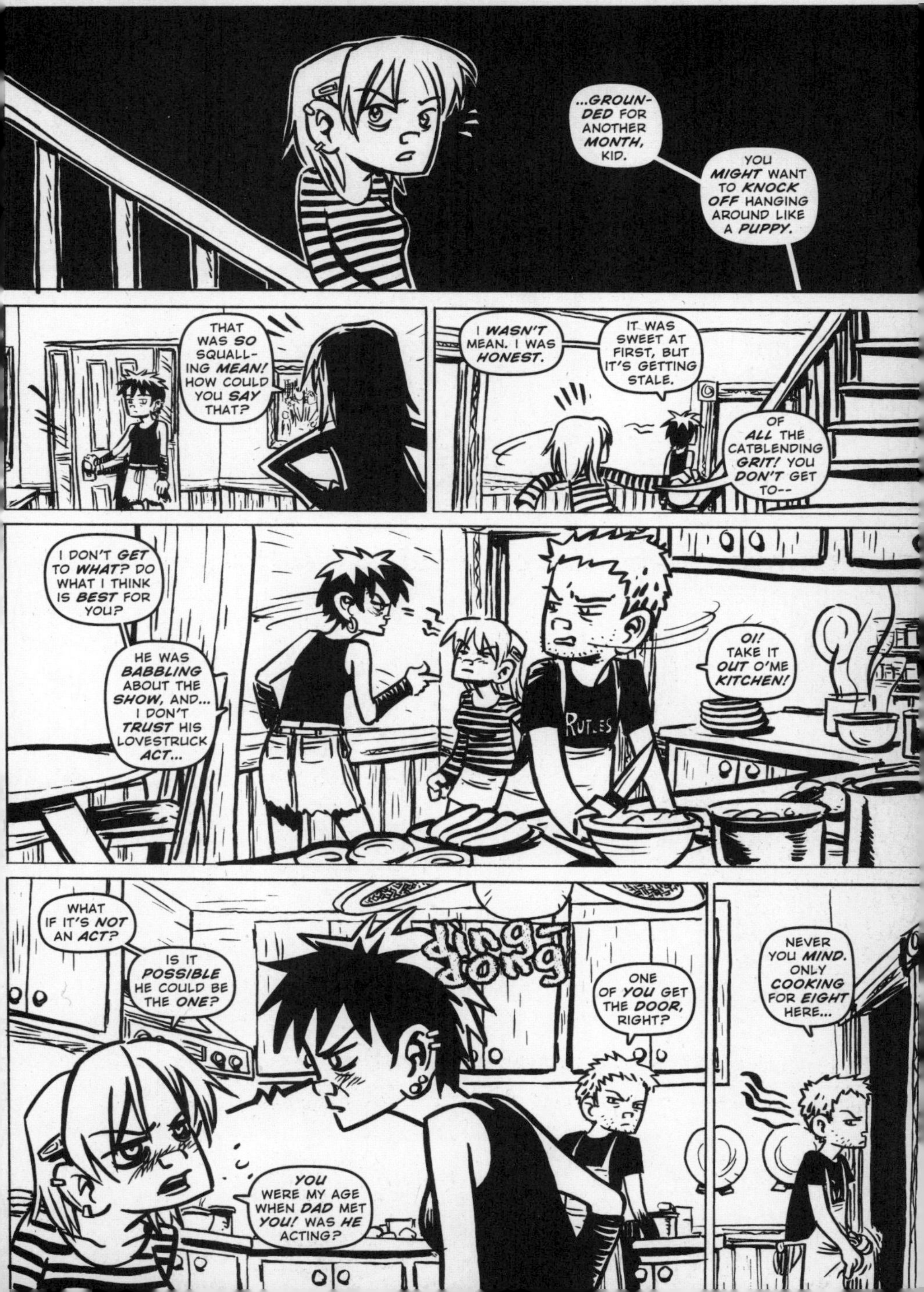
...GROUNDED FOR ANOTHER MONTH, KID.
YOU MIGHT WANT TO KNOCK OFF HANGING AROUND LIKE A PUPPY.
THAT WAS SO SQUALLING MEAN! HOW COULD YOU SAY THAT?
I WASN'T MEAN. I WAS HONEST.
IT WAS SWEET AT FIRST, BUT IT'S GETTING STALE.
OF ALL THE CATBLENDING GRIT! YOU DON'T GET TO--
I DON'T GET TO WHAT? DO WHAT I THINK IS BEST FOR YOU?
HE WAS BABBLING ABOUT THE SHOW, AND... I DON'T TRUST HIS LOVESTRUCK ACT...
OI! TAKE IT OUT O'ME KITCHEN!
RUTLES
WHAT IF IT'S NOT AN ACT?
IS IT POSSIBLE HE COULD BE THE ONE?
ding-dong
YOU WERE MY AGE WHEN DAD MET YOU! WAS HE ACTING?
ONE OF YOU GET THE DOOR, RIGHT?
NEVER YOU MIND. ONLY COOKING FOR EIGHT HERE...

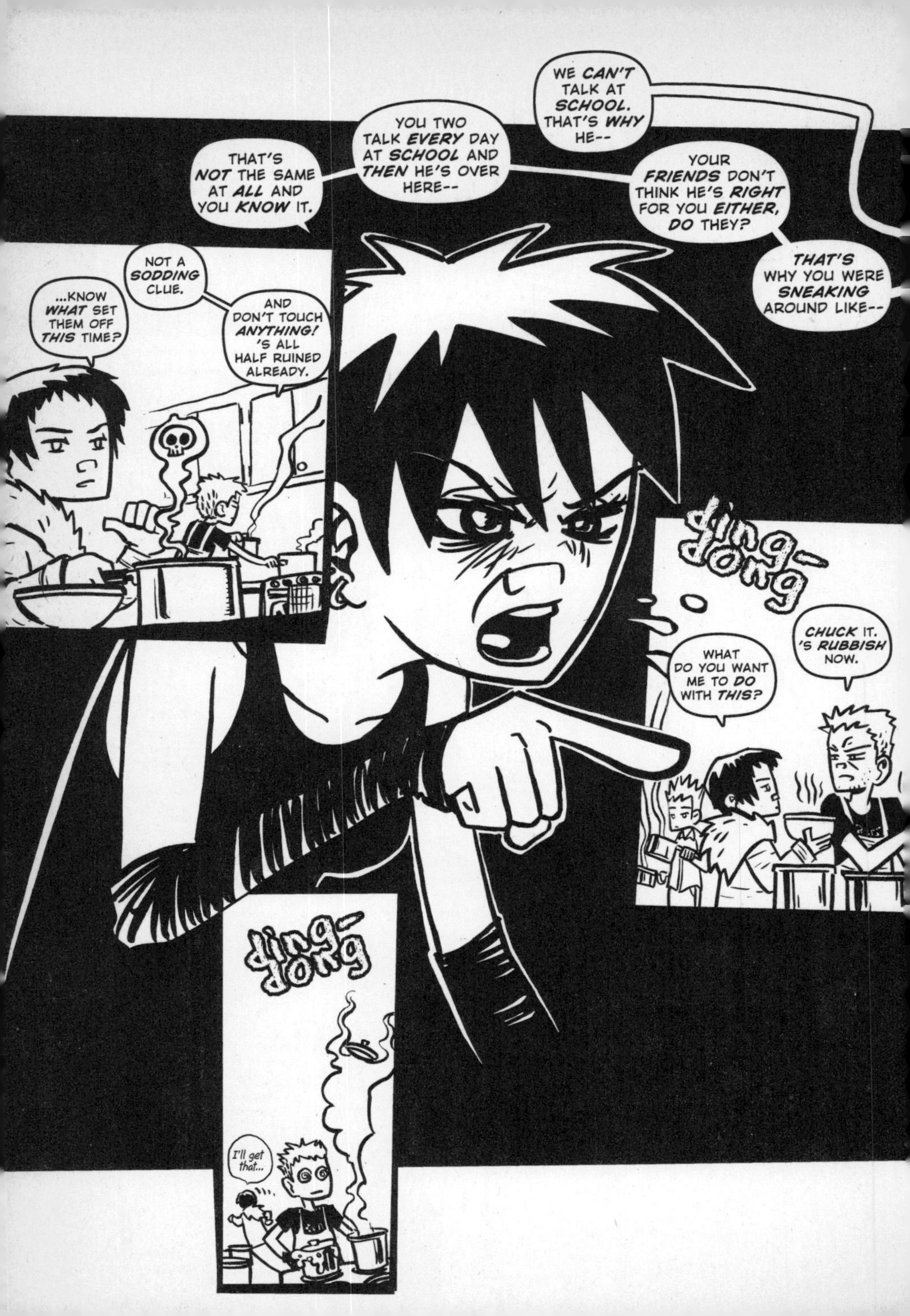
THAT'S NOT THE SAME AT ALL AND YOU KNOW IT.
YOU TWO TALK EVERY DAY AT SCHOOL AND THEN HE'S OVER HERE--
WE CAN'T TALK AT SCHOOL. THAT'S WHY HE--
YOUR FRIENDS DON'T THINK HE'S RIGHT FOR YOU EITHER, DO THEY?
THAT'S WHY YOU WERE SNEAKING AROUND LIKE--
...KNOW WHAT SET THEM OFF THIS TIME?
NOT A SODDING CLUE.
AND DON'T TOUCH ANYTHING! 'S ALL HALF RUINED ALREADY.
DING-DONG
WHAT DO YOU WANT ME TO DO WITH THIS?
CHUCK IT. 'S RUBBISH NOW.
DING-DONG
I'll get that...

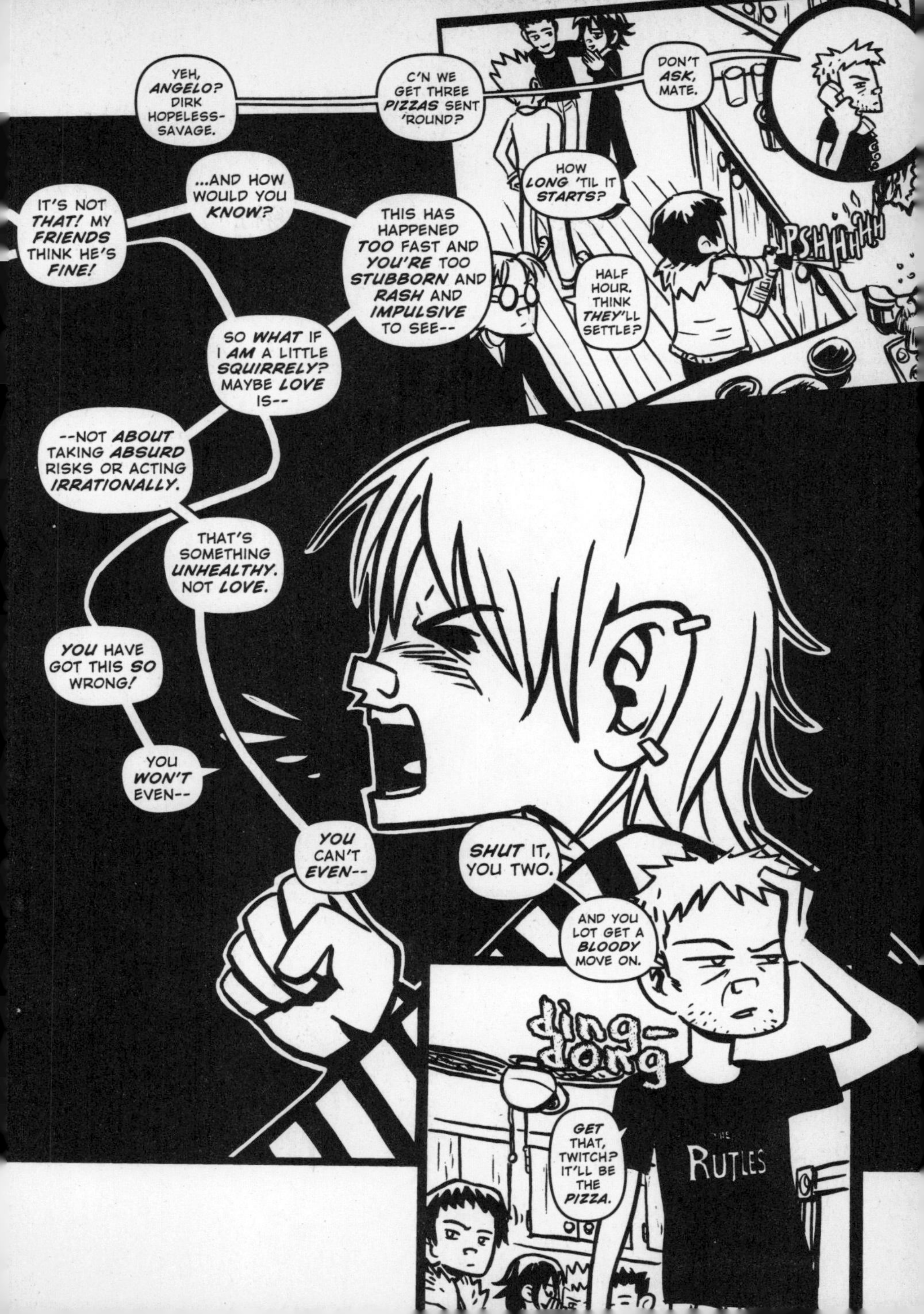
YEH, ANGELO? DIRK HOPELESS-SAVAGE.
C'N WE GET THREE PIZZAS SENT 'ROUND?
DON'T ASK, MATE.
HOW LONG 'TIL IT STARTS?
HALF HOUR. THINK THEY'LL SETTLE?
PSHHHHH
IT'S NOT THAT! MY FRIENDS THINK HE'S FINE!
...AND HOW WOULD YOU KNOW?
THIS HAS HAPPENED TOO FAST AND YOU'RE TOO STUBBORN AND RASH AND IMPULSIVE TO SEE--
SO WHAT IF I AM A LITTLE SQUIRRELY? MAYBE LOVE IS--
--NOT ABOUT TAKING ABSURD RISKS OR ACTING IRRATIONALLY.
THAT'S SOMETHING UNHEALTHY. NOT LOVE.
YOU HAVE GOT THIS SO WRONG!
YOU WON'T EVEN--
YOU CAN'T EVEN--
SHUT IT, YOU TWO.
AND YOU LOT GET A BLOODY MOVE ON.
ding-dong
GET THAT, TWITCH? IT'LL BE THE PIZZA.
THE RUTLES

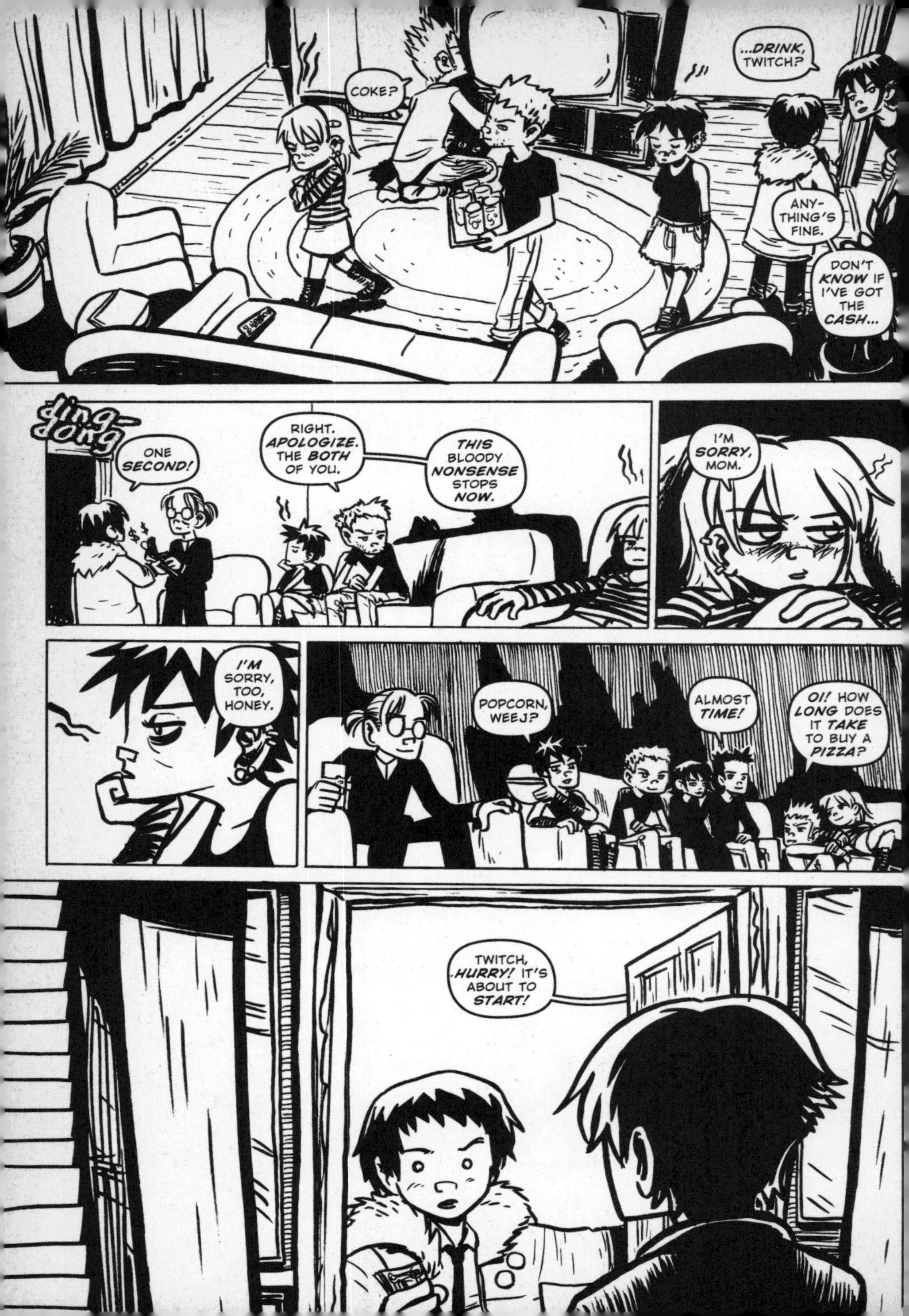
COKE?
...DRINK, TWITCH?
ANY-THING'S FINE.
DON'T KNOW IF I'VE GOT THE CASH...
ding-dong
ONE SECOND!
RIGHT. APOLOGIZE. THE BOTH OF YOU.
THIS BLOODY NONSENSE STOPS NOW.
I'M SORRY, MOM.
I'M SORRY, TOO, HONEY.
POPCORN, WEEJ?
ALMOST TIME!
OI! HOW LONG DOES IT TAKE TO BUY A PIZZA?
TWITCH, HURRY! IT'S ABOUT TO START!

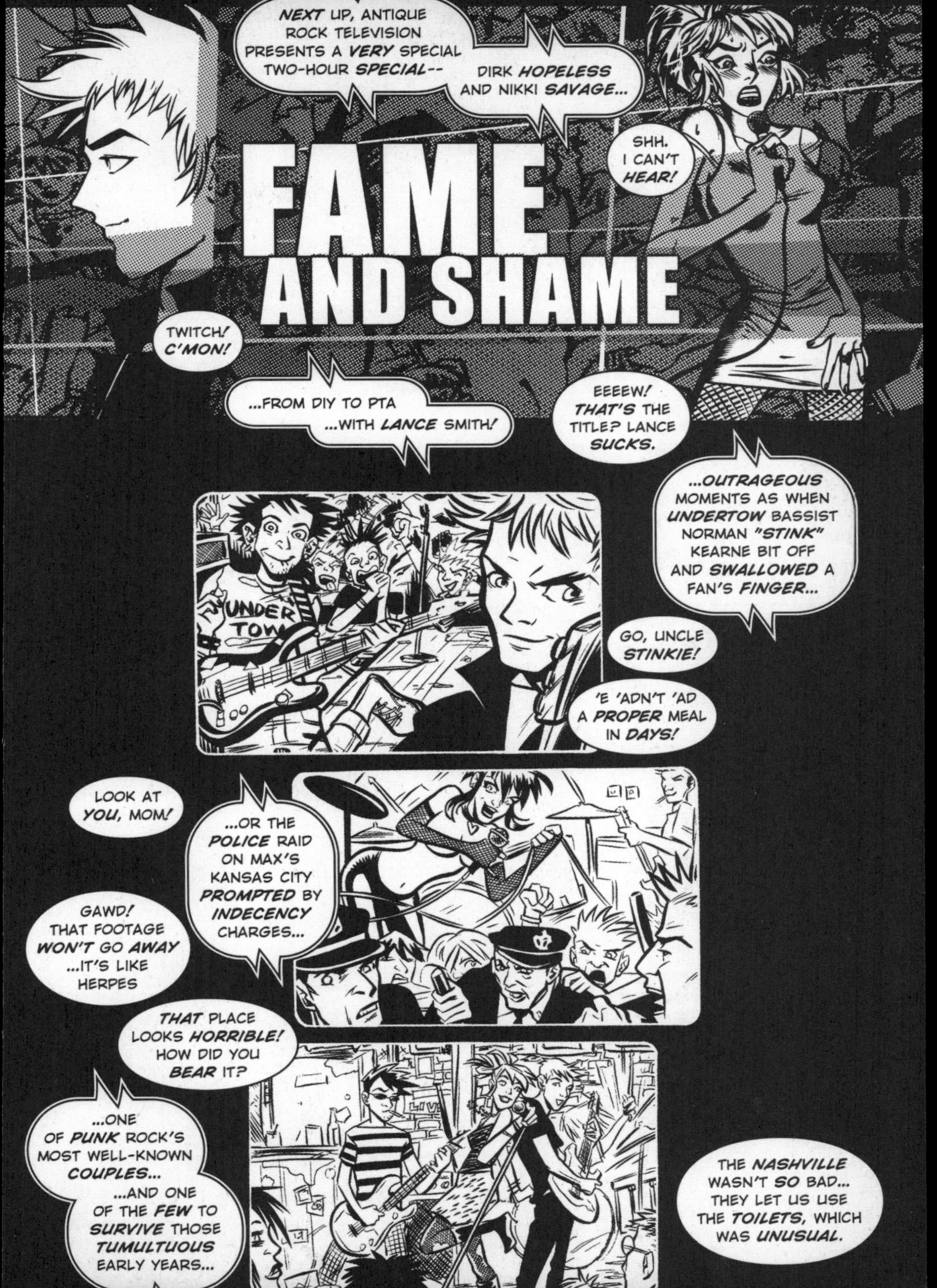
NEXT UP, ANTIQUE ROCK TELEVISION PRESENTS A VERY SPECIAL TWO-HOUR SPECIAL--
DIRK HOPELESS AND NIKKI SAVAGE...
SHH. I CAN'T HEAR!
FAME AND SHAME
TWITCH! C'MON!
...FROM DIY TO PTA ...WITH LANCE SMITH!
EEEEW! THAT'S THE TITLE? LANCE SUCKS.
...OUTRAGEOUS MOMENTS AS WHEN UNDERTOW BASSIST NORMAN "STINK" KEARNE BIT OFF AND SWALLOWED A FAN'S FINGER...
UNDER TOW
GO, UNCLE STINKIE!
'E 'ADN'T 'AD A PROPER MEAL IN DAYS!
LOOK AT YOU, MOM!
...OR THE POLICE RAID ON MAX'S KANSAS CITY PROMPTED BY INDECENCY CHARGES...
GAWD! THAT FOOTAGE WON'T GO AWAY ...IT'S LIKE HERPES
THAT PLACE LOOKS HORRIBLE! HOW DID YOU BEAR IT?
...ONE OF PUNK ROCK'S MOST WELL-KNOWN COUPLES... ...AND ONE OF THE FEW TO SURVIVE THOSE TUMULTUOUS EARLY YEARS...
THE NASHVILLE WASN'T SO BAD... THEY LET US USE THE TOILETS, WHICH WAS UNUSUAL.

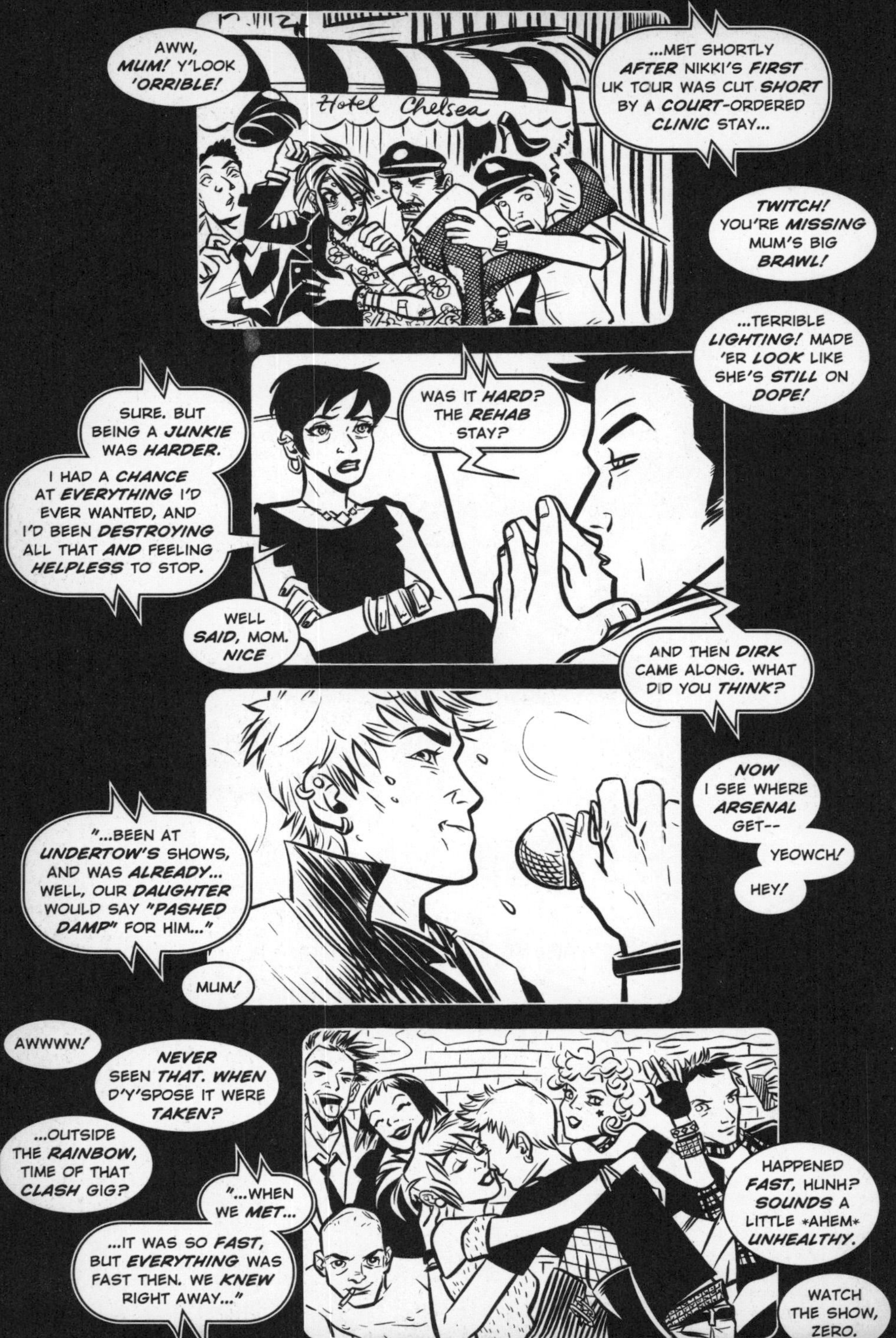
AWW, MUM! Y'LOOK 'ORRIBLE!
Hotel Chelsea
...MET SHORTLY AFTER NIKKI'S FIRST UK TOUR WAS CUT SHORT BY A COURT-ORDERED CLINIC STAY...
TWITCH! YOU'RE MISSING MUM'S BIG BRAWL!
...TERRIBLE LIGHTING! MADE 'ER LOOK LIKE SHE'S STILL ON DOPE!
WAS IT HARD? THE REHAB STAY?
SURE. BUT BEING A JUNKIE WAS HARDER.
I HAD A CHANCE AT EVERYTHING I'D EVER WANTED, AND I'D BEEN DESTROYING ALL THAT AND FEELING HELPLESS TO STOP.
WELL SAID, MOM. NICE
AND THEN DIRK CAME ALONG. WHAT DID YOU THINK?
"...BEEN AT UNDERTOW'S SHOWS, AND WAS ALREADY... WELL, OUR DAUGHTER WOULD SAY "PASHED DAMP" FOR HIM..."
MUM!
NOW I SEE WHERE ARSENAL GET--
YEOWCH!
HEY!
AWWWW!
NEVER SEEN THAT. WHEN D'Y'SPOSE IT WERE TAKEN?
...OUTSIDE THE RAINBOW, TIME OF THAT CLASH GIG?
"...WHEN WE MET...
...IT WAS SO FAST, BUT EVERYTHING WAS FAST THEN. WE KNEW RIGHT AWAY..."
HAPPENED FAST, HUNH? SOUNDS A LITTLE *AHEM* UNHEALTHY.
WATCH THE SHOW, ZERO.

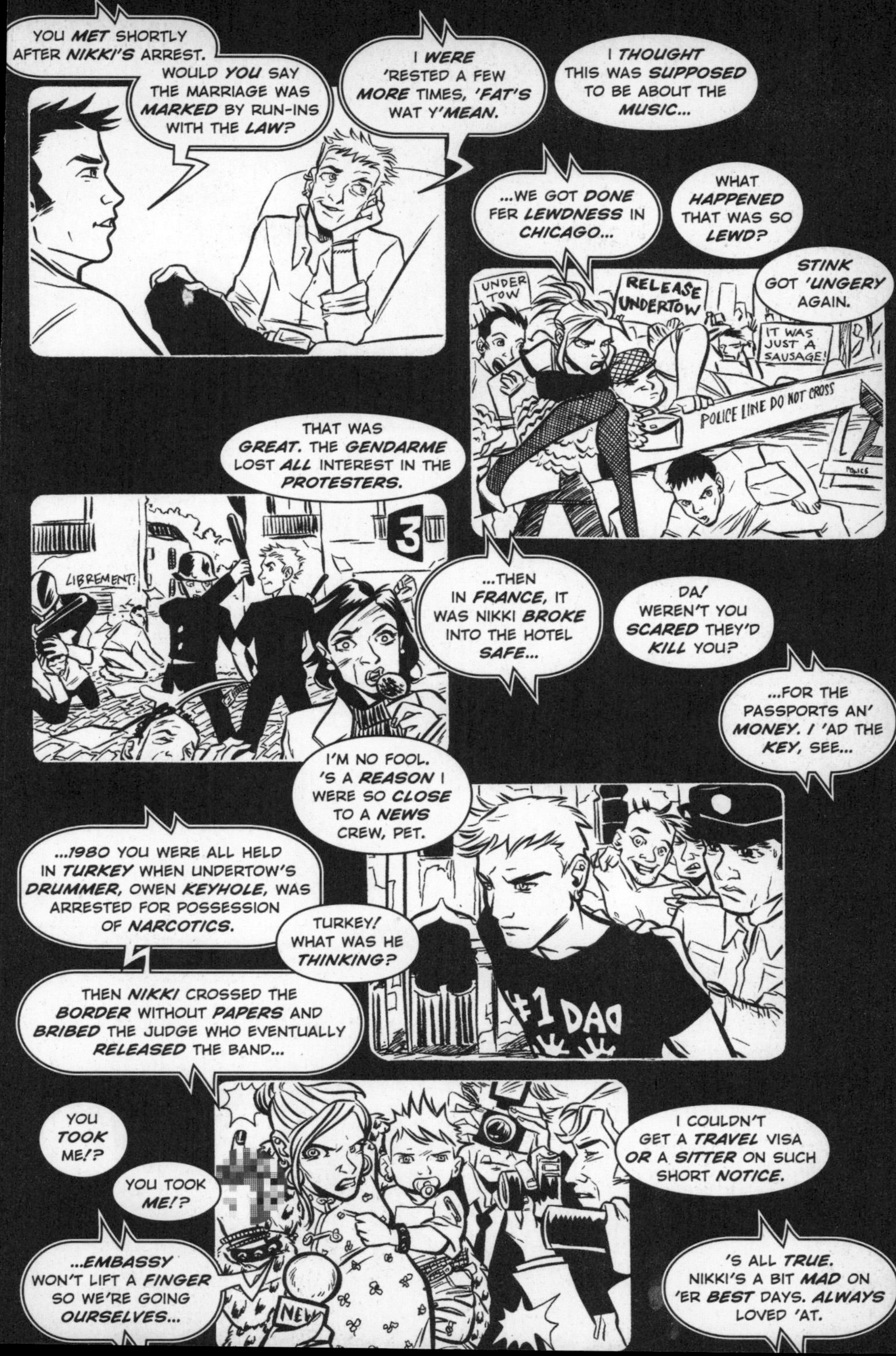
YOU MET SHORTLY AFTER NIKKI'S ARREST.
WOULD YOU SAY THE MARRIAGE WAS MARKED BY RUN-INS WITH THE LAW?
I WERE 'RESTED A FEW MORE TIMES, 'FAT'S WAT Y'MEAN.
I THOUGHT THIS WAS SUPPOSED TO BE ABOUT THE MUSIC...
...WE GOT DONE FER LEWDNESS IN CHICAGO...
WHAT HAPPENED THAT WAS SO LEWD?
STINK GOT 'UNGERY AGAIN.
UNDER TOW
RELEASE UNDERTOW
IT WAS JUST A SAUSAGE!
POLICE LINE DO NOT CROSS
THAT WAS GREAT. THE GENDARME LOST ALL INTEREST IN THE PROTESTERS.
LIBREMENT!
3
...THEN IN FRANCE, IT WAS NIKKI BROKE INTO THE HOTEL SAFE...
DA! WEREN'T YOU SCARED THEY'D KILL YOU?
...FOR THE PASSPORTS AN' MONEY. I 'AD THE KEY, SEE...
I'M NO FOOL. 'S A REASON I WERE SO CLOSE TO A NEWS CREW, PET.
...1980 YOU WERE ALL HELD IN TURKEY WHEN UNDERTOW'S DRUMMER, OWEN KEYHOLE, WAS ARRESTED FOR POSSESSION OF NARCOTICS.
TURKEY! WHAT WAS HE THINKING?
#1 DAD
THEN NIKKI CROSSED THE BORDER WITHOUT PAPERS AND BRIBED THE JUDGE WHO EVENTUALLY RELEASED THE BAND...
YOU TOOK ME!?
YOU TOOK ME!?
I COULDN'T GET A TRAVEL VISA OR A SITTER ON SUCH SHORT NOTICE.
...EMBASSY WON'T LIFT A FINGER SO WE'RE GOING OURSELVES...
NEW
'S ALL TRUE. NIKKI'S A BIT MAD ON 'ER BEST DAYS. ALWAYS LOVED 'AT.

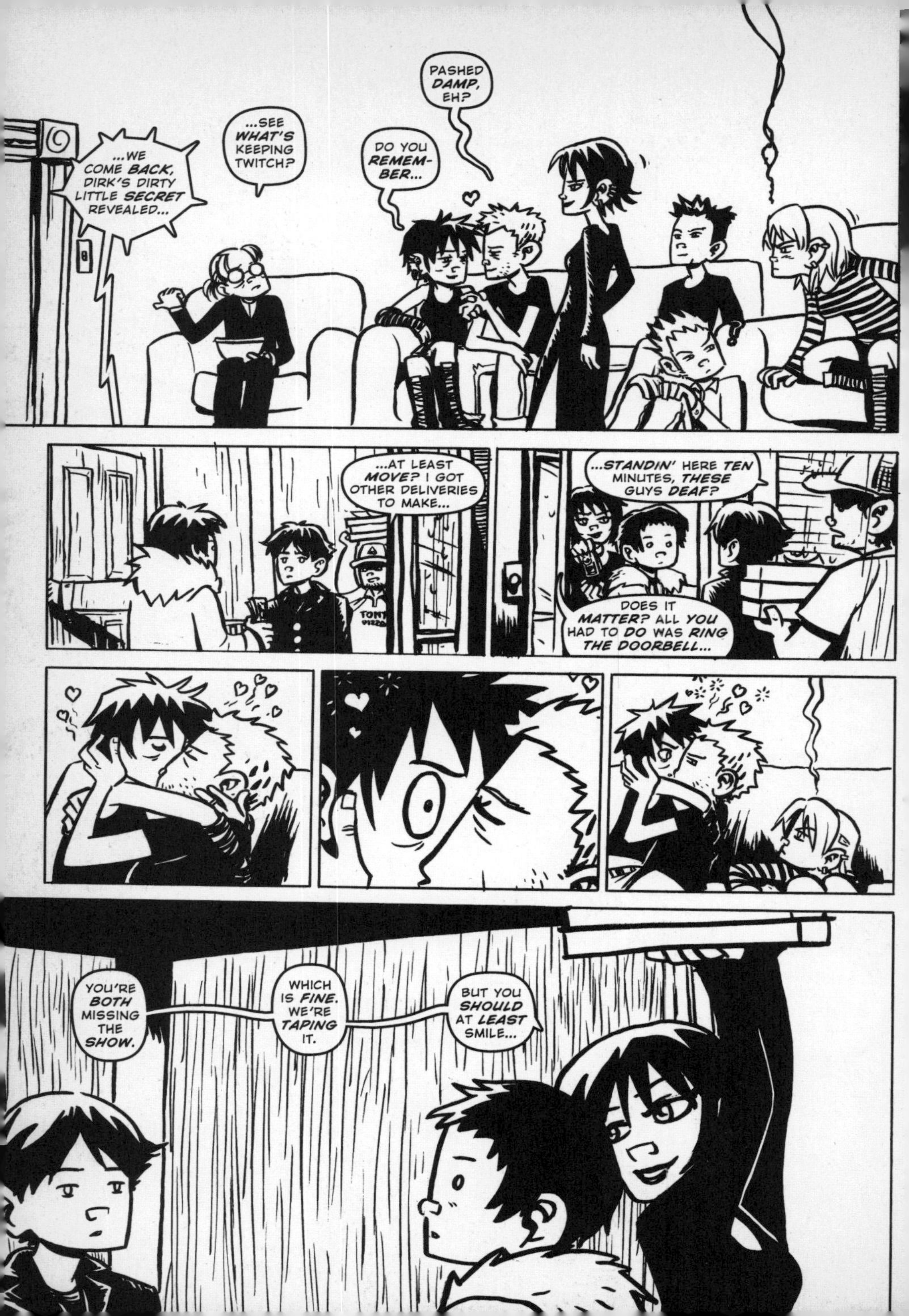
...WE COME BACK, DIRK'S DIRTY LITTLE SECRET REVEALED...
...SEE WHAT'S KEEPING TWITCH?
DO YOU REMEMBER...
PASHED DAMP, EH?
...AT LEAST MOVE? I GOT OTHER DELIVERIES TO MAKE...
...STANDIN' HERE TEN MINUTES, THESE GUYS DEAF?
DOES IT MATTER? ALL YOU HAD TO DO WAS RING THE DOORBELL...
YOU'RE BOTH MISSING THE SHOW.
WHICH IS FINE. WE'RE TAPING IT.
BUT YOU SHOULD AT LEAST SMILE...

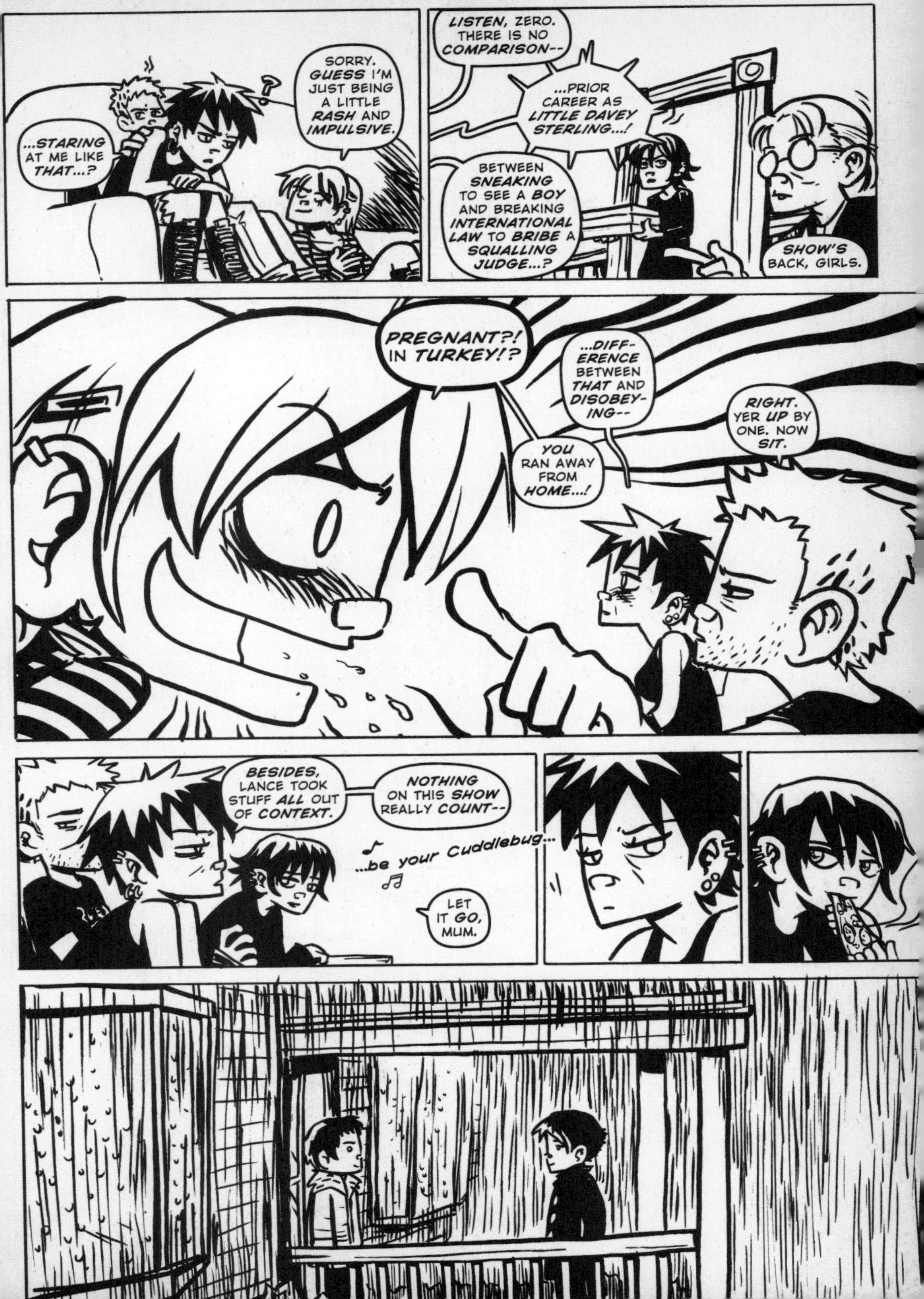
...STARING AT ME LIKE THAT...?
SORRY. GUESS I'M JUST BEING A LITTLE RASH AND IMPULSIVE.
LISTEN, ZERO. THERE IS NO COMPARISON--
...PRIOR CAREER AS LITTLE DAVEY STERLING...!
BETWEEN SNEAKING TO SEE A BOY AND BREAKING INTERNATIONAL LAW TO BRIBE A SQUALLING JUDGE...?
SHOW'S BACK, GIRLS.
PREGNANT?! IN TURKEY!?
...DIFF-ERENCE BETWEEN THAT AND DISOBEY-ING--
YOU RAN AWAY FROM HOME...!
RIGHT. YER UP BY ONE. NOW SIT.
BESIDES, LANCE TOOK STUFF ALL OUT OF CONTEXT.
NOTHING ON THIS SHOW REALLY COUNT--
...be your Cuddlebug...
LET IT GO, MUM.

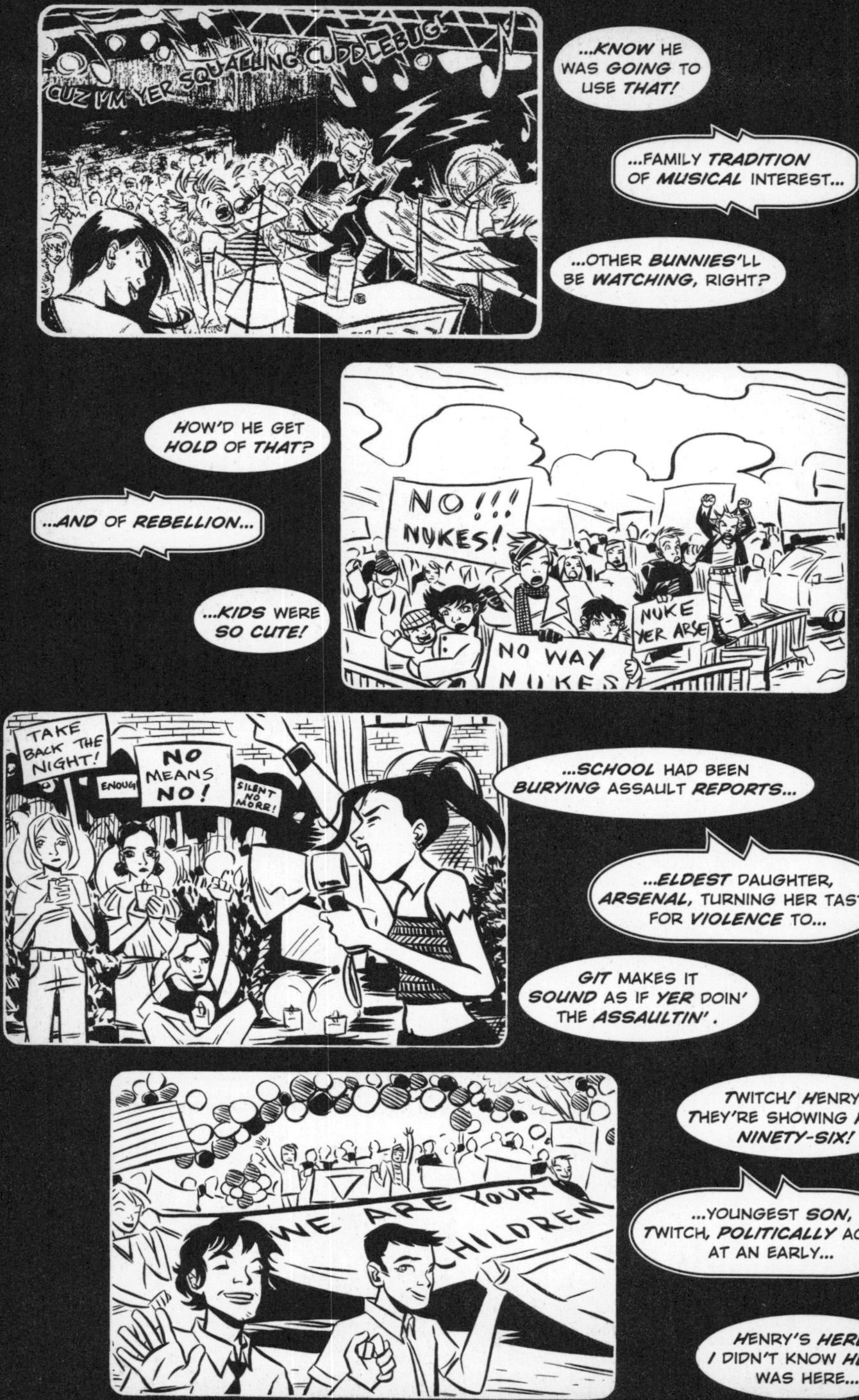
CUZ I'M YER SQUALLING CUDDLEBUG!
...KNOW HE WAS GOING TO USE THAT!
...FAMILY TRADITION OF MUSICAL INTEREST...
...OTHER BUNNIES'LL BE WATCHING, RIGHT?
HOW'D HE GET HOLD OF THAT?
...AND OF REBELLION...
...KIDS WERE SO CUTE!
NO!!! NUKES!
NUKE YER ARSE
NO WAY NUKES
TAKE BACK THE NIGHT!
ENOUG
NO MEANS NO!
SILENT NO MORE!
...SCHOOL HAD BEEN BURYING ASSAULT REPORTS...
...ELDEST DAUGHTER, ARSENAL, TURNING HER TASTE FOR VIOLENCE TO...
GIT MAKES IT SOUND AS IF YER DOIN' THE ASSAULTIN'.
WE ARE YOUR CHILDREN
TWITCH! HENRY! THEY'RE SHOWING PRIDE NINETY-SIX!
...YOUNGEST SON, TWITCH, POLITICALLY ACTIVE AT AN EARLY...
HENRY'S HERE? I DIDN'T KNOW HENRY WAS HERE...

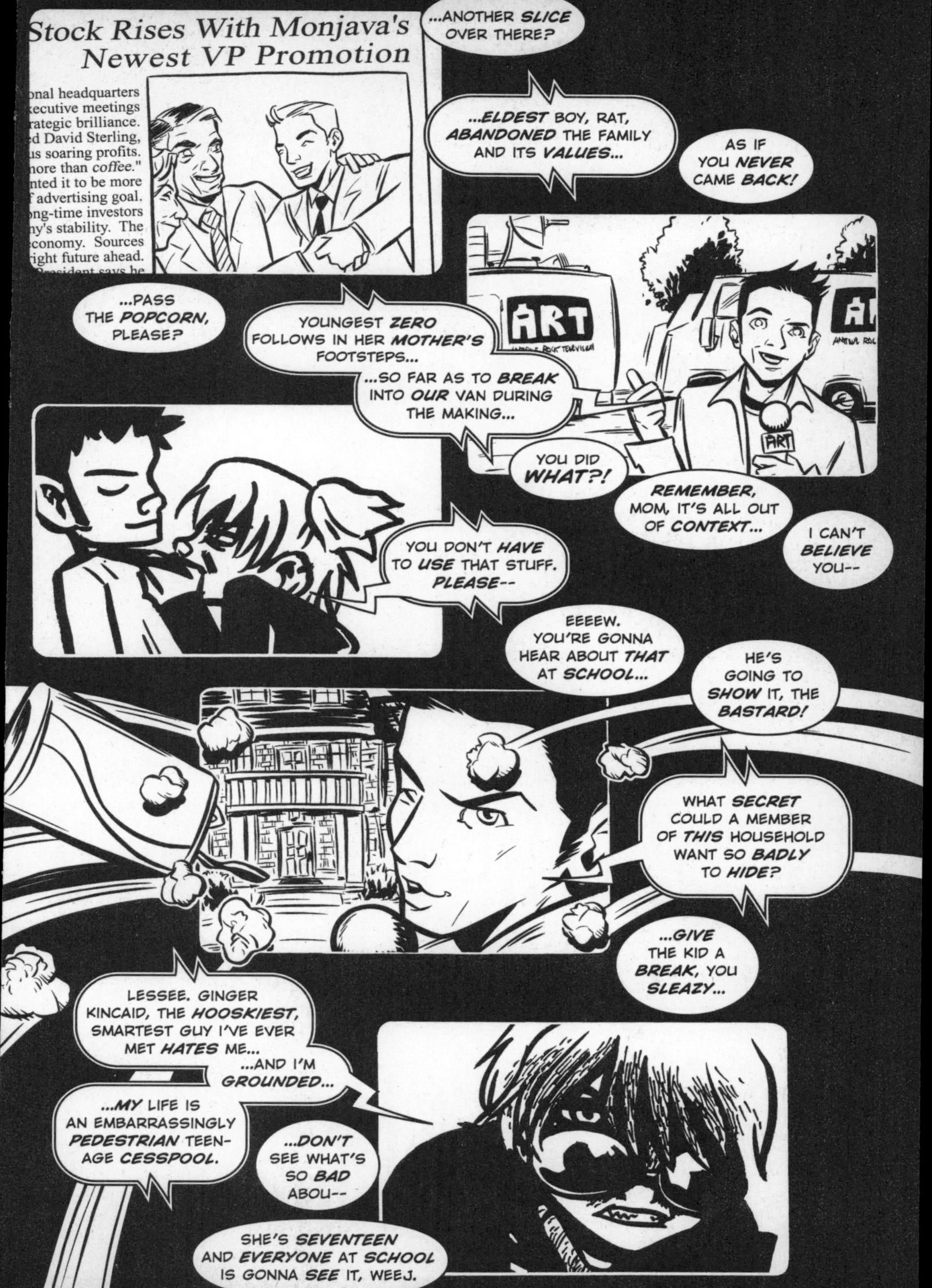
Stock Rises With Monjava's Newest VP Promotion
onal headquarters
xecutive meetings
rategic brilliance.
ed David Sterling,
us soaring profits.
more than coffee."
nted it to be more
f advertising goal.
ong-time investors
ny's stability. The
economy. Sources
right future ahead.
...ANOTHER SLICE OVER THERE?
...ELDEST BOY, RAT, ABANDONED THE FAMILY AND ITS VALUES...
AS IF YOU NEVER CAME BACK!
...PASS THE POPCORN, PLEASE?
YOUNGEST ZERO FOLLOWS IN HER MOTHER'S FOOTSTEPS...
...SO FAR AS TO BREAK INTO OUR VAN DURING THE MAKING...
ART
YOU DID WHAT?!
REMEMBER, MOM, IT'S ALL OUT OF CONTEXT...
I CAN'T BELIEVE YOU--
YOU DON'T HAVE TO USE THAT STUFF. PLEASE--
EEEEW. YOU'RE GONNA HEAR ABOUT THAT AT SCHOOL...
HE'S GOING TO SHOW IT, THE BASTARD!
WHAT SECRET COULD A MEMBER OF THIS HOUSEHOLD WANT SO BADLY TO HIDE?
...GIVE THE KID A BREAK, YOU SLEAZY...
LESSEE. GINGER KINCAID, THE HOOSKIEST, SMARTEST GUY I'VE EVER MET HATES ME...
...AND I'M GROUNDED...
...MY LIFE IS AN EMBARRASSINGLY PEDESTRIAN TEEN-AGE CESSPOOL.
...DON'T SEE WHAT'S SO BAD ABOU--
SHE'S SEVENTEEN AND EVERYONE AT SCHOOL IS GONNA SEE IT, WEEJ.

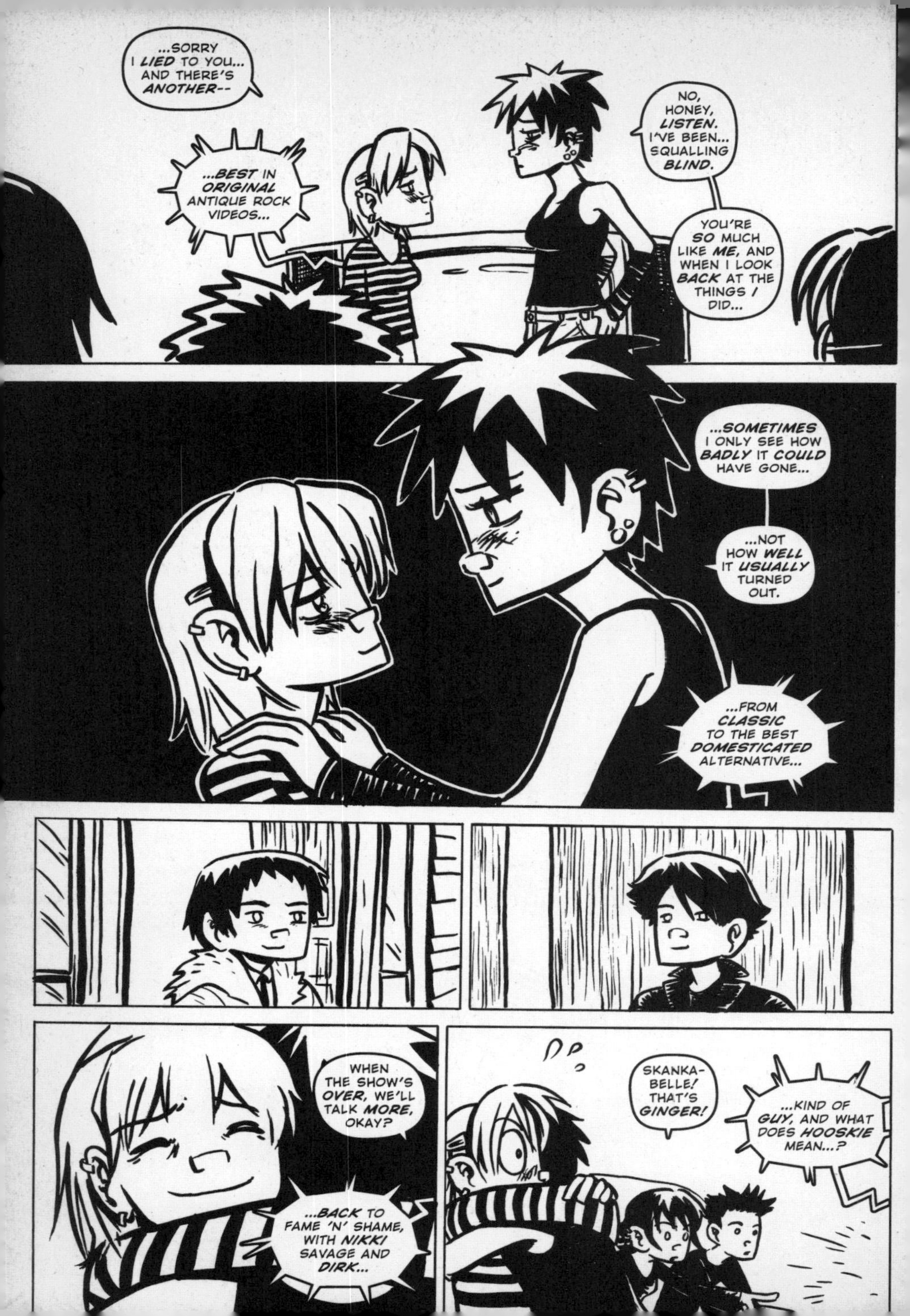
...SORRY I LIED TO YOU... AND THERE'S ANOTHER--
...BEST IN ORIGINAL ANTIQUE ROCK VIDEOS...
NO, HONEY, LISTEN. I'VE BEEN... SQUALLING BLIND.
YOU'RE SO MUCH LIKE ME, AND WHEN I LOOK BACK AT THE THINGS I DID...
...SOMETIMES I ONLY SEE HOW BADLY IT COULD HAVE GONE...
...NOT HOW WELL IT USUALLY TURNED OUT.
...FROM CLASSIC TO THE BEST DOMESTICATED ALTERNATIVE...
WHEN THE SHOW'S OVER, WE'LL TALK MORE, OKAY?
...BACK TO FAME 'N' SHAME, WITH NIKKI SAVAGE AND DIRK...
SKANKA-BELLE! THAT'S GINGER!
...KIND OF GUY, AND WHAT DOES HOOSKIE MEAN...?

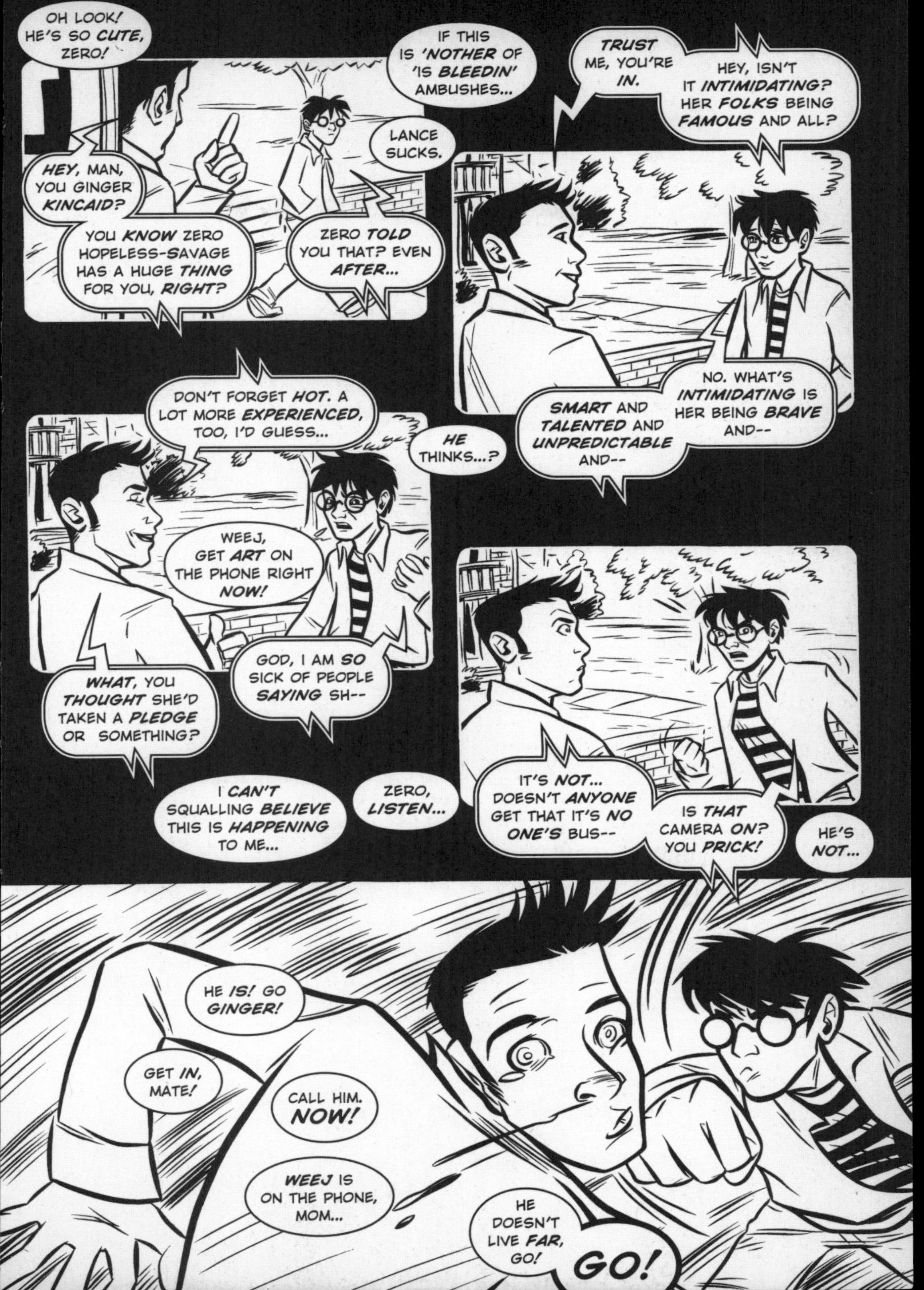
OH LOOK! HE'S SO CUTE, ZERO!
IF THIS IS 'NOTHER OF 'IS BLEEDIN' AMBUSHES...
LANCE SUCKS.
HEY, MAN, YOU GINGER KINCAID?
YOU KNOW ZERO HOPELESS-SAVAGE HAS A HUGE THING FOR YOU, RIGHT?
ZERO TOLD YOU THAT? EVEN AFTER...
TRUST ME, YOU'RE IN.
HEY, ISN'T IT INTIMIDATING? HER FOLKS BEING FAMOUS AND ALL?
NO. WHAT'S INTIMIDATING IS HER BEING BRAVE AND--
SMART AND TALENTED AND UNPREDICTABLE AND--
DON'T FORGET HOT. A LOT MORE EXPERIENCED, TOO, I'D GUESS...
HE THINKS...?
WEEJ, GET ART ON THE PHONE RIGHT NOW!
WHAT, YOU THOUGHT SHE'D TAKEN A PLEDGE OR SOMETHING?
GOD, I AM SO SICK OF PEOPLE SAYING SH--
I CAN'T SQUALLING BELIEVE THIS IS HAPPENING TO ME...
ZERO, LISTEN...
IT'S NOT... DOESN'T ANYONE GET THAT IT'S NO ONE'S BUS--
IS THAT CAMERA ON? YOU PRICK!
HE'S NOT...
HE IS! GO GINGER!
GET IN, MATE!
CALL HIM. NOW!
WEEJ IS ON THE PHONE, MOM...
HE DOESN'T LIVE FAR, GO!
GO!

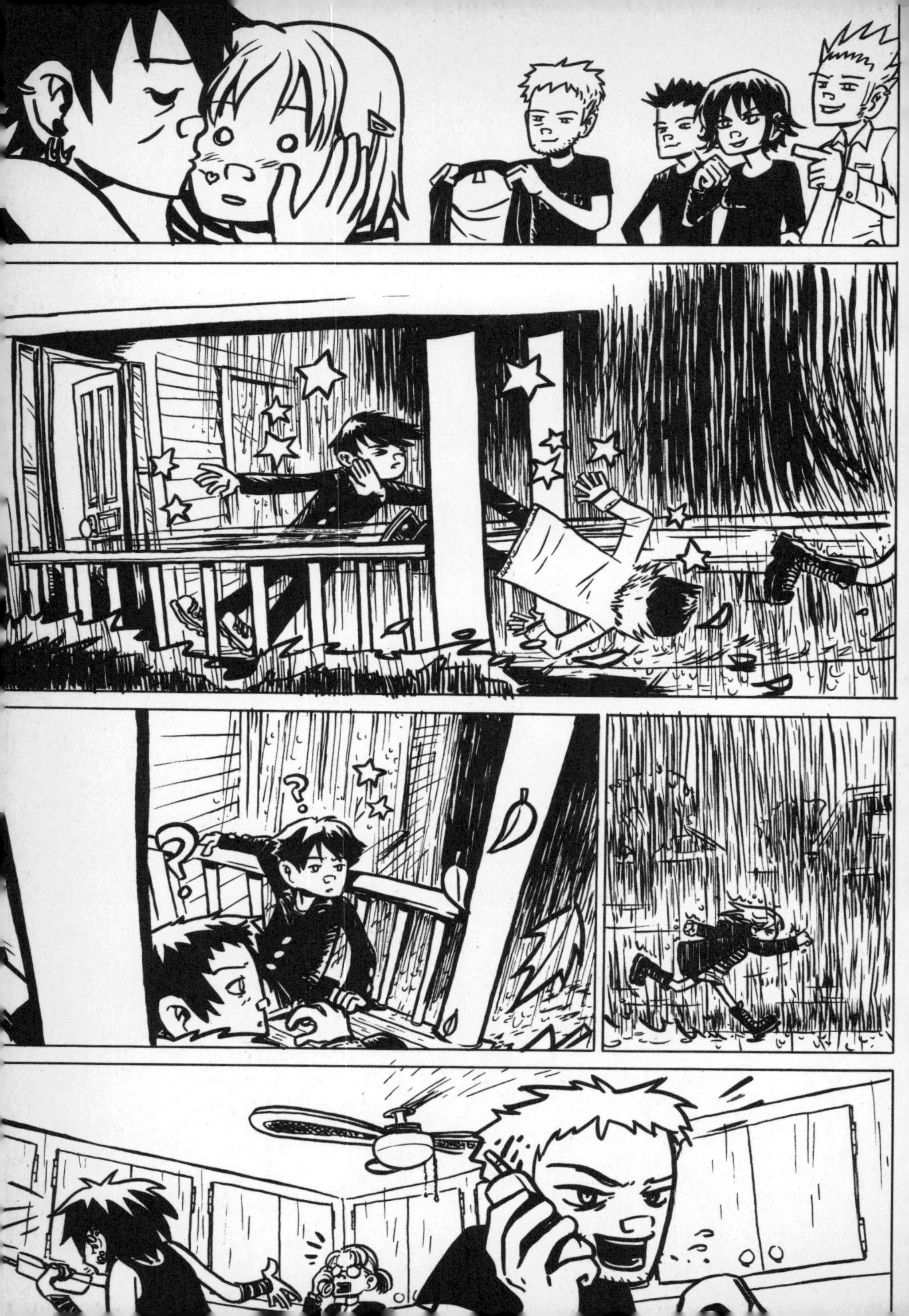

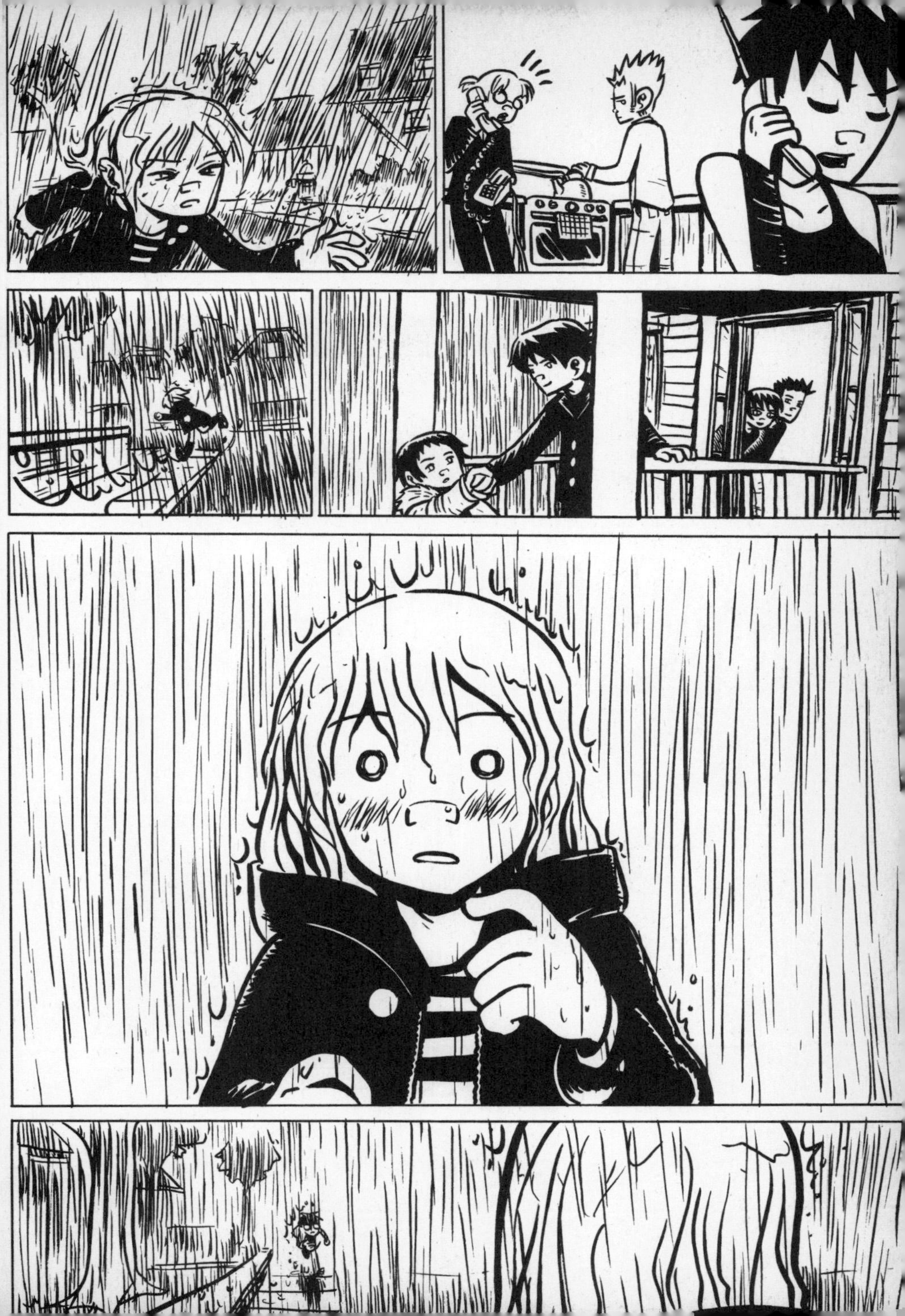

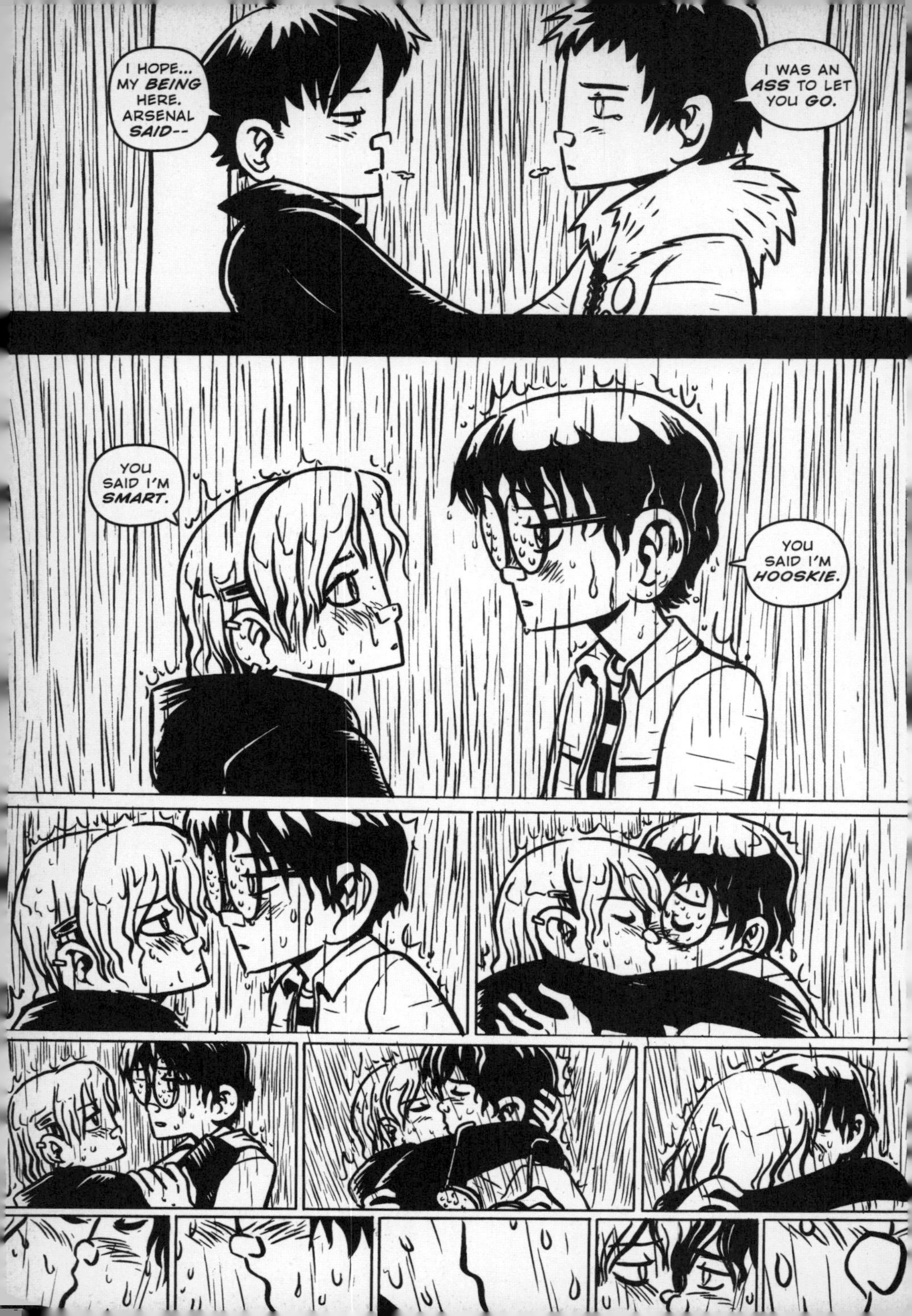
I HOPE... MY *BEING* HERE. ARSENAL *SAID*--
I WAS AN *ASS* TO LET YOU *GO*.
YOU SAID I'M *SMART*.
YOU SAID I'M *HOOSKIE*.

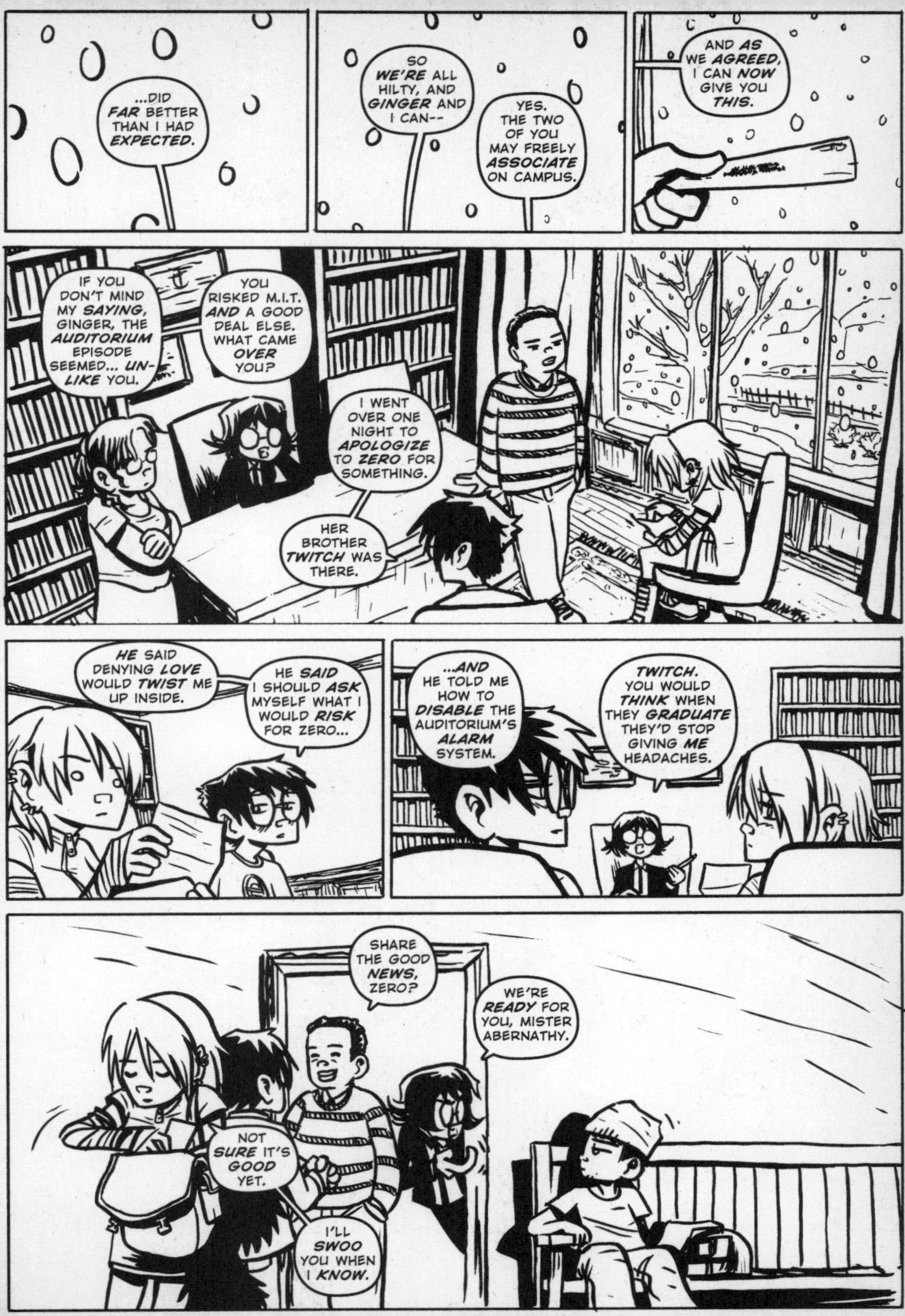
...DID FAR BETTER THAN I HAD EXPECTED.
SO WE'RE ALL HILTY, AND GINGER AND I CAN--
YES. THE TWO OF YOU MAY FREELY ASSOCIATE ON CAMPUS.
AND AS WE AGREED, I CAN NOW GIVE YOU THIS.
IF YOU DON'T MIND MY SAYING, GINGER, THE AUDITORIUM EPISODE SEEMED... UN-LIKE YOU.
YOU RISKED M.I.T. AND A GOOD DEAL ELSE. WHAT CAME OVER YOU?
I WENT OVER ONE NIGHT TO APOLOGIZE TO ZERO FOR SOMETHING.
HER BROTHER TWITCH WAS THERE.
HE SAID DENYING LOVE WOULD TWIST ME UP INSIDE.
HE SAID I SHOULD ASK MYSELF WHAT I WOULD RISK FOR ZERO...
...AND HE TOLD ME HOW TO DISABLE THE AUDITORIUM'S ALARM SYSTEM.
TWITCH. YOU WOULD THINK WHEN THEY GRADUATE THEY'D STOP GIVING ME HEADACHES.
SHARE THE GOOD NEWS, ZERO?
WE'RE READY FOR YOU, MISTER ABERNATHY.
NOT SURE IT'S GOOD YET.
I'LL SWOO YOU WHEN I KNOW.

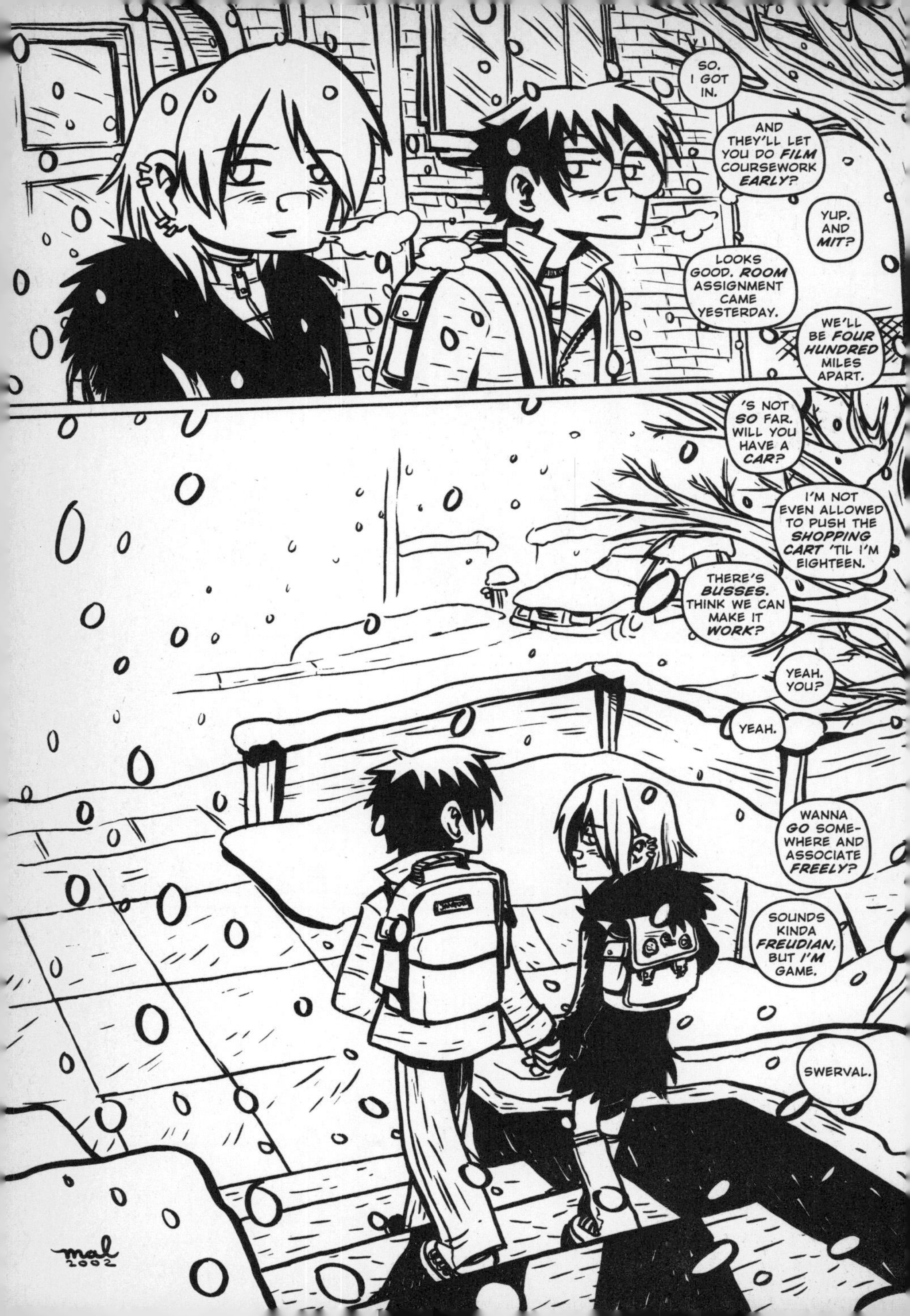
SO. I GOT IN.
AND THEY'LL LET YOU DO FILM COURSEWORK EARLY?
YUP. AND MIT?
LOOKS GOOD. ROOM ASSIGNMENT CAME YESTERDAY.
WE'LL BE FOUR HUNDRED MILES APART.
'S NOT SO FAR. WILL YOU HAVE A CAR?
I'M NOT EVEN ALLOWED TO PUSH THE SHOPPING CART 'TIL I'M EIGHTEEN.
THERE'S BUSSES. THINK WE CAN MAKE IT WORK?
YEAH. YOU?
YEAH.
WANNA GO SOME-WHERE AND ASSOCIATE FREELY?
SOUNDS KINDA FREUDIAN, BUT I'M GAME.
SWERVAL.
mal 2002

THE
END

Bios

JEN VAN METER made her comic book debut alongside Buffy the Vampire Slayer, scripting that character's first-ever comic book story for the *Dark Horse Presents Annual 1998*. She followed it up with a collaboration with Frank Quitely in Vertigo's horror anthology *Flinch*, a script for DC's *Gotham Knights*, a segment of Marvel's *Captain America* #50, and the licensed comic book tie-in *The Blair Witch Project*, the best-selling single issue in Oni Press' history. *Hopeless Savages* is her first creator-owned work (if you don't count her son, Elliot), and its first series was nominated for an Eisner in 2002. Her most recent releases include a *Batman* Elseworlds book for DC called *Golden Streets of Gotham*, the third chronicle of the Hopeless-Savage family, *Too Much Hopeless Savages!*, and a second child.

BRYAN O'MALLEY is from Canada and in addition to his handling art chores here, he has inked an issue of *Queen & Country* and letters *Blue Monday*, *Jason and the Argobots* and a variety of other things. Bryan's own *Lost at Sea* appeared in the *Oni Color Special 2002* and will be an original graphic novel from Oni in 2003. He also created the comic strip *Style*, which has run at onipress.com. And as if that wasn't enough, one can always find more from Bryan on the internet at radiomaru.com.

Born in West Germany, CHRISTINE NORRIE has lived many places but fondly claims St.Louis as her hometown, the place she grew to love comic books. She moved to New York in the late nineties, worked in the business end of comic book publishing for DC Comics, and later became a freelance illustrator. Since the debut of the first *Hopeless Savages* series, she's been nominated for many awards including the prestigious Eisner Award, the Russ Manning Award, and was a recipient for the New York City Comic Book Museum's Award for Breakout Artist of 2002. Christine Norrie is the comic artist for *Redbook* magazine's *Q&A with John Gray: You and Him* and *Spy Kids* for Disney, and just published her first graphic novel, *Cheat*. She is currently at work on the next *Hopeless Savages* series and another, slightly cheerier, romance for Oni Press. She resides in the historic North Shore of Staten Island with her husband and their parakeet, rabbit, three cats, and the ever-marvelous dog, Orwell. She was joined on *Ground Zero* by her sister, CATHERINE NORRIE, who previously has worked in graphic design. This is Catherine's first comic book work.

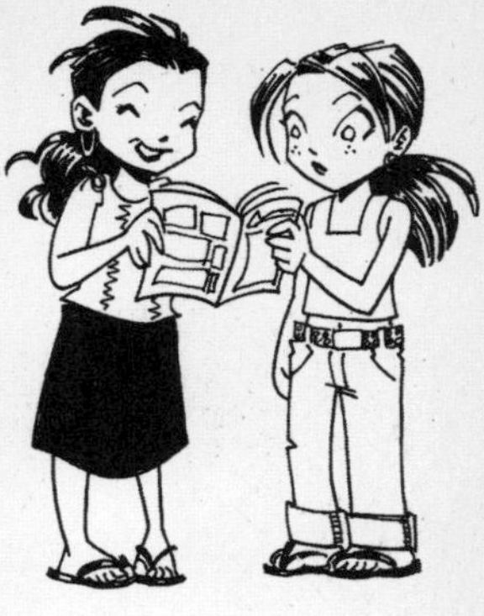

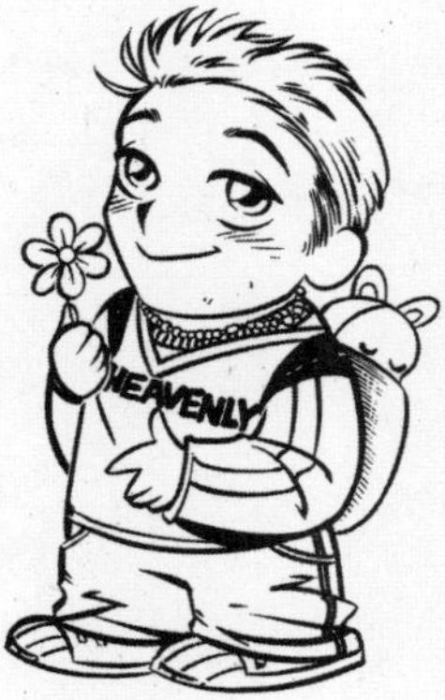
HEAVENLY

ANDI WATSON is the creator of *Skeleton Key, Geisha, Slow News Day, Dumped,* and *Breakfast After Noon*. He also scripted the *Buffy the Vampire Slayer* comics for two years, has optioned *Skeleton Key* for a cartoon series,designed animated advent calendars for AOL.co.uk, and had one of his cover images appear fleetingly in the background of teen flick *Coyote Ugly*. In the year 2001, Andi and *Breakfast After Noon* were nominated for an Eisner Award for Best Limited Series, the second nomination for the artist (he previously received notice for the collection of *Geisha* in 2000). He is currently hard at work on a brand-new series, *Love Fights*, for Oni Press,who are also releasing an expanded edition of *Geisha*. Despite his brushes with fame, he remains remarkably down to earth.

CHYNNA CLUGSTON-MAJOR is the talented cartoonist behind the award-nominated series, *Blue Monday*—available in two trade paper backs, *The Kids are Alright* and *Absolute Beginners*, and a series of holiday-themed one-shots that will be collected into the book *Inbetween Days* in the fall of 2003. She has also done work for Dark Horse's *Buffy the Vampire Slayer* comics, Paul Dini's *Jingle Belle*, and Marvel's *Ultimate Marvel Team-Up*. When not drawing, she is usually shouting at neighborhood children from her studio window or cooking up the best tacos known to man. Her next project is *Scooter Girl*, a six-issue miniseries scheduled for release from Oni Press in May 2003.

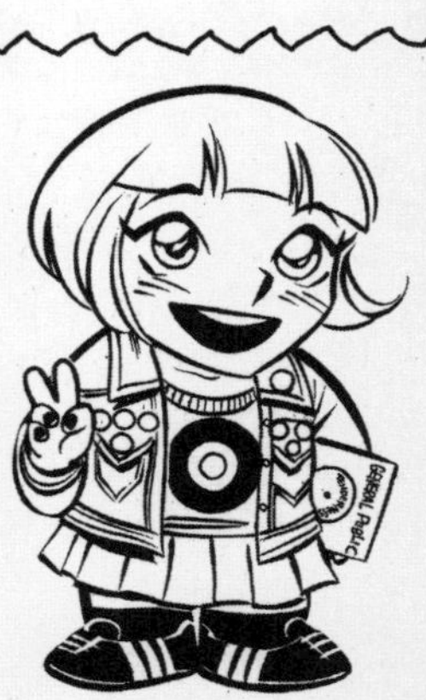

Acknowledgments

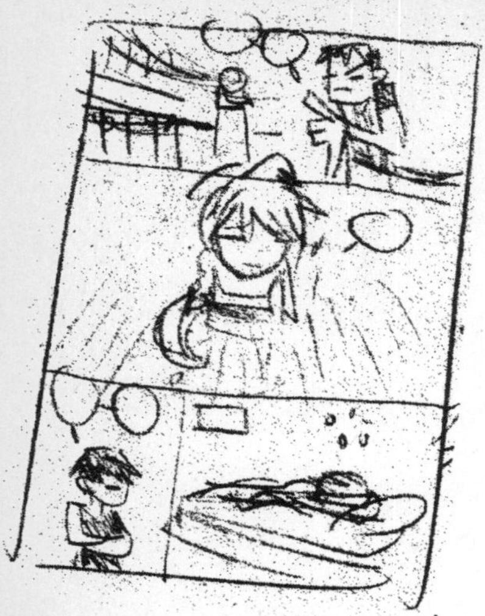

Jen thanks:

The artists who made this book possible; Terry's covers, the flashback art by Andi, Christine and Chynna, and the amazing work of Bryan O'Malley all make me so proud of and for this story. Jamie, Joe and James at Oni Press, for making it happen and for their dear friendship. Steve Woodcock for his help with the chem. and calc. homework. As always, my friends and family, who make it all possible, most especially Greg and Elliot.

Bryan thanks:

I'd like to dedicate my work on this book to Jen, Christine, Chynna, Andi, Jamie, Joe, James, Kelley, Keith, and all the other cool people that made it all happen. I had a lot of fun and I hope we can still be friends. Extra special thanks to Christopher Butcher for putting up with me during this period. I was inconsolable. He also helped on the book, I think; I can't remember. I was on drugs.

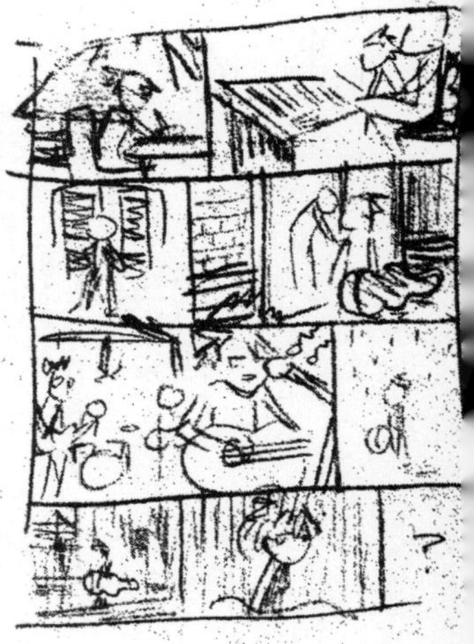

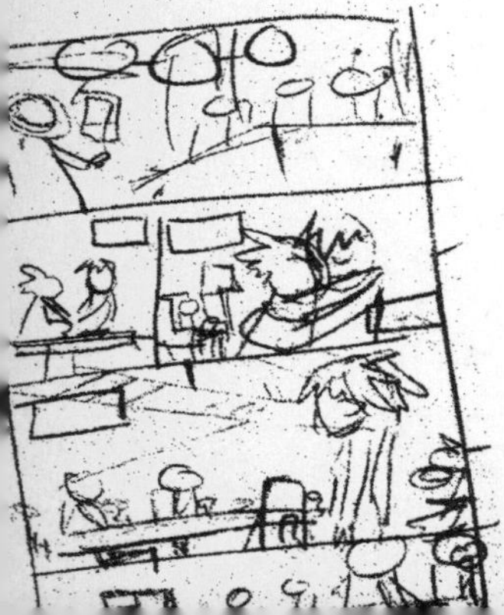

Jamie thanks:

Andrew Wheeler for helping us put our best foot forward; Catherine Norrie for bailing us out; Andy Greenwald and Kieron Gillen for opening up their address books; and Marie Du Santiago for her sartorial splendor and kindness.

************ sketches and things ************

Thumbnails and character sketches by Bryan Lee O'Malley.

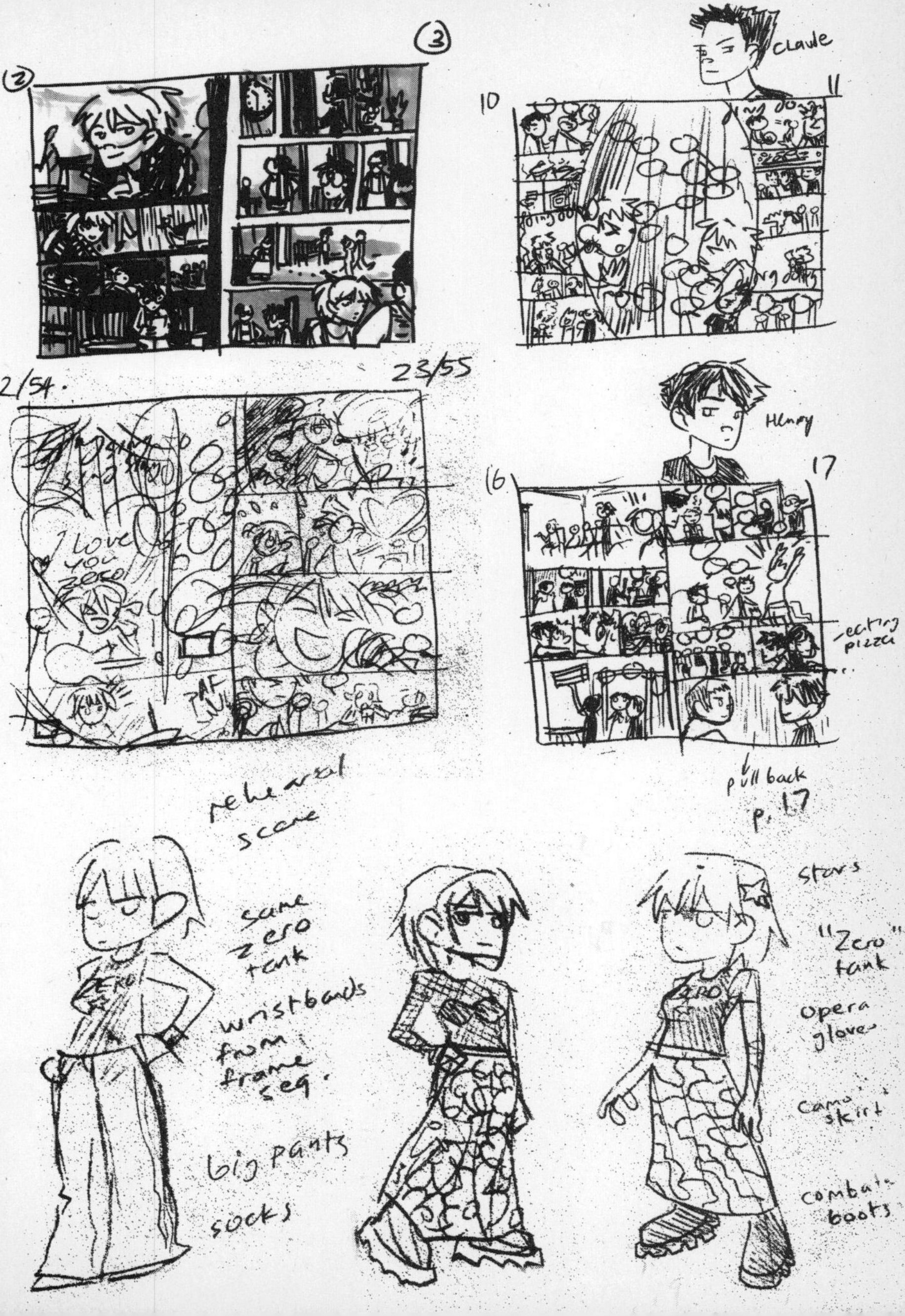

2
3
Claude
10
11
22/54
23/55
I love you Zero
Henry
16
17
eating pizza
pull back
p. 17
rehearsal scene
same zero tank
wristbands from frame seq.
big pants
socks
stars
"Zero" tank
opera glove
camo skirt
combat boots

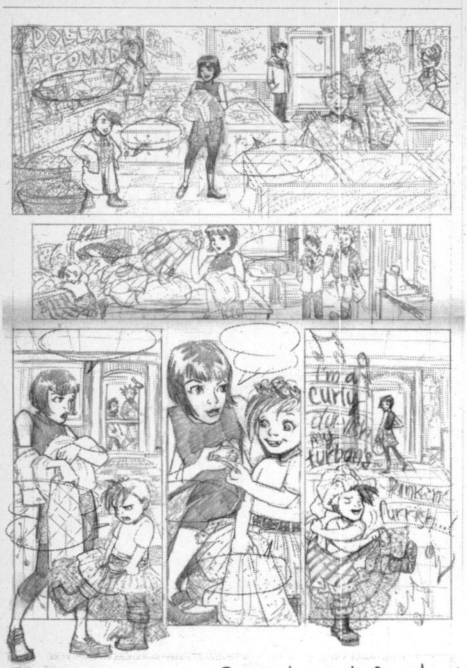

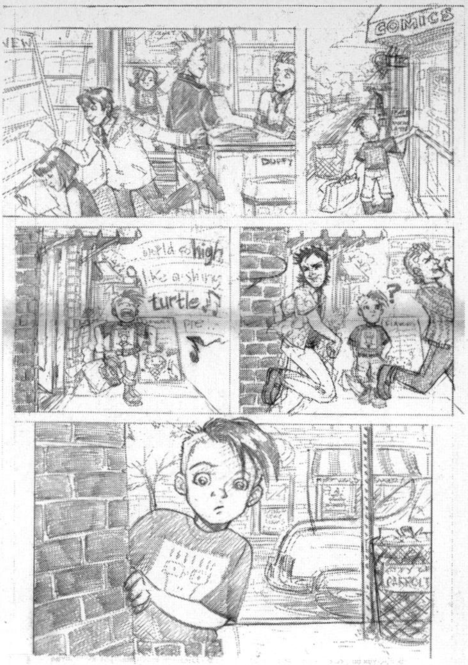
COMICS

Original pencils for chapter 2 by Christine Norrie.

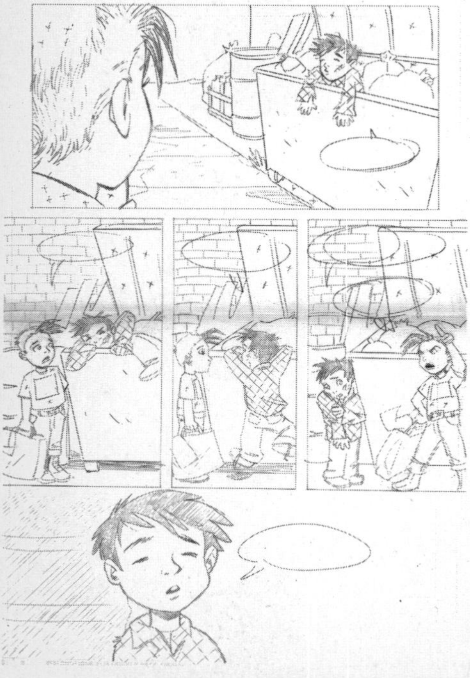

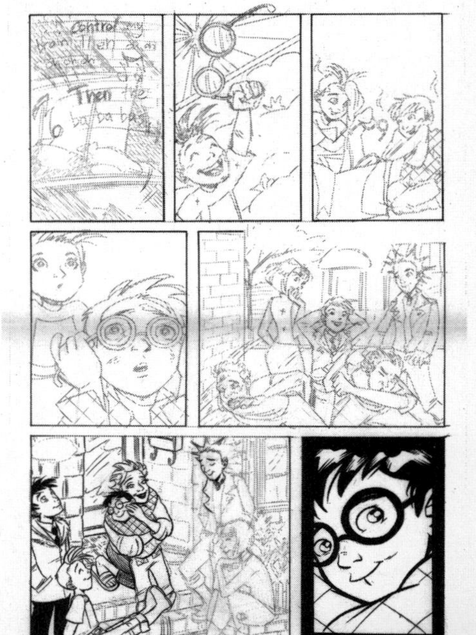

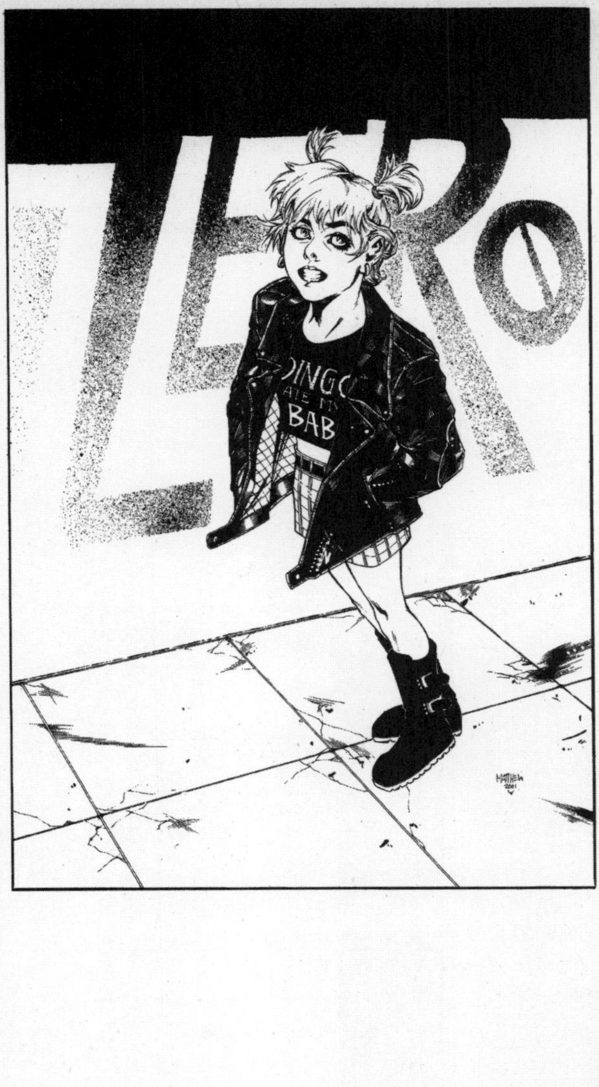
ZERO
DINGO ATE MY BAB
MATTHEW 2001

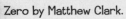

Zero by Matthew Clark.

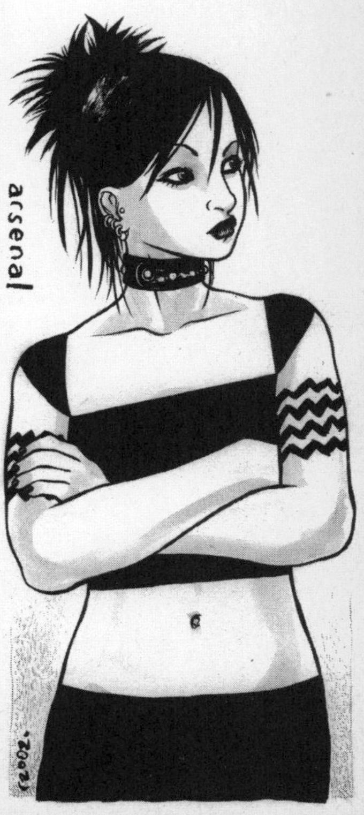
arsenal

Arsenal by Ross Campbell.

Other books from the creators of *Hopeless Savages* and Oni Press...

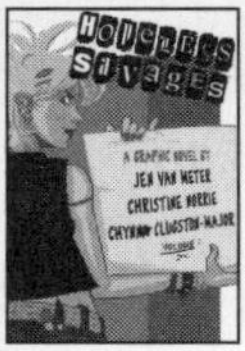
Hopeless Savages

HOPELESS SAVAGES, Vol 1
by Jen Van Meter,
Christine Norrie,
& Chynna Clugston-Major
136 pages,
black-and-white interiors
$11.95 US
ISBN: 1-929998-75-9

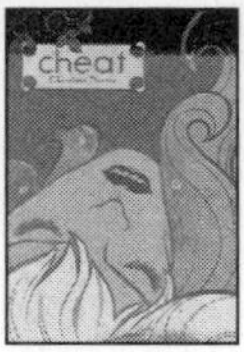
cheat

CHEAT™
by Christine Norrie
72 pages,
black-and-white interiors
$5.95 US
ISBN 1-929998-47-3

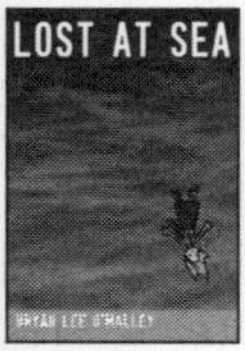
LOST AT SEA

LOST AT SEA™
by Bryan Lee O'Malley
168 pages,
black-and-white interiors
$11.95 US
ISBN: 1-929998-71-6

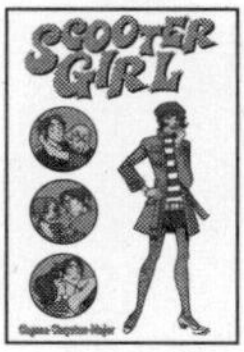
SCOOTER GIRL

SCOOTER GIRL™
by Chynna Clugston-Major
168 pages,
black-and-white interiors
$17.95 US
ISBN: 1-929998-88-0
Available May 2004!

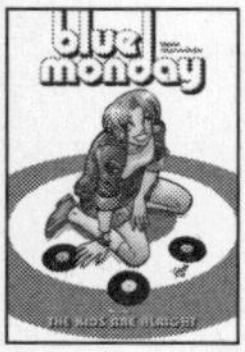
blue monday

BLUE MONDAY, Vol. 1:
THE KIDS ARE ALRIGHT™
by Chynna Clugston-Major
136 pages,
black-and-white interiors
$10.95 US
ISBN: 1-929998-62-7

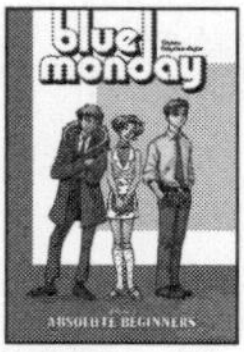
blue monday
ABSOLUTE BEGINNERS

BLUE MONDAY, Vol. 2:
ABSOLUTE BEGINNERS™
by Chynna Clugston-Major
128 pages,
black-and-white interiors
$11.95 US
ISBN 1-929998-17-1

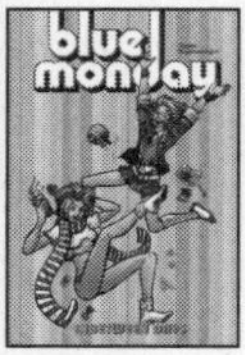
blue monday

BLUE MONDAY, Vol. 3:
INBETWEEN DAYS™
by Chynna Clugston-Major
120 pages,
black-and-white interiors
$9.95 US
ISBN: 1-929998-66-X

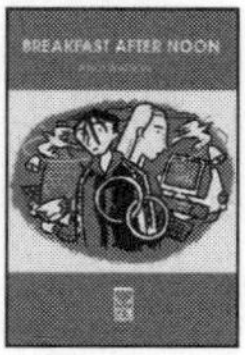
BREAKFAST AFTER NOON

BREAKFAST AFTER NOON™
by Andi Watson
208 pages,
black-and-white interiors
$19.95 US
ISBN: 1-929998-14-7

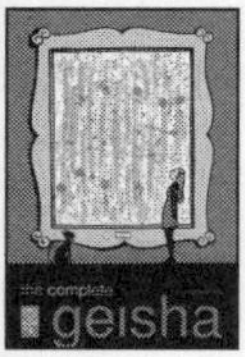
the complete
geisha

THE COMPLETE GEISHA™
by Andi Watson
152 pages,
black-and-white interiors
$15.95 US
ISBN: 1929998-51-1

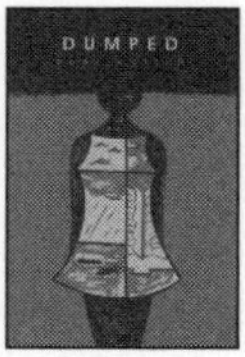
DUMPED

DUMPED™
by Andi Watson
56 pages,
black-and-white interiors
$5.95 US
ISBN: 1-929998-41-4

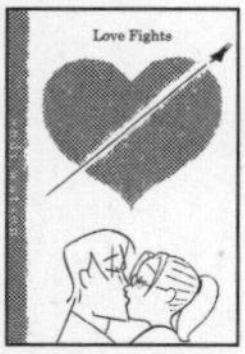
Love Fights

LOVE FIGHTS™ vol. 1
By Andi Watson
168 pages,
black-and-white interiors
$14.95 US
ISBN: ISBN 1-929998-86-4
Available April, 2004!

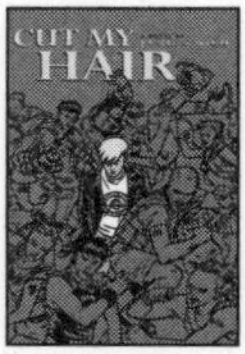
CUT MY HAIR

CUT MY HAIR™
by Jamie S. Rich
w/ Chynna Clugston-Major,
Scott Morse, Judd Winick,
& Andi Watson
236 pages, black-and-white
text with illustrations
$15.95 US
ISBN: 0-9700387-0-4

Available at finer bookstores and comic book shops everywhere.
For a comics store near you, call 1-888-COMIC-BOOK or visit www.the-master-list.com.
For more information on Oni Press publications, go to www.onipress.com.